AF412682

Postmodernism's Role in Latin American Literature

Postmodernism's Role in Latin American Literature

The Life and Work of Augusto Roa Bastos

Edited by Helene Carol Weldt-Basson

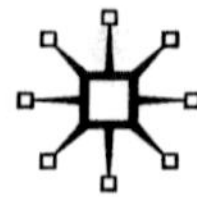

POSTMODERNISM'S ROLE IN LATIN AMERICAN LITERATURE
Copyright © Helene Carol Weldt-Basson, 2010.

First published in 2010 by PALGRAVE MACMILLAN® in the United States—a division of St. Martin's Press LLC, 175 Fifth Avenue, New York, NY 10010

Where this book is distributed in the UK, Europe and the rest of the world, this is by Palgrave Macmillan, a division of Macmillan Publishers Limited, registered in England, company number 785998, of Houndmills, Basingstoke, Hampshire RG21 6XS.

Palgrave Macmillan is the global academic imprint of the above companies and has companies and representatives throughout the world.

Palgrave® and Macmillan® are registered trademarks in the United States, the United Kingdom, Europe and other countries.

ISBN: 978-0-230-61766-7

Library of Congress Cataloging-in-Publication Data

Postmodernism's role in Latin American literature : the life and work of Augusto Roa Bastos / [edited by] Helene Carol Weldt-Basson.
     p. cm.
   ISBN 978-0-230-61766-7 (alk. paper)
   1. Roa Bastos, Augusto Antonio—Criticism and interpretation.
2. Postmodernism (Literature)—Latin America. I. Weldt-Basson, Helene Carol, 1958-

PQ8259.R56Z83 2010
863'.64—dc22   2009044755

Design by Scribe Inc.

First edition: July 2010

10 9 8 7 6 5 4 3 2 1

Printed in the United States of America.

I would like to dedicate this book to the memory of three very important people in my life, all of whom I lost over the past few years: my father, Bernard Weldt (1918–2007), who inspired me to love books and to strive for perfection; my sister-in-law, Marsha Goldstein Basson (1959–2008), whose courage and spirit are a model to live by for all who knew her; and finally, of course, Augusto Roa Bastos (1917–2005), my favorite author, whose works this volume commemorates. All of them will live forever in my heart.

CONTENTS

Acknowledgments

First and foremost, I would like to thank all the contributors to this volume for their outstanding work and unfailing cooperation in putting the collection together in an expeditious and meticulous fashion.

Second, I thank my husband, Marc, who first suggested the idea of writing a commemorative essay collection honoring the work of Augusto Roa Bastos.

As always, I would like to thank my family—my mother, my sister Rita, and my children, Rebecca and Marshall, for their unfailing support.

Finally, I would like to thank the following publishers for permission to reprint excerpts from their works:

SON OF MAN. Copyright © 1988 by Monthly Review Press. Reprinted by permission of Monthly Review Press Foundation.

YO EL SUPREMO. Copyright © 1983 by Ediciones Cátedra. Reprinted by permission of Ediciones Cátedra.

CHAPTER 1

THE LIFE AND WORKS OF AUGUSTO ROA BASTOS[1]

Helene Carol Weldt-Basson

"Las formas desaparecen, las palabras quedan, para balbucear lo indecible."
"Forms disappear, words remain, to babble the unsayable."

—Roa Bastos, *Metaforismos*

AUGUSTO ROA BASTOS'S BIOGRAPHY

Augusto Roa Bastos was born in Asunción, Paraguay, on June 13, 1917, to Lucio Roa and Lucía Bastos. Shortly after his birth, his father, a cultured man, was forced to close his exportation business and seek employment in a sugarcane factory in the small village of Iturbe in the province of Guairá. Roa was one of three siblings; he had one younger and one older sister. At the age of eight, the author was sent back to Asunción to live with his uncle, Hermenegildo Roa, a well-educated priest who opened up his extensive library to his young nephew. Hermenegildo Roa was later to become the inspiration for

---

[1] The following works were consulted in the elaboration of this summary of Roa Bastos's life: Augusto Roa Bastos, *Centro Virtual Cervantes,* Trinidad Barrera, "Augusto Roa Bastos: la ejemplaridad de la escritura," 19–37; Caleb Bach, "Augusto Roa Bastos: La realidad superada"; Eduardo Galeano, "Su voz cantó como ninguna el desgarramiento del Paraguay"; Milda Riva, "Bio-bibliografía de Augusto Roa Bastos," 330–369.

Roa's story "El viejo señor obispo," included in his first book of short stories, *El trueno entre las hojas* (Thunder Among the Leaves; 1953), just as his childhood village of Iturbe was to become the center of many of his novels and tales.

Roa Bastos wrote his first short story, "Lucha hasta el alba," in 1931, when he was fourteen years old. This autobiographical tale about a boy who rebels against his authoritative father remained unpublished until 1979, when it appeared in the journal *Texto Crítico* and was subsequently published in one of his short story collections, *Antología personal* (Personal Anthology; 1980).

Augusto was in high school in the Colegio de los Padres de San José when the Chaco War broke out in 1932. The following year, he left school to become a rearguard stretcher-bearer during the conflict. The Chaco War was a border dispute between Paraguay and Bolivia over oil territory, fomented by the U.S.-based Standard Oil Company's interests in the region. In 1935, after the war—won by Paraguay—Roa worked in a bank and wrote articles for the Paraguayan newspaper *El País*. Although he never completed high school, Roa Bastos was an avid reader and self-educated, erudite man.

Roa Bastos's literary career gained momentum in 1937, when he won the Premio del Ateneo de Asunción for his first novel, *Fulgencio Miranda*. Despite winning the contest, Roa Bastos never published this work, which unfortunately remains lost to this day. In 1939, Roa married his first wife, Ana Lidia Mascheroni, a union that produced two children, Carlos and Mirta. He already had an older son, Augusto, from a prior relationship with María Isabel Duarte. In 1942, he published his first book, a poetry collection titled *El ruiseñor de la aurora y otros poemas* (*The Nightingale of Dawn and Other Poems*). Although he is primarily known for his narrative, he would later publish another poetry book, *El naranjal ardiente: Nocturno paraguayo, 1947–1949* (*The Burning Orange Grove: Paraguayan Nocturne, 1947–1949*; 1960) and two small groupings of poems in journals. "*El genesis de los Apapokuva*" (*The Genesis of the Apapokuva*; 1971) appeared in the Paraguayan journal *Alcor II*, while his last series of poems, "*Silenciario*" (*Observing Silence*) appeared in *Cuadernos Hispanoamericanos* in 1983. He also published two anthologies with poems that previously appeared in books and journals: *Poemas reunidas* (*Collected Poems*; 1995) and *Poesía* (Poetry; 1999).

In 1942, Roa also became a full-time editor and writer for *El País*. He was sent to England as a war correspondent toward the end of World War II in 1945. Roa Bastos collected the articles he wrote in this capacity in the volume *La Inglaterra que yo vi* (*The England that I Saw*; 1946), another piece of writing of which no copy can be found.

Roa Bastos returned to Paraguay after the war, but—for political reasons—was forced into exile in 1947 under the Perón-supported presidency of Higinio Morínigo. Natalicio González, one of Morínigo's ministers, whose cultural works had been criticized by Roa in several of his articles, ordered Roa captured as a Communist subversive. Roa was allegedly guilty because of the work he produced as a writer for the Paraguayan newspaper *El País*, although, in truth, González's actions were motivated mostly by personal rancor. Before his exile to Argentina, Roa's first play, *Mientras llegue el día* (*While Day Arrives*), debuted in 1946. Other plays written by the author include the following: *La carcajada* (*The Laugh*; written with his mother in 1930), *La residenta* (*The Resident*; 1940), *El niño del rocío* (*The Boy of the Dew*; 1940), and a theater version of the novel *Yo el Supremo* (*I The Supreme*; 1991). While in Buenos Aires, the writer worked a series of odd jobs that included insurance agent, radio announcer, and screenplay writer. Before his departure in 1976, Roa Bastos produced many of his literary works, including several short story collections—*El trueno entre las hojas* (*Thunder Among the Leaves*; 1953), *El baldío* (*The Vacant Lot*; 1966), *Los pies sobre el agua* (*Feet on the Water*; 1967), *Madera quemada* (*Burnt Wood*; 1967), *Moriencia* (*Slaughter*; 1969), *Cuerpo presente y otros textos* (*Lying in State and Other Texts*; 1971)—and his two most famous novels, *Hijo de hombre* (*Son of Man*; 1960) and *Yo el Supremo* (*I The Supreme*; 1974). Roa Bastos revised and republished the first of these two novels in 1982, and was able to complete the second one with the assistance of a Guggenheim grant.

During this Argentine period, the Paraguayan writer divorced his first wife. In 1976, after the military coup by Jorge Videla, Roa Bastos was fortuitously offered the opportunity to become a Professor of Latin American Literature and Guarani at the University of Toulouse, in Toulouse, France. *I The Supreme* had been placed on Argentina's list of prohibited books, and shortly after the author's departure for France, Roa Bastos's apartment was ransacked by the Argentine government, thus suggesting he narrowly escaped becoming one of the country's many "disappeared" political activists and intellectuals.

Roa Bastos remained in France for many years, from 1976 until 1996. The author was offered Spanish citizenship in 1983, and French citizenship in 1985. After the fall of the government of the dictator Alfredo Stroessner, in 1989, the author's revoked Paraguayan citizenship was returned to him, and he was able to travel freely back and forth to his country. During his years in France, Roa married Iris Giménez, a professor of Nahuatl and ancient Mexican civilizations, with whom he raised three children: Francisco, Silvia, and Aliria. The two separated, and Roa returned to Paraguay in 1996, where he lived until his death. During the last years of his life, Roa Bastos collaborated with Paraguay's new democratic government, serving as a member of the special "Truth and Justice Commission" that studied human rights violations during the Stroessner period, and becoming a member of the Partido Encuentro Nacional—from 1997 through 2000—in support of democratic consolidation in the country (although he later abandoned this group). He suffered many health problems in the last few years, including several operations: two on the heart (1999 and 2002) and one on the prostate (2004). He died on April 26, 2005, four days after surgery from a head injury occasioned by a fall.

During the last decade or so of his life, Roa Bastos published four novels: *Vigilia del almirante* (*The Admiral's Vigil*; 1992), *El fiscal* (*The Prosecutor*; 1993), *Contravida* (*Counterlife*; 1994), and *Madama Sui* (*Madame Sui*; 1996). Other works published during his period in France are *Cándido López*, a limited edition collection of the Argentine painter's scenes of the Triple Alliance War, including a novella by the author titled "El sonámbulo," ("The Sleepwalker") published by Franco María Ricci in Italy in 1976; *Las culturas condenadas* (*The Condemned Cultures*; 1978), which is a compilation of texts about Guarani civilizations; *Antología personal* (*Personal Anthology*; 1980), and *Contar un cuento y otros relatos* (*To Tell a Story and Other Tales*; 1984). After his return to Paraguay in 1996, Roa Bastos published the following works: *Poemas recogidas* (*Collected Poems*; 1995), *Metaforismos* (*Metaphorisms*; 1996), *Poesía* (*Poetry*; 1999), *Los conjurados del Quilombo del Gran Chaco* (*The Conspirators of the Shanty of the Greater Chaco*; 2001), and *Cuentos Completos* (*Complete Short Stories*; 2003). In addition, Roa Bastos wrote three children's books: *El pollito de fuego* (*The Little Chick of Fire*; 1974), *Los juegos 1: Carolina y Gaspar* (*The Games 1: Carolina and Gaspar*; 1979), and *Los juegos 2: La casa de invierno-verano* (*The Games 2: The Winter-Summer House*; 1981). Moreover, he authored many essays on Latin American literature and culture and about thirteen screenplays. After his death, three unpublished works were discovered in his computer. The first, *Pancha Garmendia y Elisa Lynch* (*Pancha Garmendia and Elisa Lynch*), an opera libretto, was recently published (2006) by Servilibro in Paraguay. There are reportedly two other works that will be released at a future date: "Hijo del fuego" ("Son of Fire"), based on the Chamacoco and Macá Indians of Paraguay, and "Isadora Duncan," a novel about the famous ballerina.

Roa Bastos was the winner of many literary prizes. In addition to his first literary contest in Asunción, in which he won first place for best novel with *Fulgencio Miranda*, Roa won *El Concurso Internacional de Novelas de Editorial Losada* (1959; The Losada Publishing House's International Novel Competiton), the *Premio de Las Letras Memorial de América Latina* in Brazil (1988; Memorial Prize of Latin American Letters), and the *Premio Cervantes* (Cervantes Prize) in Spain (1989), the latter of which is the most prestigious literary prize of the Spanish-speaking world.

Roa Bastos was not only an important writer, but also a great man who hoped to change and better society through his literary works. Sabas Martín claims he found the following declaration by Roa: "Yo, Augusto Roa Bastos, amanuense supremo de la Historia, ficcionador perpetuo de la realidad, proclamo que las palabras cuentan como actos: viajan al núcleo central de las cosas para encontrar esa verdad muy escondida a veces" ["I, Augusto Roa Bastos, supreme amanuensis of History, perpetual fiction writer of reality, proclaim that words count as acts: they travel to the central nucleus of things to find that truth that at times is very hidden"] (Martin 29; my translation). In the following pages, we will examine this legacy of "acts" by the writer that have left their impact on the world—the words that remain, through which he so eloquently "babbles" to us the unsayable.

ROA BASTOS AND POSTMODERNISM

It is difficult to speak of Roa Bastos's work in terms of generalizations and unifying characteristics, especially since the author's narrative trajectory has been one of a "poetics of variations" or constant rewriting of his fiction. Fragments of *Yo el Supremo* were published in journals prior to the novel's appearance, as were several short stories that were later rewritten and incorporated into his short story volumes. In 1982, Roa Bastos rewrote his first novel, *Hijo de hombre*, originally published in 1960. An earlier, unpublished version of *El fiscal* was destroyed, and the novel was rewritten and published in 1993. The two sections of *Los conjurados del Quilombo del Gran Chaco* written by Roa Bastos are reworkings of sections of *El fiscal*. These examples illustrate that Roa Bastos's *oeuvre* is conceived of as a process in constant flux as opposed to a fixed corpus of writing. This ongoing transformation to which he has subjected his works yields a hidden benefit to the reader and critic. It allows them to observe a theory of literary construction implied by patterns of changes, and this theory is inextricably linked to what can be termed a postmodern vision of both fiction and history.

Postmodernism is a term that has undergone much discussion by theoreticians who study literature, architecture, painting, and film, among other disciplines. A discussion of the various debates surrounding postmodernism could indeed constitute the content of a book in itself, and for this reason, I will be forced to limit my discussion of postmodernism to some very general concepts. Linda Hutcheon focuses her work on achieving a definition of postmodernism in literature. A careful reading of *A Poetics of Postmodernism* (1988) allows us to extract the following four principal concepts. First, postmodernism is a contradictory phenomenon that both appropriates and subverts characteristics of its precursor, modernism. It rejects the elitism and political conservatism of modernism, as well as its notion of the autonomy of art, in favor of cultural democratization (use of pop culture) and a contestatory stance toward the totalizing artistic vision conveyed by modernism. Second, postmodernism is both historical and political in essence and cannot be separated from these two dimensions. Third, postmodernism is self-reflexive by nature and views all knowledge as human construct. Thus, postmodernism questions the mimetic relationship between language and reality, as well as the supposedly transparent relationship between history and reality, exposing the subjectivity behind historical discourse. Indeed, postmodernism challenges all discourses with pretensions to absolute truth, or what Jean-Francois Lyotard—another great theorist of postmodernism—calls incredulity toward all master or metanarratives. Fourth, postmodernism is centered on the notion of difference as opposed to that which is universal—it recognizes heterogeneity, distinctions of class, race, gender, and sexual orientation, and deconstructs binary oppositions that schematize human nature (Hutcheon 3–53; Lyotard 34).

The postmodern project of questioning language, reality, history, and limiting dichotomies clearly implies a political commitment on the part of the postmodern author. Consequently, anyone familiar with Roa Bastos's life and work can readily perceive the connections between postmodern art and the writer's *oeuvre*. In the following pages, I will examine how postmodernism evolves throughout the course of Roa Bastos's writing.

THE POETRY

Roa Bastos initiated his literary career as a poet, although there are only a handful of articles written by literary critics on his poetical works. Roa Bastos's first collection of poetry, *El ruiseñor de la aurora* (1940), is essentially an imitation of Spanish Baroque lyric poetry, with the notable influence of Garcilaso and Quevedo (Bordoli Dolci 97; Villar Luis 197). Roa Bastos's subsequent poetry places him within the Paraguayan "Grupo del 40" (Group of the Forties), along with Josefina Plá and Hérib Campos Cervera. Their poetry movement is noted for its character of social protest, and this is the principal element that can be observed in Roa Bastos's subsequent collection, *El naranjal ardiente Nocturno paraguayo 1947–1949* (1960). Written by the author in exile, Bordoli Dolci notes that the poetry of *El naranjal ardiente* is full of nostalgia and sentiment, in addition to its marked tone of social criticism (Bordoli Dolci 97). *El naranjal ardiente* includes several poems written by Roa in Guarani, an important aspect of his work studied by Tracy K. Lewis in "Poetry's Expository Function in Contexts of Linguistic Inequality: the Guarani Verse of Augusto Roa Bastos," included in this volume. Lewis's chapter elucidates the relationship between the lack of expository prose in the corpus of published, written Guarani texts, and the function of denunciation of social evils in Roa Bastos's Guarani poetry. Although it might be a gigantic leap to refer to Roa Bastos's poetry as postmodern, its connection to historical circumstances is an incipient clue to the direction his work will follow in the future. Moreover, "El genesis de los Apapokuva" ("The Genesis of the Apapokuva"; 1971) is a small group of poems (e.g., "El principio," "El primer hombre," "Nacimiento de Kuña," "Castigo de Kuña," and "La destrucción") inspired by Guarani myth, in which Roa Bastos accentuates the oral and performative qualities of his poetry through repetitions, epithets, and Guarani words, in ways that connect it to the postmodern project of questioning the validity of written discourse and illustrating the uneasy relationship between signifier and signified in writing. Finally, Roa Bastos's "Silenciario" continues the line of social protest (in such poems as "Destino" ["Destiny"] and "Serrallo" ["Brothel"]), the nostalgia of exile ("Apátrida" ["Stateless Person"]), and the postmodern preoccupation with writing (for example, "Margen" ["Margin"]), all of which characterized his previous poetry.

THE SCREENPLAYS

Over the years, especially during his exile in Buenos Aires, Roa Bastos worked as a screenplay writer. His screenplays include "*El trueno entre las hojas*" (1955; based on his own short story by that title), "La sangre y la semilla" ("The Blood and The Seed"; 1959), "La sed" ("Thirst", 1960, based on a chapter from his novel *Hijo de hombre*), "Shunko" (1960), "El terrorista" ("The Terrorist"; 1962), "El último piso" ("The Last Floor"; 1962), "La boda" ("The Wedding"; 1963), "Alias Gardelito" (1966), "El señor presidente" ("Mr. President"; 1966), "Castigo al traidor" ("Punishment to the Traitor", 1965; based on Roa Bastos's short story "Encuentro con el traidor"), "Soluna" (1968), "Don Segundo Sombra" ("Mr. Second Shadow"; 1969), "La cosecha" ("The Harvest"; 1970), and "La Madre María" ("Mother Maria"; 1974; [Etcheverry 129–43; Blas Matamoro 91–105). In the chapter "Augusto Roa Bastos and Argentine Film," David William Foster illustrates the profound relationship between Roa Bastos's varied film projects and his commitment to both social protest and the valuation of indigenous cultures. Foster's chapter is an important survey of Roa Bastos's filmography since very little has been written about this aspect of his work.

THE SHORT STORIES

Roa Bastos initiates his published narrative fiction within the short story genre. Although Roa Bastos's first collection of short stories, *El trueno entre las hojas* (1953), is written within the context and techniques of the literary regionalism that characterized Latin American literature during the first half of the twentieth century, the astute reader can already perceive Roa Bastos's postmodern questioning of reality through his use of what is generally referred to as magical realism. Magical realism, like postmodernism, is a poorly defined and widely used term that means different things to different critics. Adalbert Dessau defines it as the popular, mythical vision of the peasants mixed with the narration of historical events (Dessau 351–58). Many of Roa Bastos early stories, notably "Carpincheros" ("Capybara Hunters"), "El ojo de la muerte" ("The Eye of Death"), "La rogativa" ("The Rogation"), "La tumba viva" ("The Living Tomb"), and "El trueno entre las hojas" ("Thunder Among the Leaves") counterpoise seemingly fantastic or mythical interpretations of events to realistic explanations of the same. Some critics, such as Sibylle Fischer, insist that Roa Bastos clearly rejects mythical interpretations of events in *El trueno entre las hojas*, and instead employs myths as purely socio-historical elements that symbolize the plight of the peasants and ultimately reinforce realistic interpretations of occurrences (Fischer 173). Despite Fischer's assertion, there are clearly stories in the collection that do not privilege one interpretation over the other, but instead, in an incipient postmodern fashion, allow the mythical and "realistic" viewpoints to "dialogue" with one another, thus exposing the ultimate subjectivity of reality. For example, in "La rogativa," Felipe Taavy claims that the drought will end when the blue tiger urinates. Indeed, when he brings news of this event to Poilú, it begins to rain in the story, suggesting the possible veracity of the mythical viewpoint. Meanwhile, the townspeople believe that their religious prayers have ended the drought and give thanks to God in the final scene. Finally, there remains the possibility that the drought ends at this particular moment in the story by mere coincidence. The reader is never explicitly offered confirmation of what triggers the event and consequently, what is emphasized in the story is the ultimate subjectivity of reality.

El trueno entre las hojas has sometimes been criticized as political propaganda because many of its stories, such as the one that bears the same title as that of the collection, focus on the division between rich bosses and poor workers. These stories present somewhat stereotyped characters like the purely evil factory owners, Simón Bonaví and Harry Way. However, despite occasional defects of this nature, the stories are without a doubt poetically constructed to present a complex view of Paraguay's social and linguistic reality. The stories, written in Spanish, are peppered with Guarani phrases that depict the importance of bilingualism in Paraguay. Moreover, the complex interplay of Guarani myth and Paraguayan history introduces symbolism and other literary subtleties. A good example of this is the story "Carpincheros." In this text, a German immigrant girl, Gretchen, becomes obsessed with the *carpincheros*, who are men that live on rafts in the water. She refers to these men as "men from the moon," a reference that, at first glance, seems arbitrarily chosen. However, those familiar with Guarani myth discover a symbolic dimension to this part of the story. According to versions of how the sun and the moon came to exist presented in the *Pequeño Decameron Nivaklé* (*Small Decameron Nivaklé*), the sun and the moon were originally two brothers on earth. One brother, Jincucla'ai, became the sun, while the other brother, Jive'cla, became the moon. While the sun is described as selfish and gluttonous, the moon is portrayed as generous, sharing his food with others and illuminating the way at night: "Siempre daba la impresión que tenía deseos de hacer algo diferente. Un hombre solía comentar que Jive'cla no era tacaño, pues repartía las presas de caza que había cobrado entre sus vecinos" (He always gave the impression that he desired to do something different. One man used to comment that Jive'cla was not a cheapskate, since he distributed the prey he hunted among his neighbors; 53).[1] The moon brother is clearly the hero of the Guarani myth, saving his children from the sun brother, who attempts to burn them to death. This mythic connection develops the opposition constructed in both "Carpincheros" and "El trueno entre las hojas" between the *carpincheros*, who are free men on the water, and the factory workers enslaved by the owners, Simón Bonaví and Harry Way. The factory is associated with violence, death, and in "El trueno entre las hojas," a disastrous fire from which the *carpincheros* (termed men on the moon by Gretchen) save the factory workers. Thus, the positive association attributed to the moon in the Guarani myths about the moon and the sun symbolically resurfaces in these texts, and the dramatic rescue from the fire in "El trueno entre las hojas" parallels Jive'cla's salvation of his children from the burning sun by transforming into the moon and cooling them with his frost. In general, this blending of mythical and historical context in *El trueno entre las hojas* may be thought of as a precursor to the postmodern bent of Roa Bastos's posterior fiction.

Roa Bastos's next collection of stories, *El baldío* (1966), written while he was in exile in Buenos Aires, represents a striking shift from the regionalist context of *El trueno entre las hojas*. In *El baldío*, the theme of exile pervades many of the texts, and the principal scenario moves from rural Paraguay to Buenos Aires. Although there are still references to Guarani words and myths, they are radically reduced in comparison to *El trueno entre las hojas*, and the book's themes may be considered more universal in nature. Most critics agree that it is in *El baldío* where the postmodern character of Roa Bastos's fiction becomes evident. Stories such as "Borrador de un informe" ("Draft of a Report") counterpoise different versions of what has occurred. The fact that there are multiple versions questions the concepts of "reality" and "history." In this story, the narrator offers two versions of events in which a blind woman is murdered. He counterpoises his unofficial story, in which he admits responsibility for murdering the woman, and his official report, in which he implicates another character in this crime. Although it is clear to the reader that the official has lied in his report, the story still exposes the ways in which the narration of events is subject to interpretation and falsification. In this book, two chapters focus on postmodernism in *El baldío*. In "Postmodernism and its Signs in 'Juegos nocturnos' by Augusto Roa Bastos," Fernando Burgos analyzes two important stories from the second edition of this collection (first published in Moriencia three years earlier) in terms of the notion of rhizomatic writing developed by Gilles Deleuze and Félix Guatttari and the deconstruction of time suggested by the philosopher Henri Bergson. According to Burgos, the mixture of conscious and subconscious states in the story is indistinguishable, thereby creating a deterritorialized space in which the duration of time is nullified. Time is conceived of as a conglomeration of presents, a subjective interiorization on the part of the individual. Burgos illustrates how this conception of time ties into the story's rhizomatic narrative structure. A rhizome, a term borrowed from botany, is "a rootlike stem under or along the ground, ordinarily in a horizontal position, which usually sends out roots from its lower surface and leafy shoots from its upper surface" (*Webster's* 1556). Burgos discusses how Deleuze and Guattari employ the rhizome as a postmodern figure and then demonstrates how Roa Bastos adopts this figure in his narrative structure of indivisible space and time: "The comprehension of the rhizome as an incessant activity of growth in diverse and uncontrollable directions and in permanent movement not only configures a provocative metaphor for understanding postmodernism, but also an extraordinarily productive space for the exegesis of Roa Bastos's work."[2] Similarly, Fátima Nogueira, in "Rhizomatic Writing in Augusto Roa Bastos's Short Stories," analyzes "Contar un cuento" ("To Tell A Story"), "El y el otro" ("He and the Other"), and "El aserradero" ("The Sawmill")—all from *El baldío*—in terms of the figure of the rhizome. Nogueira focuses on the rhizome as an intratextual figure that establishes relationships between Roa Bastos's short stories and novels, as opposed to a figure descriptive of internal narrative or temporal structure.

Roa Bastos's third and fourth collections of short stories, *Los pies sobre el agua* (1967) and *Madera quemada* (1967) mostly include previously published stories. *Los pies sobre el agua* introduces three new tales: "Niño-Azoté" ("Samanea Tubulosa"), "Nonato" ("Unborn"), and "Ajuste de cuentas" ("Settling Accounts"). The aforementioned chapter by Nogueira also analyzes the postmodern character of the last of these stories. *Madera quemada* presents two new pieces: "Kurupí," which was later reworked and included as a chapter in the rewritten version of *Hijo de hombre* in 1982, and "Bajo el Puente" ("Under the Bridge"). Both "Nonato" and "Bajo el Puente" are subsequently incorporated into Roa Bastos's fifth short story collection, *Moriencia* (1969), and these two stories also constitute important episodes in Roa Bastos's novel, *Contravida* (1994).

Moriencia, like *El trueno entre las hojas*, incorporates a markedly mythical interpretation of reality. Martin Lienhard suggests that the term "intertextuality" should not be limited to the relationship between written texts, but rather should be extended to account for interconnections between written texts and other discourses such as oral legend. Lienhard analyzes *Moriencia* in terms of the traces of Guarani myth within the narration, an effort that establishes the relationship of this collection to *El trueno entre las hojas,* where we already observed such traces within the stories "Carpincheros" and "El trueno entre las hojas." According to Lienhard, the stories that compose *Moriencia* are constructed through an artisanal tradition that denies the creativity of the individual artist. Each of the first five stories of *Moriencia* evolves not toward an ending, but rather toward a beginning. Lienhard cites the example of "Moriencia" ("Slaughter"), the first story in the collection, in which the reader knows from the outset that the protagonist, Chepé Bolívar, is dead, and that the story consists of various contradictory versions that explain how the occurrences surrounding his death began (Lienhard 151). This evolution toward the beginning is also found in "Nonato," where the protagonist, the schoolteacher, devolves from a grown man to the status of unborn child. This regression toward the origins is clearly characteristic of mythological tales. Moreover, elements such as the mortar, the drum, and the canoe, which appear in these stories, are linked to Guarani oral tradition (Lienhard 151–53). According to Lienhard, stories like "Nonato" present the unfolding of a protagonist—Cristaldo, in this case—into two characters: the mother and the unborn child, and this is a sign of "la imposibilidad de reproducer la realidad de los hechos mediante los códigos de la ficción" (the impossibility of reproducing the reality of events through the code of fiction) (Lienhard 156). In other words, once again, the mythic dimension presented in Roa Bastos's texts is not an attempt at providing picturesque details, but is rather a sign of a postmodern vision of reality in which disputing viewpoints are allowed to sound in order to stress the subjectivity of all narratives.

Antología personal (1980) and *Cuentos completos* (2003) also contain only a few new stories. *Antología personal* is the first volume in which Roa Bastos's very first short story, originally published in the journal *Texto Crítico* (*Critical Text;* 1979), appears. It is a tale of a young boy's struggle with writing and his father's attempts to dominate him. In *Cuentos Completos,* there are six stories that never appeared in any of Roa Bastos's short story collections: "La cita" ("The Appointment"), "Chico-Coa" ("Coconut Plantation Boy"), "El Crack" ("Crack"), "Función" ("Performance"), "El país donde los niños no querían nacer" ("The Country Where Children Didn't Want to be Born"), and "Cuando un pájaro entierra sus plumas" ("When a Bird Buries its Feathers"). Of these, the most interesting are the last two, both of which implement the narrative movement and Guarani oral context suggested by Lienhard with regard to *Moriencia*. "El país donde los niños no querían nacer" is a story about a young prince who seeks revenge on the evil emperor who murdered his father. The emperor has the young prince killed, and as a result, in protest, all the children of the country refuse to be born. The population of the country diminishes over time. One day, a young boy, referred to as Nada (which is Adán, or Adam, spelled backward in Spanish), wanders into the country. An old woman narrates to him the history of the country and then sends him off to a garden, where he meets "Ave" (which is Eva, or Eve spelled backward in Spanish). There, Nada kills a serpent while Ave eats an apple from the tree. Thus, these two characters reenact the myth of Adam and Eve and the creation of the world. They briefly signify an opportunity for the world to positively reinvent itself. However, Nada and Ave's repetition of the actions of Adam and Eve causes the sun to disappear and darkness to envelop them. The narration suggests the repetition of the guilt of original sin and thus the repetition of a world in which there will be murderous emperors, such as the one who killed the kind prince at the beginning of the story. Although this tale focuses on Christian, rather than Guarani, myth, it clearly mimics the mythic movement from end to origins and a mythic, cyclical time.

The second story, "Cuando un pájaro entierra sus plumas," incorporates many Guarani mythic beliefs, including the healing power of the hummingbird. In this tale, the protagonist's godmother wishes to construct a protective relic for him using a hummingbird. However, when the boy kills the hummingbird with his slingshot, instead of hunting it with palm leaves, the godmother revives it and sets it free. The relic is never created and, at the story's end, the boy dies while trying to fly through the air like a bird. The story highlights the Guarani mythic belief in the protective value of the hummingbird, and constitutes another example of how mythic beliefs (the boy dies because he lacks the protective hummingbird relic) intersect with other interpretations of reality (the boy dies because no human being can fly).

In summary, although Roa Bastos's short stories were written over a span of fifty years, most of them share a postmodern questioning of man's ability to know reality, whether through a focus on myth versus history or a recounting of different versions of the same occurrence. The interconnectedness of characters and events among many of his narratives reinforce the postmodern rhizomatic model suggested— and aptly analyzed by Burgos and Nogueira in this volume—with regard to the author's short story production.

THE NOVELS

Hijo de hombre

Roa Bastos's first published novel is *Hijo de hombre*, which appeared in 1960 during the early Latin American Boom period. Although Roa Bastos's early works are associated with the boom, he did not receive the international attention granted to other boom writers, such as Gabriel García Márquez and Carlos Fuentes. *Hijo de hombre* is a political novel about the exploitation of the poor Paraguayan peasants and the cycle of revolutions aimed at bringing social justice to them. It is also about the dilemma faced by the Latin American intellectual who attempts to identify with the poor people but cannot fully do so because of his bourgeois origins. The novel is highly symbolic, paradoxically employing biblical elements to express a Marxist message.

If we were to simply consider this first version of *Hijo de hombre*, we would no doubt classify it as a book with modernist tendencies. The metanarrative of a socialist utopia looms behind the revolutionary "ciclos en espiral" ("spiral cycles") of which the narrator speaks toward the end of the novel and which is illustrated by the string of revolutions narrated during the course of the text. However, in 1982, Roa Bastos published a second, revised version of *Hijo de hombre*, in which numerous important changes were incorporated. First, the novelist added a tenth chapter—section nine, titled "Madera quemada"—which was formerly the short story "Kurupí" (which he originally conceived of as a section of *Hijo de hombre*). The addition of this section is significant because it introduces a new narrator, a nun who witnesses the life and death of the political boss, Melitón Isasi. This introduction of a new and different viewpoint on events is one of many elements that point toward the evolution of *Hijo de hombre* into a postmodern text. Elsewhere, I discuss the specific changes that Roa Bastos effects in the new version of *Hijo de hombre*.[3] Some of these alterations clearly relate to the author's postmodern vision. For example, in the 1982 text, Roa Bastos eliminates obvious political messages and symbols, such as a passage in which we are told that Gaspar Mora's guitar playing was "la voz de innumeros y anónimos martirizados" ["the voice of innumerable and anonymous martyred people"] (my translation, 20). The new version also adds several paragraphs to Miguel Vera's diary in the section "Destinados" ("Doomed Men") that question the relationship between written language and its referents and praise the authenticity of oral expression. We are told that writing is a "viejo vicio" (old vice) or "una manera de buscar el lugar que se llevó nuestro lugar" (A way of searching for the place that took our place away; my translation; 236). These passages are similar to those that appear in Roa's subsequent novel, *Yo el Supremo,* and clearly exhibit the postmodernist preoccupation with language as representation.

Similarly, the second version of *Hijo de hombre* amplifies historical themes to suggest the postmodern connection with history and politics. Fiction is not an isolated, self-contained world (although it never was for Roa Bastos, even in the original *Hijo de hombre*), but rather a medium that connects to historical context and questions it. The later version of *Hijo de hombre* subverts the original positive mention of the historical figure Father Fidel Maíz as a brilliant orator by now presenting him as a bloodthirsty prosecutor of conspirators against Francisco Solano López during the Triple Alliance War.[4]

Despite *Hijo de hombre's* modernist vision of socialist utopia, the novel offers a surprisingly postmodern view of women. This aspect of the novel is studied in detail in two of the chapters in this book. First, Katie MacLean's "Gender and the State: Transgression and Integration in *Hijo de hombre*" examines how the initial impression of female characters in the novel as a series of traditional earth mothers or Christian Marys is eventually subverted through the portrayal of working women. She offers the example of María Regalada, who, as keeper of the town cemetery, becomes a custodian of history and rebels against repressive state operations by, among other things, aiding the revolutionary Cristóbal Jara. Thus, María Regalada adopts a traditionally male role within the novel. Moreover, MacLean argues that the character Sor Micaela evolves from the traditional female role of nun to a powerful contributor to the writing of history. Similarly, María Encarnación (Salu'i), originally a prostitute and a nurse, breaks the binary opposition between masculine and feminine by dressing up as a male soldier to participate in Jara's mission of bringing water to the Chaco soldiers. MacLean illustrates how these female characters evolve from typically feminine roles to integration into the structures of male power. This breaking of boundaries between such binary oppositions as male and female is a classic element of postmodern fiction.

My chapter "All Women Are Whores: Prostitution, Female Archetypes, and Feminism in the Works of Augusto Roa Bastos" also focuses on the ways in which Roa Bastos subverts binary oppositions in his construction of female characters. The chapter examines how, despite the fact that many of Roa Bastos's female characters are prostitutes, his texts ultimately do not subscribe to a stereotyped, traditional view of women. Indeed, the chapter examines how Roa Bastos deconstructs the metanarratives of female archetypes as defined by Neumann and

Jung, that polarize women as either virgins or prostitutes, nurturing Sophias or devouring witches. The author's blending of archetypal stereotypes deconstructs traditional dichotomies, as does his employment of the archetype of the sacred prostitute, a figure that combines virgin and prostitute, loving and evil females, in the character of Salu'i.

In summary, *Hijo de hombre* may be seen as a novel that, despite its modernist philosophy, has incipient postmodern elements that prefigure Roa Bastos's later fiction.

Yo el Supremo

In 1974, Roa Bastos published his masterpiece, *Yo el Supremo*, based on the life of the nineteenth-century Paraguayan dictator, José Gaspar Rodríguez de Francia. The novel is constructed as a postmodern dialogue of discourses in the form of the dictator's dictation to his secretary, Policarpo Patiño, his private notebooks (including the logbook), the "Circular Perpetua" (Perpetual Circular; the dictator's narration of Paraguayan history), the notes of a compiler who assembles the dictator's papers, dialogues between the dictator and other characters, the tutorial voice of the dictator's father, the pasquinade that opens the novel and another document titled "Pueyrredon's Draft," footnotes (that frequently cite historical sources), and an unknown handwriting. These different voices intersect in a Bakhtinian dialogic fashion[5] and present a contradictory view of the dictator. He is presented as both an obsessive, power-hungry man who abused the authority given to him by the common people who elected him dictator for life, and as an astute politician, genuinely dedicated to better the plight of the common man, who recognized the imperialist threat of the countries surrounding Paraguay and managed to preserve the nation's independence through its isolation. What distinguishes Roa Bastos's dictator novel from the others published at about the same time by Carpentier and García Márquez is his focus on a specific historical figure (rather than a composite dictator) and his postmodern indictment of the written history or "black legend" surrounding Dr. Francia. While criticizing the dictator's abuse of power, the novel—following a current of revisionist history initiated by the historian Julio César Chaves in the 1960s—nonetheless manages to show some positive aspects of El Supremo's character and dictatorship. The novel, as its final compiler's note states, stresses the ultimate subjectivity of all discourse, due to its necessary dependence on the written word, by indicating to us that the story that should have been narrated by the compiler's notes has not, in fact, been successfully narrated.

It would be impossible to delve into the complexities of *Yo el Supremo* in an introduction of this sort. However, this book fortunately includes two outstanding analyses of the novel that elucidate some of its key postmodern aspects. First, Gustavo Verdesio's "Verba Volant, Scripta Manent: Orality and Literacy in *I the Supreme*" is an excellent example of how *Yo el Supremo* questions the validity of written discourse through traces or residues of orality that appear in the novel. Verdesio explores the use of carnivalization of discourse and Guarani language and myth as forms of subversion of the written word in the novel. In addition, Verdesio examines how the indigenous peoples of Paraguay are viewed in a contradictory, postmodern light by the dictator in *Yo el Supremo*. According to Verdesio, El Supremo simultaneously evinces three attitudes toward the indigenous people: a positive attitude, including a strong belief in the power of Guarani magic, a paternalistic attitude, and a negative one of racist criticism. Once again, this intersection of contradictory viewpoints suggests a postmodern approach rather than a monolithic or monologic vision.

In "Tyranny and Foundation: Appropriations of the Hero and Rereadings of the Nation in Augusto Roa Bastos and Jean-Claude Fignolé," Javier Uriarte illustrates how *Yo el Supremo* and another dictator novel, *Moi, Toussaint Louverture*, by Jean-Claude Fignolé, appropriate and construct the figure of the national hero in ways that are linked to ideological or political projects that deal with the present and with the future of Paraguay and Haiti, respectively. Thus, the postmodern nature of these texts can be immediately apprehended since the political and historical connection is paramount to the postmodern project. Uriarte focuses on how these two novels disturb the clarity of two seminal historical figures: Dr. Francia and Touissant Louverture. He discusses how both novels, by problematizing major historical figures, question such key concepts as foundation, hero, nation, memory, dictatorship, liberation, and history.

In 1992, Roa Bastos published his first new novel in eighteen years, *Vigilia del almirante*, based on the life of Christopher Columbus. In a manner similar to his portrayal of Dr. Francia in *Yo el Supremo*, Roa Bastos engages in a postmodern fashion with the notion of the white and black legends surrounding the historical figure of Columbus, the overlap between history and fiction, and the ultimate subjectivity of both. Indeed, there is a polyphonic technique created through a "profusion of voices" that sound throughout the novel and create a complex, contradictory vision of the protagonist (Rosalía Cornejo-Parriego 453). *Vigilia del almirante* cites directly from Columbus's diary, thus mixing historical and novelistic discourse. The novel also cites from various chroniclers of America, among which figure Fernández de Oviedo, López de Gómara, and Fray Bartolomé de las Casas, all of whom offer differing opinions on the question of whether an "unknown pilot" had landed in America prior to Columbus (Weldt-Basson, "Christopher Columbus," 169–78). Joaquín Juan Penalva signals the connection between the debate presented on this topic in the novel and other sources, such as Juan Manzano Manzano's book *Colón y su secreto*, where the author defends the existence of a dying sailor who indicated to Columbus the path he should take to find America (Penalva 662).

In addition to these sources, Columbus (although never directly referred to as such in the novel) narrates his life and suggests the lack of authenticity of his own writing. He informs us that his son and Bartolomé de las Casas will rewrite his papers, the ones that are ultimately handed down to us through history. In other sections, Columbus admits that he has lied for his own personal advantage and questions the validity of all writing. In addition to Columbus's autobiographical words, the novel includes the narration of a third-person narrator-historiographer on Columbus. The multitude of opinions cited by both Columbus and the narrator ultimately stresses the impossibility of knowing who the man Columbus was and what actions he truly performed. Some critics have also suggested the identification between the narrator Columbus and Roa Bastos himself (Penalva 664; Weldt-Basson, "Christopher Columbus," 171). The narrator frequently speaks with an anachronistic voice that betrays the writer's knowledge and also many of his key preoccupations. This merging of the author with his cultural product is another postmodern characteristic that can be observed in Columbus's constant declarations about the inadequacy of writing, as well as references to what would constitute future events for Columbus, such as the existence of AIDS or the works of Juan Rulfo. *Vigilia del almirante* is one of many contemporary Latin American novels that center around Columbus, an essential figure in Latin American history.

EL FISCAL

In 1993, Roa Bastos published *El fiscal*, the final volume of what he has called his trilogy on the "monotheism of power." *Hijo de hombre* and *Yo el Supremo* are the first two books of this trilogy. An earlier version of *El fiscal*, written before the overthrow of the Stroessner dictatorship in 1989, was destroyed by the author and then rewritten a few years later. *El fiscal* is a novel that defies categorization. On the one hand, one might consider it a novel of dictatorship, since it centers on the protagonist's attempt to assassinate the Paraguayan dictator, Alfredo Stroessner, and delineates the atrocities of the Stroessner government (1954–89). On the other hand, the novel presents a complex reflection on the historical events surrounding the figure of the nineteenth-century Paraguayan president, Francisco Solano López, and the disastrous War of the Triple Alliance that Paraguay waged against Argentina, Brazil, and Uruguay. In a postmodern vein, the novel reexamines the contradictory figure of Solano López. He is simultaneously portrayed as an obsessed dictator who needlessly led his people to certain death in a suicidal war and then fled in defeat, and a self-sacrificing, Christlike hero who stood by his country to the end and was crucified by the Brazilians.

This second vision of López, although perhaps just a nationalist myth (see Guerrero's chapter in this volume), leads us to a third major theme in the novel: that of the double, a concept that intersects with postmodernism in a number of ways. The protagonist, Félix Moral, is a Paraguayan exile living in France (similar to Roa Bastos himself, with all the autobiographical overtones this implies), who determines that the defining act of his life, the one that will give meaning to his existence, will be to assassinate Stroessner and thus free the Paraguayan people from his tyranny. Following Rainer Maria Rilke's concept of "a death of one's own" (that every person should have a death that is in concordance with how he or she lived his or her particular life), Félix returns to Paraguay during an international congress, is apprehended and tortured, and finally shot while attempting to escape. His sacrifice and suffering for the good of his fellow man has Christlike overtones and suggests a parallel with the imagined crucifixion of López at Cerro-Corá.

What makes Roa Bastos's portrayal of Moral particularly compelling is the subtle ways in which he offers the reader two conflicting versions of Moral's fate. On the one hand, Moral, in a letter written to his partner Jimena, explains that he attended the first session of the international congress on September 28 and actually managed to shake the dictator's hand, injecting the poison contained in the ring he was wearing on his finger. On the other hand, the letter from his lover Jimena to Félix's mother after his death states the Félix attended the first two sessions of the congress on the first and second of September, and then disappeared on the third. The text never clarifies for the reader the dates and circumstances surrounding Félix's arrest. In a postmodern fashion, the novel allows distinct versions to contradict one another, exposing the subjectivity of history and the perhaps impossible task of unearthing an absolute truth.

The theme of the double also resurfaces in the novel's portrayal of the Argentine painter, Cándido López, who depicted scenes from the Triple Alliance War. The narrator speaks of two Cándido Lópezes, a fictitious Paraguayan painter (who depicts the Paraguayan point of view) and the historical Argentine figure, whose paintings are housed in the museum in Buenos Aires and present the perspective of an Argentine soldier.

In "All Women Are Whores: Prostitution, Female Archetypes and Feminism in the Works of Augusto Roa Bastos," I also explore how this theme of the double extends to the novel's female characters, notably Leda Kautner (who is also known as Paula Becker, a love interest of the aforementioned German poet Rilke) and the historical characters Madame Lynch and Pancha Garmendia. I show how the proliferation of doubles highlights contradictory and contrasting personality traits that deconstruct stereotyped, traditional archetypes of women and illustrate their complex, postmodern nature. Similarly, in "Rewriting in Roa Bastos's Late Fiction: 'El ojo de la luna,' *El Fiscal*, and *Los conjurados del Quilombo del Gran Chaco*," Jorge Carlos Guerrero examines several postmodern traits in *El fiscal*. The chapter centers on the relationship between a short story titled "El ojo de la luna," published by Roa Bastos in *Cuadernos Hispanoamericanos* in 1991, sections of *El fiscal* relating to the same topics dealt with in the story, and two sections of *Los conjurados del Quilombo del Gran Chaco*. *Los conjurados* is a collaborative text coauthored by Roa Bastos along with authors from Argentina, Brazil, and Uruguay, and focuses on examining the Triple Alliance War from a transcultural and integrative political perspective, as opposed to a traditional nationalist approach. Guerrero emphasizes how *El fiscal* treats the historical source of Sir Richard Burton's *Letters from the Battle-fields of Paraguay* (a nineteenth-century text focused on the Triple Alliance War) with postmodern irony, and he also delves into how the novel treats Moral's tortured death as useless martyrdom, thus representing the crisis of utopia and the impossibility of its achievement because of the complexity of both historical processes and human actions. Moreover, Guerrero's analysis of *Los conjurados*, a hybrid text that combines history and fiction—and one that most closely approximates the short story genre without neatly fitting into any literary category—also illustrates the postmodern interplay of distinct genres and disciplines.

CONTRAVIDA

In 1994, Roa Bastos published *Contravida*, a novel that bears an intratextual relationship to many of his previous works. *Contravida* includes references to Pirulí from the story by the same name and Solano Rojas from "El trueno entre las hojas" (both from Roa Bastos's first collection of short stories); Cristóbal Jara from *Hijo de hombre*; Gaspar Cristaldo from "Nonato" and "Bajo el Puente" in the collection *Moriencia*; and Pedro Alvarenga from *El fiscal*, among others. This "reworking" of Roa Bastos's previous fiction has been interpreted both positively (Pacheco 2001) and negatively (Albonico 1996) by different critics.[6] The difficulties of reading postmodern fiction, with all its inherent ambiguities, colors the reception of this complex text. A careful reading of *Contravida* reveals the same technique of simultaneously positing two or more distinct versions of events, whose ultimate "truth" or "reality" is never confirmed. In *Contravida*, an unnamed protagonist, victim of torture and prison under the Stroessner dictatorship, flees from jail. The novel concurrently develops two trips on the part of the protagonist: Andreas Bolander refers to these as an interior trip and an exterior one. According to Bolander, the train trip that the protagonist realizes to his birthplace is a journey that evolves in time, while the remembrances of the protagonist's childhood is an inner journey that evolves in the magical space of Manorá (Bolander 348–49). Indeed, *Contravida* offers two possible denouements for the protagonist. First, there are indices that suggest that the character never actually boards the train, but rather dies from a fever while lying unconscious in a pit prior to the narrated train ride. The memories of his youth and Manorá, the magical town within his hometown, Iturbe, may be unconsciously experienced while he lies dying in the pit. Second, the narrator recounts his train trip to Manorá and his ultimate consumption in flames in the tarumá tree. Elsewhere, I have shown how through a series of identifications with other revolutionary characters such as Cristóbal Jara and Pedro Alvarenga, the protagonist of *Contravida* is converted into the archetype of the revolutionary hero, whose death in the burning tree, in a manner similar to the Egyptian myth of the Phoenix, implies an eternal rebirth or return of this figure throughout Paraguayan history.[7] *Contravida* is undoubtedly a highly symbolic text that opens itself up to multiple interpretations. It is also intimately connected to Roa Bastos's last novel, *Madama Sui*, where the protagonist is similarly constructed as an archetype of the exploited Paraguayan woman.

MADAMA SUI

Madama Sui was published in 1995 and has received very little critical attention. In the preface to the book, Roa Bastos asserts that the novel is historical, focusing on one of Stroessner's favorite prostitutes. Although it is impossible to corroborate the veracity of this statement, the significance of the novel's construction is more intimately connected to its symbolic value than its potential historical referentiality. The writer constructs Madama Sui as an archetype of the exploited, Paraguayan female, who, like the archetypal protagonist of *Contravida*, meets a similar death by flames in the tarumá tree (Weldt-Basson, "Augusto Roa Bastos's *Contravida*, 100–101). The novel traces the life of the courtesan who is ostracized by society and pines for her childhood sweetheart. There are many clues that suggest that this sweetheart is in fact the protagonist of *Contravida*, who is also a revolutionary against Stroessner in the novel *Madama Sui*, and whose life, as we have seen, is symbolic of the life of every revolutionary against dictatorship. Blake Seana Locklin takes this interpretation one step further, suggesting that Sui is a symbol not only of the exploited Paraguayan woman, but of the Paraguayan nation in general, delineating an interesting connection between sexuality and politics in the novel (Locklin 123–24).

Madama Sui is the only female protagonist in Roa Bastos's novels, and her status as prostitute is the culmination of portrayals of an array of minor characters who are also prostitutes throughout Roa Bastos *oeuvre*. As previously mentioned, in "All Women Are Whores: Prostitution, Female Archetypes and Feminism in the Works of Augusto Roa Bastos," included in this volume, I examine this recurrence of women portrayed as prostitutes in Roa Bastos's fiction to show that despite the initial impression that the author is relying on the conventional binary division of women into "virgins" and "prostitutes," he actually subverts monolithic stereotypes of this nature and constructs both a feminist and postmodern view of women as both complex and ever-changing.

There are various other aspects to Roa Bastos's *oeuvre* that we are unable to cover in this introduction: his theater production, of which, with the exception of his play *Yo el Supremo*, it is almost impossible to obtain copies, and his numerous essays on Paraguayan and Latin American literature and culture, which are so extensive as to perhaps merit a separate book. However, in the following pages, the nine chapters written in tribute to the late Paraguayan writer offer the latest and most significant research on the writer's postmodern production in homage to the late author.

NOTES

1. Chase Sardi 53; the translation is mine.
2. See Fernando Burgos's article in this volume.
3. See Weldt-Basson, "A Genetic Approach."
4. See Ibid. 142–43, and Weldt-Basson, "Augusto Roa Bastos's Trilogy" 345.
5. See Weldt-Basson, *Augusto Roa Bastos's I The Supreme.*
6. See Pacheco, "Autobiografía" and Albónico, "*Contravida* de Augusto Roa Bastos."
7. See Weldt-Basson, "Augusto Roa Bastos's *Contravida.*"

WORKS CITED

Albónico, Aldo. "*Contravida*, de Augusto Roa Bastos, o el macrotesto rebajado a cajón de sastre." *Rassegna Iberistica* 57 (1996): 27–35. Print.

"Augusto Roa Bastos," Centro Virtual Cervantes. http://cvc.cervantes.es/actcult/roa/bibliografia01.htm. Web.

Bach, Caleb. "Augusto Roa Bastos: La realidad superada." http://www.ronanistik.uni-mainz.de/hisp/roa/La_realidad_superada.htm. Web.

Barrera, Trinidad. "Augusto Roa Bastos: la ejemplaridad de la escritura." *Augusto Roa Bastos: Premio "Miguel de Cervantes" 1989.* Barcelona: Anthropos, 1990. 19–37. Print. Bolander, Andreas. "Una lectura de *Contravida*, de Roa Bastos." *Alba de América: Revista Literaria* 23.43–44 (2004): 347–61. Print.

Bordoli Dolci, Ramón. "La poesía social de Augusto Roa Bastos." *Cuadernos Hispanoamericanos* 493–94 (1991): 95–100. Print.

Chase Sardi, Miugel, ed. *Pequeño Decameron Nivaclé.* Asunción: Ediciones NAPA, 1981. Print.

Cornejo-Parriego, Rosalía. "De escribas y palimpsestos: *Vigilia del Almirante*, de Augusto Roa Bastos." *Revista Canadiense de Estudios Hispánicos* 20.3 (1996): 449–62. Print.

Dessau, Adalbert. "Realismo mágico y nueva novela latinoamericana: consideraciones metodológicas e históricas." *Actas del simposio internacional de estudios hispánicos, Budapest, 18-19 de agosto de 1976.* Ed. Matyas Horanyi. Budapest: Akad. Kiado, 1978. 351–58. Print.

Fischer, Sibylle. "El trueno entre las hojas: Cultura popular y ficción o la arquelogía de lo real." *Cuadernos Hispanoamericanos* 494–94 (1991): 159–75. Print.

Galeano, Eduardo. "Su voz cantó como ninguna el desgarramiento del Paraguay." http://www.lajiribilla.com.cu/2005/n207_04/207_31.html. Web.

Gamarra Etcheverry, Hugo. "Le cinéma m'a fait naitre comme écrivain: Augusto Roa Bastos homme de cinéma." *Cinémas d'Amérique Latine* 14 (2006): 129–43. Print.

Hutcheon, Linda. *A Poetics of Postmodernism: History, Theory, Fiction*. New York: Routledge, 1988. Print.

Lienhard, Martin. "Una intertextualidad 'indoamericana' y *Moriencia*, de Augusto Roa Bastos." *Revista Iberoamericana* 50.127 (1984): 505–23. Print.

Locklin, Blake Siena. "Un país seductor y combativo: Japan as Paraguayan Paradise in *Madama Sui*." *Chasqui: Revista de Literatura Latinoamericana* 33.2 (2004): 123–37. Print.

Martín, Sabas. "Yo, Roa Bastos." *Cuadernos Hispanoamericanos* 493–94 (1991): 129–35. Print.

Matamoro, Blas. "Augusto Roa Bastos, guionista." *Cuadernos Hispanoamericanos* 493–94 (1991): 91–105. Print.

Pacheco, Carlos. "Autobiografía, intertextualidad y metaficción en *Contravida*, de Augusto Roa Bastos." *Hispanic Research Journal: Iberian and Latin American Studies* 2.3 (2001): 245–51. Print.

Penalva, Joaquín Juan. "Entre la realidad de la fábula y la fábula de la historia: *Vigilia del almirante* y la novelibridación del descubrimiento." *Río de la Plata: Culturas* 29–30 (2004): 659–71.

Riva, Milda. "Bio-bibliografía de Augusto Roa Bastos." *Cuadernos Hispanoamericanos* 493–94 (1991): 330–69. Print.

Roa Bastos, Augusto. *Metaforismos*. Buenos Aires: Seix Barral, 1996. Print.

Villar Luis, Manuel. "Los hombres: Un soneto de Augusto Roa Bastos." *Las voces del Karaí: Estudios sobre Augusto Roa Bastos*. Ed. Fernando Burgos. Madrid: Edelsa-Edi 6, viii, 1988. 197–203. Print.

Webster's New Universal Unabridged Dictionary. 2nd ed. New York: Simon and Schuster, 1979. Print.

Weldt-Basson, Helene C. "Augusto Roa Bastos's *Contravida* and *Madama Sui*: An Archetypal Interpretation." *Confluencia* 23.1 (2007): 93–106. Print.

———. *Augusto Roa Bastos's I The Supreme: A Dialogic Perspective*. Columbia: University of Missouri Press, 1993. Print.

———. "Augusto Roa Bastos's Trilogy as Postmodern Practice." *Studies in Twentieth Century Literature* 22.2 (1998): 335–55. Print.

———. "Christopher Columbus as Postmodern Construct in Carpentier's *El arpa y la sombra* and Roa Bastos's *Vigilia del almirante*." *Hispanic Journal* 18.1 (1997): 169–78. Print.

———. "A Genetic Approach to Augusto Roa Bastos's *Hijo de hombre*." *Confluencia* 11.1 (1995): 134–47. Print.

Chapter 2

Poetry's Expository Function in Contexts of Linguistic Inequality

The Guarani Verse of Augusto Roa Bastos

Tracy K. Lewis

Browsing in a bookstore some years ago in Asunción, Paraguay, I was struck by two facts: (1) the relative lack of materials in Guarani, which is spoken by the majority of the country's people, and (2) the even greater paucity of expository prose material available in that language. Given the problematical status to which non-European tongues are often confined, even where they are the dominant means of oral communication, the first observation in not surprising. The second, on the other hand, merits thinking about. My trip to the bookstore produced Guarani dictionaries and grammars, collections of Guarani folklore, some plays, and various volumes of poetry, but almost no nonfictional prose. Historical and philosophical treatises, political tracts, "how-to" books for the home, technical manuals: all these were the province of Spanish. At first, this seemed an unfortunate—but not altogether shocking—consequence of "the way things are." As time has gone on, however, I am persuaded that it bears profound implications, not only for Paraguay, but also—speaking now in the generic sense—for vast portions of the planet we inhabit. Even in countries where many can read and write the native tongue, large populations find themselves subject to a second and equally disturbing form of illiteracy—the simple unavailability of certain significant forms of written discourse.[1] The catalogue of outcomes of this situation is lengthy and tragic: ongoing dependence on "developed" societies as dispensers of the written word, relegation of "things native" to the margins of life in the modern world, academic discouragement of those who would school themselves in the only vernacular they understand well, psychological damage to the young people so affected, and so on.

My objective in this chapter is not, of course, to exhaustively deal with this immense subject, but rather to focus on a single phenomenon arising from it: the role of poetry as a substitute for certain types of expository prose in the written literature of non-European languages. Particularly in languages where a body of historical and philosophical prose has not been allowed to develop, the bard steps in as a sort of surrogate. Though I hope to present ideas that are applicable in many areas of the world, my immediate reference will be to the Guarani poetry of Paraguay's Augusto Roa Bastos. Generally accepted as one of the great Latin American authors of the twentieth century, Roa chose, early in his career, to write in Spanish. He did, however, produce a small cluster of poems in Guarani that bear his genius quite as much as his production in Spanish and that amply illustrate the "expository" function alluded to above. As such—and I am sure Roa would not have wanted it this way—these poems are part of a Guarani poetic literature that exists in the absence of expository prose in that language—a poetic literature that unconsciously coexists with the notion that non-European languages are inadequate to express certain complexities of the modern world.[2] Roa and other Guarani-language poets, one may say, are unwilling participants in, and victims of, a myth of inadequacy that is so widespread in the former colonies of Europe as to constitute an ideology of linguistic inequity. What is so often lacking in these contexts is not a native tongue of great expository power, but rather the effort on the part of writers, educators, and bureaucrats to recognize and promote that power. My treatment of Roa's verse is one of loving admiration, but I also hope to show how it poeticizes a range of historical realities that could, and should, also be expressed in the analytical manner of prose.

From the outset, an important clarification has to be made: we are *not* in any sense "blaming" Roa and other poets for this state of affairs. As we shall show, poetry in the world of Guarani writing performs some of the tasks of prose, but what has starved the latter's growth is the overall system of "linguistic apartheid"[3] that prevails in Paraguay. Indeed, by thus confining the unique expressive features of Guarani to the Soweto of a single genre, this apartheid of the word impoverishes "winners" and "losers" alike and deprives the broader society of the visions it leaves unarticulated. Poetry and prose are distinct modes, as we shall confirm, but, under normal circumstances, they should enrich each other. We can only wonder what a vibrant expository prose tradition in Guarani would look like if invigorated by the sort of expressive power found in Roa Bastos' Guarani verse, and what a similar unleashing of ghettoized perspectives around the globe would do for world culture.

An approach to poetry from the perspective of prose, however, requires some preliminary observations about the latter. I am, of course, not the first person to note the dearth of prose in Guarani. In fact, it was quite heartening to find myself preceded in this by no less than Padre Antonio Guasch, one of the world's foremost Guarani grammarians and lexicographers. (I eagerly gobbled up everything that bore his name in my bookstore jaunt.) Prefacing the brief anthology found at the end of his standard grammar *El idioma guarani*, he writes:

> Dos partes contiene nuestra colección: prosa y verso. El verso es mercancía muy abundante en nuestros días. Un muchacho de trece años ya se siente inspirado. Abundan por doquier las revistas repletas de versos.
>
> En cambio, la prosa ya es harina de otro costal. Anda muy escasa en el mercado. En guarani moderno poca prosa se ha escrito. Razón para agradecer más y más la colaboración de los noveles autores que rompen brecha . . .
>
> El *Catecismo bilingüe*, que hace poco vio la luz, y las lucubraciones que van a continuación, son los primeros jalones que el paraguayo podrá saborear. (Guasch, *El idioma guarani*, 333)

Our anthology consists of two parts: prose and verse. Verse is common currency in the Guarani-speaking world these days. Even thirteen-year-olds are inspired to try their hand, and magazines full of poems abound.

Prose, however, is another matter in Guarani. Very little of it is to be found in the market, and little has been written in modern Guarani. All the more reason to thank the pioneering efforts of new writers.

The recently published Bilingual Catechism, and the pieces which follow in this anthology, are the first landmarks of Guarani prose the average Paraguayan reader will be able to savor (my translation).

Guasch's statement is solid evidence for the concepts that begin this chapter. I note that he cites a religious work (of which, incidentally, he is the author) as one of the few prose pieces available in Guarani. In other words, when Father Guasch says that little prose is written in Guarani, in that statement, he is including what I may refer to as "sacred" or "scriptural" prose. Remove this category, and one is left with the stark void alluded to in the opening paragraph.[4]

As stated earlier, poetry (and here we include song) has filled the vacuum left by a stunted expository tradition, and has, in some sense, assumed its role. To say this, of course, calls for precision in our definition of these types of written discourse. The common understanding of expository prose is that it is nonfictional and that it explains its subject matter step by step. What is said less frequently is that "step by step" means "linear": exposition is mostly a linear process in which each element primarily derives from the one that preceded it. We note the following typical example, taken from an ecology textbook:

> Between the seas and the continents lie a band of diverse ecosystems that are not just transition zones but have ecological characteristics of their own. Whereas physical factors such as salinity and temperature are much more variable near shore than in the sea itself, food conditions are so much better that the region is packed with life . . . A rocky shore, a sand beach, an intertidal mud flat, and a tidal estuary dominated by salt marshes [constitute] four kinds of marine inshore ecosystems. The word "estuary" refers to a river mouth or coastal bay where the salinity is intermediate between the sea and fresh water, and where tidal action is an important physical regulator. (Odum 114)

The sentences grow in linear fashion from their predecessors, and though new information is added at each step, one finds little suggestion of worlds beyond the subject being developed. Those sorts of resonance, on the other hand, those echoes that break the headlong linear rush of exposition, are precisely the stuff of poetry. That same coastal ecosystem passes from the filter of the poet's mind more like a constellation of impressions than a concatenation of concepts, more like swirling foam than water jetting from a hose:

> The ebb slips from the rock, the sunken
> Tide-rocks lift streaming shoulders
> Out of the slack, the slow west
> Sombering its torch . . .
> Over the dark mountain, . . .
> Down the long dark valley along the shrunken river,
> Returns the splendor without rays. (Jeffers 6)

Thus did one poet render dusk on the California coast, filling, tidelike, the hollows of discourse with a rich suggestive eddying of metaphor and alliteration.

Of course, everyone knows that poetry and expository prose are vastly different, and the definitions I have offered here are nothing new. My comparison of a poem and a piece of textbook prose seems sophomoric, or even ludicrous, until one recalls that this very difference becomes a barrier that needlessly impoverishes written expression in so many corners of the world. The two excerpts just quoted are evidence that English, like most European languages, is privileged with a solid tradition in both genres, a solid sense that both are possible within the ample confines of the language. So solid, in fact, is this truth of our English-speaking universe that we find it difficult to contemplate the linguistic reality of billions who must learn an alien language merely to read the history of their own country, or, failing that, must seek that history hidden in the genre that is available to them, namely poetry.

Returning to the example of Guarani, I offer the case of Augusto Roa Bastos. As I said earlier, most of Roa's production—primarily novels and short stories—is in Spanish, but he did publish a handful of excellent poems in Guarani. These, along with some of his other writings, grew out of four related phenomena: (1) Paraguay's traditional concentration of land and rural wealth in the hands of a few oligarchs, (2) the brief but devastating 1947 civil war that resulted in part from this situation, (3) the subsequent growth of a large community of expatriate Paraguayans in Argentina and elsewhere, and (4) the ongoing involvement of these exiles in the political life of the country of their birth.[5] It should be noticed that I have deliberately presented these concepts in the linear manner of expository prose; the first leads to the second, which leads to the third, which produces the fourth. Taken together, that is, they constitute precisely the sort of writing one searches in vain for in Guarani.

Observe, however, the way the poetry tries to bear some of the burden of this absent tradition, the way it weaves the fragments of a line of exposition into its characteristic ferment of image and echo. The following two citations help illustrate the point:

(from "Ñemomarandu," "Self-Knowledge"[6])

(Ohecha . . . vaekue ikerape yvyjara poguasu)	(What the landowner saw . . . in his sleep)
. . . Ore roha'arôta nde kera rembe'ype kirirîhapemi . . .	. . . We'll just wait here quietly on the threshold of your sleep . . .
. . . Nde mandu'ake orerehe, ko'êrô, ko'êroitentema voi jajohecha jevyta	. . . Remember us, for when day breaks we'll see each other again

ñambojoja jevy ñande reko . . . ,	to equalize our lives . . . ,
kara.[7] (Roa 85–87)	sir.[8]

(and from "Tetâ ambue guive," "From a Far Country")

. . . Ñande retã . . .	. . . Our country . . .
iñipytûmba . . .	tapers now to darkness . . .
. . . Jaipovâne ipore'y,	. . . Let us weave the fragile thread
topa ñande rekove	which holds us to its absent presence; better
jaiko rangue tyre'y.[9] (Roa 79–80)	to end life than to live it as orphans.[10]

Though the full text of the poems cannot be given here, the portions cited perhaps suffice to show the historical phenomena embedded in Roa's original creation: rapacious landlords, restless rural masses dislodged from their land, the seeds and the aftermath of civil war, exiles still engaged in the suffering of their homeland, still waiting to return. These notions, however, come to us in the manner peculiar to poetry, with all the advantages and disadvantages that this implies. The Guarani language does splendidly lend itself to poetic expression. Its ability, unlike Spanish, to use nouns adjectivally creates powerful images, such as *tuguy ryakuâ*—"blood spoor"—and *angapy pu rendy*—"spirit-interior sound light," that is, "radiance sounding from the inner soul." And its distinction, typical of Native American languages, between a "we" that includes the addressee and a "we" that excludes him or her, makes for interesting dialogical nuances. The outraged servant in "Ñemomarandu" tells of his people's plight using the latter form, that is, excluding the landlord to whom he speaks, but he switches to the inclusive form at the poem's apocalyptic end, as if to say, "We all shall share one Earth." However, these and other characteristics of Guarani could also be applied to prose. Roa's vision of a cruel time in the life of his country is a stunning and necessary part of the literature, but this in no way justifies the linguistic context in which these poems came about, the withering of the expository genre and near eclipse of the possibility of linear written analysis in one's own tongue.

To be sure, the use of poetry in lieu of prose is an ancient phenomenon. My point, therefore, is not that this situation is unique to Guarani, but rather that it has occurred in Guarani, and probably many other non-European languages, for the reasons and with the effects outlined here. To all of this, one could object that the problem has naturally resulted from cultural and linguistic differences; that Europeans, at least since the Renaissance, have favored linear analytical thinking whereas many other peoples have not; that

Guarani and other native languages are latecomers to the business of writing; that these languages have an insufficient vocabulary to deal with many of the subjects of expository prose; and so forth. There is some small truth in these arguments, but, to my mind, they neither excuse nor fully explain the denial of a people's need to understand their world in a written language that is theirs. Father Guasch's hefty dictionary is ample evidence of Guarani's capacity to generate neologisms of all kinds, and the same adaptability can be demonstrated for any number of "third world" tongues. The problem, then, is not the fitness of Guarani and similarly repressed languages, but a lack of faith in the flourishing of their unrepressed word. What is required is the will to transcend an intellectual and political climate, and to accept that when Roa Bastos uses a concept like *pore'y*[11], the word stretches the capacity of "dominant" languages to receive it, and endows our global intellect with a new and powerful intuition, "absent presence," valid for any genre, and emblematic of much in our human condition. One can only speculate on the difference it would make if this small example were allowed to proliferate in the broad discourse of our species.

NOTES

1 David Crystal's valuable book *Language Death* gives a thorough overview of the problem of threatened and dying languages, and actually sounds an optimistic note with respect to Guarani (135). An aspect he appears not to notice, however, regarding Guarani or any other language, is the problem of literary genres detailed in this chapter.

2 Even the most passionate advocates of native-language rights often lapse into false notions of linguistic "superiority" and "inferiority," pigeonholing languages in categories of presumed suitability. Witness the case of Rafael Barrett, whose words of a century ago still express a sentiment widely held today: "Que el castellano se aplique mejor a las relaciones de la cultura moderna . . . , ¿quién lo duda? Pero, ¿no se aplicará mejor el guarani a las relaciones individuales, estéticas, religiosas, de esta raza y de esta tierra? Sin duda también." (from Barrett's *El dolor paraguayo*, quoted in Romero 13)

   We should add, however, that important elements of the Guarani-speaking intelligentsia defend their language's ability to function in every realm of discourse. Observe, for instance the words of Lino Trinidad Sanabria: "Jaikuaava'erã, ñane ñe'e guaranime ikatuha ja'e oimeháichagua temiandu; oguerekoiteha oimeraeva ambue ñe'e oguerekóva, ha michi michi, jaiko pypukuramo ipype, jahecha kuaáta ñaína ha'eveha ambue ñe'egui, oguerekopavégui tekoteveva ñambopepo haguã akãho ha apytu'u poty" (We must know that our language Guarani can express any feeling and has everything that other languages have. Indeed, as little by little we enter its depths, we will see that it is more apt than other tongues in giving wing to the flowers of our imagination and our intellect; Sanabria 85; translation mine).

3 The term has become a rallying cry of Paraguayan *campesino* organizations protesting the discrimination they, and their language, continue to suffer. For further analysis, see Susy Delgado's interview with the German scholar Wolf Lustig in the journal *Takuapu*.

4 In the *Takuapu* interview, Wolf Lustig comes close to the terminology of our essay when he speaks of his planned translation of an eighteenth-century medical manual written in Guarani: "Aunque parezca ser un tema histórico sin repercusión inmediata está relacionado con el problema actual de la diglosia: Ese hallazgo es la prueba de que el guarani se ha usado y se puede usar para expresar complicados contenidos científicos, siendo uno de los textos pragmáticos (no literarios) más amplios en lengua guarani, si exceptuamos los escritos teológicos de la misma época jesuítica. (Delgado, *Takuapu* 15)

5 As is well known, Roa was himself an anguished participant in this page in Paraguayan history, having been compelled into exile in Argentina by the events of the 1947 war.

6 The rendering of *ñemomarandu* as "self-knowledge" is admittedly a departure, since the word normally has a dictionary meaning of "notification" or "informing." I felt this was justified, given the context of the poem, and given the literal morphology of the word: *ñe* (reflexive) + *mo* (causative) + *marandu* ("informed"), that is, "making oneself informed."

7 Punctuation and orthography have been left exactly as in the original, despite differences with the conventions of current Guarani writing.

8 The translation is a free one, in which I have sacrificed literal correspondence of words for a more cogent overall interpretation.

9 Again, the text is left exactly as in the original.

10 As in the previous translation, I have taken necessary liberties with literal meaning. My thanks, in this instance, to Rubén Bareiro Saguier and Teresa Méndez-Faith for their help with certain images and phrases.

11 The word has a normal lexical equivalence of "absence" or "absent," and derives literally from the elements *pore*, "footprint," and *'y*, "not." The one who is absent is the one who is "without footprint." In my opinion, however, both contemporary Guarani sources and the long lineage of Guarani mythic thought call for the complex, seemingly contradictory rendering "absent presence." An absence keenly felt is indeed a presence, and confirms what has been a cornerstone of Guarani cosmology since long before the Spanish conquest: the coexistence of opposites in a single entity. For additional background, see my article "El fundamento guarani de la poesía de Augusto Roa Bastos," as well as the Guarani poetry of writers such as Susy Delgado and Miguelángel Meza.

Works Cited

Bareiro Saguier, Rubén. Telephone conversation. March 22, 1988.

Barrett, Rafael. *El dolor paraguayo.* Ed. Miguel Ángel Fernández. Prol. Augusto Roa Bastos. Caracas: Biblioteca Ayacucho, 1978. (A relatively recent edition; work was originally published in 1911.) Print.

Crystal, David. *Language Death.* Cambridge, England: Cambridge University Press, 2002. Print.

Delgado, Susy. *Ayvy membyre/Hijo de aquel verbo/Offspring of the Distant Word.* Trans. Susan Nash Smith. Asunción: Arandurã, 2003. Print.

———. "Wolf Lustig: 'En el Paraguay no se respetan los derechos lingüísticos de la mayoría" (interview). *Takuapu* 3.1 (June 2007), 14–17. Print.

Fundación Yvy Marâe'õ. "Guarani: To the Swedish Assembly of Finland." E-mail forwarded to the author by Betsy Partyka. September 30, 2007. Print.

Guasch, Antonio. *El idioma guarani: gramática y antología de prosa y verso.* Asunción: Ediciones Loyola, 1983. Print.

———. *Diccionario castellano-guarani, guarani-castellano.* Asunción: Centro de Estudios Paraguayos Antonio Guasch, 1998. Print.

Jeffers, Robinson. *Selected Poems.* New York: Vintage Books, 1965. Print.

Lewis, Tracy K. "El fundamento guarani de la poesía de Augusto Roa Bastos." *Takuapu,* mayo 2005, 8–9. Print.

Méndez-Faith, Teresa. Personal conversation. March 1988. Print.

Meza, Miguelángel. *Ita ha'eñoso/Ya no está sola la piedra.* Asunción: Alcándara Editora, 1985. Print.

Odum, Eugene. *Ecology.* New York: Holt, Rinehart and Winston, 1963. Print.

Okaraygua Ñemongu'e Paraguáipe-Movimiento Campesino Paraguayo. "Paraguái: Chokokue Atykuéra-Organizaciones Campesinas." E-mail forwarded to the author by Betsy Partyka, March 30, 2007. Print.

Roa Bastos, Augusto. *El naranjal ardiente (Nocturno paraguayo) 1947–1949.* Asunción: Alcándara Editora, 1983. Print.

Romero, Roberto. "El idioma guarani en el proceso de la cultura paraguaya." *Ñande reko,* 3 (1986): 9–15. Print.

Sanabria, Lino Trinidad. *Taruma poty.* Asunción: Biblioteca Paraguaya de Antropología, 1995. Print.

C H A P T E R   3

Augusto Roa Bastos and Argentine Film

David William Foster

A paradigm shift in the Argentine film industry occurred in 1956.[1] In that year, the director, actor, and film writer Armando Bo (1914–81) introduced his lover, Isabel Sarli (1935), to the Argentine public.[2] Correctly judging that the Argentine filmgoing public was ready for a sexpot in the image of Bridgette Bardot and various American models, Bo (who himself acted in more than fifty potboilers) went on to work with Sarli in twenty films between 1956 and 1979. After Bo's death, Sarli (who is still alive), except for some minor roles, never filmed again. Armando Bo had a perfect formula: Sarli's body was voluptuous to a degree unimagined before in Argentine cinema; Sarli, although she expressed reservations in written sources, was willing to display her body in remarkable ways, including full frontal nudity and the self-manipulation of her breast; Bo was willing to put together production projects based on the money of any and all comers, which gave Sarli maximum international exposure, including the United States; and, finally, Bo never let the exigencies of coherent plot development stand in the way of Sarli's disrobing.

The year 1956 also constituted a paradigm shift in the way in which Sarli's debut as an actress brought, for the first time to the Argentine screen, a wholly sexualized female body, one in which the actress exercised some control over the meaning of her parts and one in which the famed star was no longer the vaporous or stagey allegory of a masculinist view of the world. Latin America had a long tradition of female heroines in fiction and, subsequently, in films and film versions of novels in which women were allegorical stand-ins for the masculinist business of life. By contrast, raw sexuality was the real stuff of life for Sarli, and if there is much about her repetitive roles that is self-parodying and unrelieved kitsch, the spectator never loses sight of the fact that the woman writhing in pleasure on the bed is nothing more nor less than just that: a real woman.

However, what most contributed to the Bo-Sarli duo getting off to a good professional start was the fact that their inaugural film, one that went on to become an important entry in the list of the best Argentine films ever, was that it was *El trueno entre las hojas*, the title story of Augusto Roa Bastos's prizewinning 1953 collection of the same name.[3] Roa would go on to write fourteen film scripts based on his stories and fragments of his novels.[4] Although Roa, Bo, and Sarli would rejoin to work on *Sabaleros* in 1958, after that date, Roa went on to other projects that never again included either Bo or Sarli. The couple was exploring formulas of international funding and thematic variations that cannot have appealed to Roa, who adhered throughout his life to an austere socialist ideology that had little use for profits gained on the basis of exploitation of the flesh.

However, the simple fact is that Roa undertook a brilliant adaptation of his story for Bo's film.[5] In the story, workers in Paraguayan tea plantations are effectively tortured into compliance with the prevailing system. Roa eschews the facile dream of a spontaneous worker's revolt that will kill the bosses and put the means of production into the hands of those who produce it. Instead, in this capstone story of a collection of seventeen texts, Roa envisions the slow accumulation of a rage drawn from all the elements, but originally of the "thunder among the leaves," that will, in time, lead to a social revolution in which the peasant is vindicated for his sufferings.

In Bo's film, the Sarli character is a young and exuberant woman who soon grasps that her older husband, the plantation owner, will not be able to satisfy her lusts for long. Turning to a handsome city man (Bo himself), who has mistakenly signed on with peons more accustomed to the harshness of life in the outback, she attempts to seduce him. When he spurns her advances because he sees her only getting in the way of the organization of the peasants he is spearheading, she denounces him to her husband, who subjects him to the most brutal tortures at his disposal. Regretting her betrayal, she attempts to intercede on his behalf, which only further enrages his husband, and he kills her. Bo's character, who from the abyss of his torment had began to doubt the success of a peasant rebellion, now arises with renewed vigor, the image of the woman before him, and leads the peasants to the destruction of the plantation.

Although one might well argue that, once again, we are in the face of a redemption against patriarchal bestiality through the agency of the feminine principle, the film never loses sight of the fact that Sarli's character is very much flesh and blood, and that, unlike virginal waifs who inspire through the exercise of disembodied virtue, Sarli's woman is very much at one with the forces of nature. *El trueno entre las hojas* contains the first scenes of frontal nudity in Argentine film-making, as we see Sarli's character displaying her body in full communion with nature.[6]

In any case, the teaming of the Paraguayan writer Roa Bastos with Isabel Sarli and Fernando Bo in the production of Roa Bastos's and Sarli's inaugural film project is a singular event in Argentine filmmaking. The final product is a rather stunning cinematographic accomplishment.

In 1961, the Argentine master Lucas Demare (1914–81) released *La sed*, based on the seventh segment, "Destinados," and the eighth segment, "Misión," of the novel *Hijo de hombre*.[7] In reality, this film is known by three titles. Often, the name of the novel, *Hijo de hombre*, is used, while frequently the subtitle, *Choferes del Chaco*, is employed to identify the film. "Destinados" is the least narrative segment of *Hijo de hombre*, consisting of a series of dated diary entries beginning on New Year's Day, 1932, with the last one dated September 29, while "Misión" is perhaps one of the most expressionistic segments of *Hijo de hombre*.

Since the Chaco region is arid terrain, sustaining only minimal life, one of the most challenging problems for both Bolivian aggressors and Paraguayan defenders was the lack of water and the accompanying torture of thirst. Many forms of human torture are described in Roa's fiction, but none is as fearsome as thirst. Roa's chapter, which begins with the height of the summer heat at the center of the continent, is organized around the delirium that thirst produces and the futile attempts to effect a distribution of water. The chauffeurs of water carts would assume a mythic stature of conquerors of the desert, if their efforts in the end made any difference. As such, thirst, and the failure to quench that thirst, are signs of the fratricidal folly of war. Indeed, as a consequence of his own experiences in the Chaco, Roa became a pacifist.

The organizing motif of the film is the blinding thirst of a battalion of soldiers lost in the Chaco wasteland, which is dominated by the smell of kerosene that led to the false attribution of petroleum deposits. Here, thirst is described as the "white death" from which, in the absence of water, there is no release. The film is narrated by Miguel Vera, whose diary entries constitute the chapter *Hijo de hombre*, on which the script is based. Miguel Vera is, in the novel, an imperfect narrator, fatally flawed by his personal demons and by his imperfect humanity. In the novel, fragments narrated by Vera alternate with fragments focused on Crístobal Jara. The Christological allusion of the latter character's name underscores the way in which he is the paradigmatic son of man, a man whose deep humanity conjugates the Paraguayan people. The opening of Demare's film with Vera's narration affords it the tone of a humanity lost in time. As Vera says early in the film, "En pocos días, hemos retrocedido millares de años" ("In a few days, we have receded millions of years").[8]

The message of the battalion's isolation within enemy lines (near the city of Boquerón) reaches the Paraguayan command post, and a special detail from which it is likely that one may never arrive or return, is commissioned. The mission will be led by Cristóbal Jara, played by the important Spanish actor Francisco Rabal, who, at the time, was working in exile in Argentina, and who later went on to fulfill a legendary film career. Thus begins the long odyssey through the desert. The slow pace of the water trucks, whose overheating radiators appear to be consuming almost as much water as the tanks carry, provides numerous opportunities for narratives regarding personal motivations, conflicts, acts of heroism, and, above all, sheer human survival in the face of the daunting desert and the attacking Bolivian planes. It is in this context that Jara, asked whether he believes in miracles by a prostitute who has turned nurse, and who sneaked aboard the convoy to be with him, utters one of the guiding refrains of Roa Bastos's writing: "Lo que no puede hacer el hombre, nadie más puede hacerlo" (What man can't do, no one can do).[9] Speaking of his mission, he underscores the way in which individuals who are victims of a senseless war are still able to engage in heroic acts in defense of what is most essentially human. The novel suggests that perhaps sheer endurance, within the community of human beings, is the greatest heroic act of all.

La sed (to use the title that matches the dominant image) is visually stunning, both in the images of the desert wastelands and the grinding effect it has on the soldiers. When Jara's water tank finally makes it through to the outpost, its wheels in flames from the friction of the desert sand, it has all been for naught because Vera is the lone survivor of the long wait. Jara does not know this, however. His wrists tied by barbed wire to the steering wheel of his truck so as not to lose control, he crashes into a tree, lunges forward in death, and sets off the truck's horn. Rather than announcing the arrival of salvation, the lone squawk of the horn in the middle of the desert marks the absolute desolation of man becoming one with the desert in death. This film must surely be counted as one of the great Argentine accomplishments of the early sixties, and is unquestionably one of the best of Roa's scripts that he saw produced.

Roa's other major project of the early 1960s was to work with the outstanding Argentine actor and director Lautaro Murúa in the filmmaking of Jorge W. Ábalos's 1949 fictionalized memoir, *Shunko*. The film was released in 1960.[10] *Shunko* was an ideal vehicle for Roa's sociocultural interests. Ábalos, who was a renowned entomologist, also served as a rural schoolteacher in the far northwestern Argentine province of Santiago del Estero, an area, at the time, of essentially indigenous culture, where the Quichua language predominated[11] and where there were only fragmentary and superficial contacts with the modernity of the capital. This was a region of premodern agrarian existence that, nevertheless, was disrupted by the incursions of modernity. In the case of Roa's own Paraguay, these conditions meant that the international corporations exploited the *Ilex paraguayensis* crops through the abject and absolute enslavement of indigenous Guarani workers. While exploitation on such a vast scale did not occur in Santiago del Estero, Roa was, nevertheless, committed to the dignity of indigenous life in the South American interior. He chronicled the pathos of its destruction, shading often into tragedy, by an encroaching modernity that exploited and corrupted, but rarely ameliorated, the lives of the original peoples. This is the main point of Hugo Gamarra's documentary on Roa's Paraguay, *El portón de los sueños* (1996).

One of the principles of modernity that reached out in varying degrees from Buenos Aires was Domingo Faustino Sarmiento's much touted project for universal childhood education that would be "*libre, laica y obligatoria*" ("free, secular, and mandatory"). Undoubtedly, such a project played a major role in the creation of a modern Buenos Aires by promoting the assimilation of immigrant children to parameters of national identity. However, the effect that such a project had is questionable as one moved farther and farther away from the metropolitan center to the rural periphery. The image of the rural schoolteacher, carrying the fruits of civilization to the farthest reaches of the new nation, is a staple of many of the cultures of the American states. For example, witness the icon of the one-room schoolhouse frontier teacher in the United States (e.g., Edward Eggleston's classic, *The Hoosier School-Master*, 1871), the *maestro rural* in postrevolutionary

Mexico (e.g., Emilio Fernández's 1930 *Río Escondido*, with María Félix as the missionary *maestra rural*), and Ábalos's *Shunko*, which has gone on to become a juvenile classic in Argentine schools.

Shunko, in Quichua, means the "littlest one," and refers to the youngest of the charges taken on by the narrator, who is sent out to provide rudimentary education to Indian children in Santiago del Estero. Ábalos's story is told in retrospect, as he recalls, with deep tenderness from his humble apartment back in Buenos Aires, the multiple facets of his interactions with the children and their parents and the inevitable cultural conflicts that ensue from the confrontation between modernity and millenary ways of life. The important point for Ábalos, and one on which Roa's film script capitalizes, is that the process of education that ensues is not merely the substitution of Quichua by Spanish, the so-called primitive with the modern, or a tribal point of view with a national one, but rather the honest exchange that occurs between his students and a teacher who senses he has more to learn from them than they from him. This attitude is the basis of the heartfelt love that develops between them. Ábalos's recollections after his return to Buenos Aires focus on the sustained investment, from within the core of the modern, in the dignity, humanity, and sincere emotions of the children whose lives he was sent to change. That the children change him more than he changes them is part of the cultural nostalgia that is the principal ideological thrust of the memoir and that gives it its depth and importance.

Lautaro Murúa's relatively short film (only seventy-two minutes) is a visual gem. One of the most handsome actors of his day in Argentine filmmaking, Murúa is cast in conjunction with a group of twenty adorable preteen-aged girls and boys, mostly of indigenous descent, although there appears to be a smattering of immigrant children as well. The teacher, who is never identified directly by name, arrives at the beginning of the school year (March) in a mule-drawn cart, dressed formally with a jacket and tie. As he assimilates more into the life of the remote village, which has never had a school before, he graduates to short-sleeved shirts and then more peasant garb, such that when some female colleagues arrive from the capital to invite him and his students to participate in a combined end-of-the-year scholastic event, they titter between themselves over his impoverished appearance.

Shunko makes use of visual detail to underscore the relatively harmonious integration of the Sarmientine educational system within the rural context. In this case—and unusual for Roa's writing—the script dwells on the smoothing out of cultural conflicts (including linguistic ones between Quichua and Spanish) that might threaten to undermine the teacher's educational mission. Indeed, there is a more apparent edge of conflict (again, paradigmatically, the linguistic one, which is difficult to reproduce in the film[12]) in Ábalos's novel than there is in Murúa's film.

Of course, one expects Roa Bastos to demonstrate a profound sympathy for indigenous ways of life, and *Shunko* represents the complementing of his native Guarani culture with a benevolent view of northern Argentine Quichua society. In another film project, *Soluna*, not analyzed here, he works with the Maya-Quiché culture of Miguel Ángel Asturias's acclaimed theatrical text, published in 1955 in Buenos Aires. In *Shunko*, there are two sequences that are of particular eloquence in demonstrating an accommodation between modern and original peoples' interpretation of natural events.

The first concerns a lunar eclipse. In one of the best visual moments in the film, we see the townspeople beating their empty mortars with pestles in a rhythmic ritual against the lunar-lit landscape. The next day, the teacher asks his students if they saw the lunar eclipse the night before; they claim not to know what he is talking about. However, when he begins to explain the phenomenon through a scientific demonstration, they suddenly react with familiarity about the event, although Shunko says, "Aquí sabemos de otra manera" (Here we know in another way). In order to obtain the full information on that "other way," which involves the beating of the empty mortars to stop the death of the moon, teacher and students adjourn to the hut of the old woman Doña Jacinta, who patiently explains, in Quichua, the legend of the moon's consumption in the interplay between el Padre Sol y la Madre Luna. This is the one time in Murúa's film in which there is an extended use of subtitles to capture the sense of the woman's animistic explanation in Quichua, but it is an effective device here that reinforces different ways of interpreting the processes of the natural world, in this case reinforced by the different spheres of meaning of the two languages.

The other incident of interest in this regard concerns the little shepherdess, Ana Vieyra, who falls down a ravine to her death trying to protect one of her stray animals. After the teacher, the townspeople, and the students have completed the construction of a rustic schoolhouse (which proudly flies the Argentine flag), the teacher and his students hear a knocking sound in the wall of the schoolroom. The teacher claims that it must be a rodent, and he starts shifting books and papers so it will reveal itself. However, the students immediately proffer their own—in their view, superior—correct interpretation: "'Es Ana, señor,' insiste Pancho. 'Todos sabemos que es ella'" ("'It is Ana, sir,' Pancho insists. 'We all know that it is her'"). Claiming to have heard her knocking for several days, the children go on to explain that Ana wishes to reclaim her reader, which she left behind when she fell into the ravine. Out of reverential respect for Ana and the explanation of his students, the teacher solemnly places the book on a bonfire that will carry its ashes to her. This scene of unquestioning respect for the interpretation given by the students for the noises they have heard is underlain by a scandalous disjunction: the need to preserve scarce and respected sources of knowledge, in the form of government-issued books. There is also the need, whether the teacher sees it as symbolic or literal, to acquiesce to his students' higher cultural knowledge that contradicts explanations of the natural order represented by the burned book.

In the sociocultural domain of *Shunko*, there can be no compromising with the need to forge a continuous cloth of indigenous and modern beliefs, and the success of the teacher, borne out by the expressions of affection and sadness at his departure at the end of the school year, lies in his ability to skillfully and sensitively mediate between the two belief systems. Clearly, there is something like a sentimental nostalgia on the part of the teacher as he recollects his experiences with Shunko and the other children. However, Murúa's film, with Roa's script, is an important moment of appeal to social accord, midway between the collapse of Peronismo in 1955 and the rise of the authoritarianism and neofascism in the mid-sixties that drove Roa Bastos from Argentina in 1976.

Roa again had the opportunity to work with a legendary figure of the Argentine stage and cinema, the great comedienne Niní Marshall, in *Ya tiene comisario el pueblo* (1967). Comedy was not exactly Roa's preferred cultural genre, having too much of a somber regard in general for the deep social conflicts of injustice, oppression, and extermination in Latin America that could hardly be resolved through the comedic gesture. Yet it is significant that his intervention in the genre involved such an important figure as Marshall, with a text based on a play by the Argentine Claudio Martínez-Payva that had already been transferred to the screen (by Martínez Payva himself, along with Eduardo Morera, in 1936).[13]

Although I have no information as to how Roa became involved in this project and exactly how he felt about working on a comedy—apparently the only one of the two dozen films in which he participated—it is possible to see some resonance of this project with Roa's personal commitments, since the film turns on the figure of a cowardly, yet overbearing, village police sergeant whose antics, while tinged with comedy, have serious implications in terms of human rights abuse. Police sergeants, *comisarios*, are the lowest common denominator of local law and order in Argentina, something along the lines of the legendary porcine country sheriff of the unreconstructed U.S. South, a social icon that enjoys as many comic representations (the primus inter pares of the "good ole boys") as menacingly tragic ones (the most public face of authoritarian control in the Old South). Both dimensions are present in *Ya tiene comisario el pueblo* (The Village Already Has a Police Sergeant), although, in the final analysis, what prevails are the echoes of authoritarian dictatorship in Argentina, such as the sort that came to power in July through a military coup in 1966, just months before the film's release in January 1967. It would not be likely that the coup had any influence on the final form of the film, and it is more plausible to speak of a tradition of arbitrary authoritarianism in Argentina as the model for the film and the play behind it, just as much as the coup is the political embodiment of a sustained backdrop of authoritarianism in Argentine social history.

The film is an awkward series of anecdotes propelled by the efforts of the *Comisario*, Sargento Lorenzo Paniagua, played by the memorable character actor Ubaldo Martínez, to find new victims for "el desplume" (literally, the plucking—that is, their fleecing by his corruption). The townspeople seem to drift along with his antics, aided by his five stooges of guards and minor officers, and the most distinguishing feature of their lives is the ragtag municipal band that weaves in and around the humble installations of the forgotten town of Monte Olbidado [*sic*]; the film was made in a small town in the province of Jujuy. Paniagua is minimally restrained, however, by his wife, Doña Sofocación (played with provincial imperiousness by Niní Marshall), who struggles to keep his larceny in check, but mostly takes her frustrations out on the foodstuffs that pass over the chopping block of her kitchen. There is much that is farcical about this whole mélange, punctuated about every ten minutes by someone bursting into song, although the lyrics may strategically allude to the injustices of life, which officials like the *Comisario*, who self-characterizes himself as "Sargento, en ejercicio del Poder Ejecutivo" (Sergeant, exercising Executive Power), are adept at compounding. As the opening song of the film, which plays while the credits roll, says, evil always trumps virtue.

Yet, the *Comisario* meets his match in the person of a venerable Gaucho. El Negro, in full regalia as a throwback to the Gauchos de Güemes, who fought against the Spaniards in Alto Perú in the struggle for independence in the early nineteenth century, frustrates the police sergeant's attempt to shake down the cardplayers in the local tavern with the pretext that they are an insult to decency since they are drinking and gambling rather than working in support of progress. When the Gaucho humiliates the *Comisario*, returns their money to the gamblers, and invites everyone to a round at his expense, the film is affirming the right of popular action to go against constituted authority and the phony ideologies, such as patriotism and progress, on which their arbitrary authoritarianism is grounded. A scene like this is hardly a culminating moment in what is a mishmash of local color, musical interludes, and farcical and foregrounding actions whose silliness is an aesthetic end in itself rather than part of a tight semiotic of social meaning. However, it does propel the film in terms of the use of comedy to articulate perspectives of injustice with which Argentine audiences can readily relate. In this sense, the satiric characterization of the person of the *Comisario*, who is unlikely ever to disappoint in his venality, gives *Ya tiene comisario el pueblo* an edge lacking in the American cowboy musicals that are undoubtedly one of its models.[14]

There are several more run-ins with El Negro and his wife, when a crowning of the queen of the grape harvest (another of Paniagua's schemes to raise money for his coffers) is punctuated by the attempt by a frustrated pretender to kidnap the queen—an attempt that is thwarted by an impromptu display of popular justice led by El Negro. Yet in the end, the *Comisario* is redeemed when he is forced by an inspector, who arrives to examine the books of the commissary, to legally marry Doña Sofocación before a priest, in exchange for not pressing charges. In the process, Paniagua submits to the superior morality of his wife. This sort of bucolic resolution is certainly at odds with Roa Bastos's general view of how justice works. The fact that this—of all of the films on which he worked—was the greatest box office success is very much of a cruel irony that leads one to suspect that he had little creative control over *Ya tiene comisario el pueblo*.[15] By that time, in any event, Roa is pretty much at the end of his career as a scriptwriter. He only worked on two more films, the already discussed *Shunko* (1969), and, after a hiatus of five years, finally, *La Madre María* (1974). In 1976, the *Proceso de Reconstrucción Nacional* (Process of National Reconstruction) came to power, with a full display of neofascist ideology, and Roa Bastos promptly departed for Toulouse, France, ending the nineteen years of his residency in Argentina.

I would like to close this discussion of Roa's work as a scriptwriter by stepping back to 1961 in order to discuss *Alias Gardelito*, perhaps one of the best films he worked on and one of the very few of his films readily available in DVD format. *Alias Gardelito* won the 1962 Condor de Plata award for the best film of the year. The Condor award is Argentina's equivalent of the Oscar. Based on a short novel by the Argentine writer Bernardo Kordon (who collaborated on the script), and directed by the masterful Lautaro Murúa, with whom Roa worked on *Shunko* (Murúa has a minor role in *Alias Gardelito*), the film is valuable for the interpretation of an Argentine common man in the transition period between the authoritarian government of Juan Domingo Perón (overthrown by the military in 1955) and the emergence of the string of military dictatorships that held sway between 1966 and 1983.

Alias Gardelito is a superb example of the Argentine interest in the film noir mode. If we understand noir, which usually, but not always, means working in black and white, to be a film narrative focusing on the underbelly of urban life and projecting a strong message with regard to corruption, immoral interpersonal relationships, and the social life of bourgeois society as a turbulent cesspool, it is not difficult to find a host of excellent Argentine examples. These examples range from the high period of noir (the 1940s and 1950s) to the 1960s. Indeed, the need to examine the consequences of military dictatorships in Argentina, especially their devastating effect on the fabric of social life, tinges even recent films with a neo-noir quality. If noir in the United States, Britain, and France, the major sites of noir production, dealt with relatively stable societies socially and politically, the effects of authoritarian governments and their reinforced versions in the form of military dictatorship made noir a particularly resonant film mode in countries like Argentina, as did the recent fascist experience in Italy and Germany. Although Argentine noir does not always directly refer to either the Peronista period (1946–55) or to subsequent military dictatorships (1966–73, 1976–83), it is difficult not to perceive their shadow in the pertinent texts.

This is the case with *Alias Gardelito*, whose context is the late 1950s through the very early 1960s. This is a time when Argentina experienced the repercussions of the profound decline of the Peronista experiment, the overthrow of President Perón, the imposition of a military stewardship, and the precarious attempts at institutional democracy. These attempts failed and led to a series of brutal military dictatorships from 1966 through 1973. Although the country, and especially Buenos Aires, retained a certain level of economic comfort, the period after 1955 saw attempts by the military and its supporters to undo the Peronista experiment in national socialism, and there is an unquestionable level of social instability as a consequence.

This is particularly evident in Murúa's film, where the protagonist, Toribio, is witness to diverse manifestations of social violence, unemployment, vengeful behavior, and an overall degree of breakdown of interpersonal relationships that point to the attempt to provide an interpretation of meaningless and aimless communal life. The echo of Peronismo is specifically present in the film through the character Toribio, a provincial outsider who has come to the city to attempt to make it as a singer. Hence, the title's reference, *Gardelito*, to Carlos Gardel, the French-born Argentine singer who, in the 1920s and 1930s, made tango lyrics an international phenomenon and sparked interest in the tango as a dance form. Toribio is, therefore, an example of the impoverished provincials who are drawn by the bright lights of Buenos Aires to the capital city in the hope of finding a better life. Peronismo turned this hope into an organized program in the attempt to make Buenos Aires even more proletarian by providing cheap labor in the push for industrial development. Most of those who arrived under Perón's plan, and those who arrived after on their own, were content to find employment in menial jobs or (semi)skilled occupations. However, others had higher aspirations suitable for the considerable degree of social mobility that Buenos Aires offered. Eva Duarte, "Evita," who subsequently became Perón's first lady, is an icon of such possibilities, and it is for this reason that Toribio's career plans are not as preposterous as they might be in other Latin American societies.

Yet Murúa's film makes it clear from the start that Toribio's experiences in the big city will end violently, and the film efficiently establishes the mix of the lack of self-knowledge, incompetence, and swaggering bravado that characterize Toribio's character as he moves heedlessly and blithely into the Porteño underworld. He eventually becomes involved in a smuggling operation, and his clumsy attempt to cheat his bosses leads to his death. He ends up as another piece of human garbage on the bleak Porteño cityscape. Toribio is a loser, and Murúa's film makes judicious use of an antipícaro characterization for him: he is consistently incapable of constructing strategies for survival in Buenos Aires. If foreign immigrants sought to "hacer la América" in Argentina, internal immigrants sought to "hacer Buenos Aires" in the country's capital, and Toribio is an Argentine everyman whose trajectory of experiences in Buenos Aires attests to the impossibility for most of doing so, at least during the period following Peronismo.

Where Roa's influence on the film is particularly evident is in the relentless characterization of Toribio as the Argentine everyman caught in the web of social decay represented by post-Peronista Buenos Aires. While the images of the film show the measure of cosmopolitanism the city had confirmed by midcentury, the deportment of the citizenry in their interpersonal relationships (the tone of which is set by the cold and uncaring way in which his relatives in the city receive him, an unwelcome burden on their domestic economy) underscores a society that has broken down as regards the quality of communal life. It is not that the film suggests some golden Argentine past of benevolent human intercourse: Buenos Aires has always been a tough town. Rather, Peronismo had created, through its multiple layers of demagoguery and heavy-handed national socialism, a promise of a better future and social accord for the Argentine people. The decay of Peronismo was devastating, both in the short run of institutional instability and in the long run of authoritarianism and, ultimately, neofascist dictatorships. Neither Kordon, Roa, or Murúa could have known how ugly life would get in Argentina by the late 1970s, but the Roa-Kordon script very much shows their commitment to a socialist critique of what Buenos Aires had become by the late 1950s. In this sense, *Alias Gardelito* stands as one of Roa Bastos's most eloquent screenplays, while the film stands as one of the monuments of Argentine filmmaking in the 1960s.

It is regrettable that so many of the films Roa Bastos worked on as a screenwriter are unavailable in any format. Many of the important works of Argentine filmmaking are slowly being reissued in DVD format, and perhaps more of Roa's film work will become available and in better quality formats than I have had at my disposal for this chapter. In the case of Roa's films, aside from his personal recognition of how much working in film enhanced the visual quality of his narrative fiction, he had the advantage of being involved with the industry at a time when important literary works were still being used as the basis of film scripts, and when actors and directors now recognized as the best of Argentine film history had important roles to play. In addition to his own exceptionally fine writing, Roa Bastos worked with literary texts by Bernardo Kordon, Jorge W. Ábalos, future Noble Laureate Miguel Ángel Asturias, Claudio Martínez Payva, Andrés Lizarraga, and Mario Halley Mora. The directors with whom he worked included such masters as Lucas Demare, Manuel Antín, and Lautaro Murúa, not to mention the iconoclastic Armando Bo. Finally, among the important actors for whom Roa wrote are: Tita Merello, Niní Marshall, Sergio Renán, Graciela Borges, Virginia Lago, Norma Aleandro, Lautaro Murúa, and the inestimable Isabel Sarli.

In sum, Roa Bastos's work as a screenwriter, while hardly on the same artistic level as his magnificent narrative fiction, is nevertheless a signal contribution to Argentine filmmaking. Few other Latin American writers can boast of having been so near the center of a major national film industry for so long.

Notes

1. I wish to acknowledge the important contribution made to this paper by Santiago Juan-Navarro, who procured access to several of the films discussed in this essay. My research assistant Kyle Black provided bibliographic support.

2. This discussion of *El trueno entre las hojas* is drawn from my essay "Las lolas de la Coca."

3. See Foster, *Augusto Roa Bastos*, for a discussion of Roa's major literary works.

4. See Rojo, "Eisenstein," regarding the importance of the visual in Roa's film scripts and the influence of his experiences in filmmaking on his writing, particularly the novel *Yo el Supremo* (1974). Etcheverry, "A mí el cine me hizo nacer como escritor," provides an overview of Roa's film career.

5. As will be apparent throughout this chapter, I do not subscribe to the imperative to compare a film with its presumed literary pretext, but rather subscribe to a poststructuralist view of independent texts, as formulated by scholars like Cahir. The two texts can be mutually referred to, but the filmic version is neither authorized nor discredited by reference to an alleged "original" literary text.

6. In actuality, the nudity here is that of a white woman. The appearance of indigenous women with their breasts on view is not taken into account as significant in the ideology of corporal revelation of the period.

7. Roa discusses the relationship between this film and his novel in Augusto Roa Bastos, *Mis reflexiones*.

8. The original quote is from Roa Bastos, *Hijo de hombre* 162.

9. The original quote is from Roa Bastos, *Hijo de hombre* 199; the English translation is from *Son of Man*, 229.

10. For information on the backgrounds and the making of the film, see Huerga. See also Medina on Ábalos's combined careers of writer and scientist-professor, and *Wikipedia*'s entry, "Shunko," for information on the novel.

11. Quichua is the name used in northern Argentina for that area's variant of the Quechua language.

12. The film does make use of the device of speech in Quichua, with translated Spanish subtitles. In the novel, there is greater room for footnoted speech and the addition of a twenty-page linguistic glossary that would be rather clumsy to handle in the film.

13. On the career of this minor playwright, see Foppa.

14. In keeping with the advances in Argentine filmmaking, it is important to note that *Ya tiene comisario el pueblo* is filmed in color; almost all of the other films on which Roa worked were filmed in black and white.

15. Significantly, Gamarra Etcheverry does not mention *Ya tiene comisario el pueblo* in his excellent analysis of Roa's film writing.

WORKS CITED

Ábalos, Jorge. *Shunko.* Buenos Aires: Losada, 1959. Print.

Cahir, Linda Costanzo. *Literature into Film: Theory and Practical Approaches.* Jefferson, NC: McFarland, 2006. Print.

Foster, David William. "Las lolas de la Coca: el cuerpo femenino en el cine de Isabel Sarli." December 13, 2008. http://web.mac.com/karpa1/Site_10/Foster-Sarli.html. Web.

———. *Augusto Roa Bastos.* New York: Twayne Publishers, 1978. Print.

Foppa, Tito Livio. "Martínez Payva, Claudio." *Diccionario teatral del Río de la Plata.* Buenos Aires: Argentores, Ediciones del Carro de Tespis, 1961. 439–40. Print.

Gamarra Etcheverry, Hugo. "A mí el cine me hizo nacer como escritor: Augusto Roa Bastos, hombre del cine. Le Cinéma m'a fait naÊtre écrivain: Augusto Roa Bastos, homme de cinéma." *Cinémas d'Amérique Latine* 14 (2006): 129–43. Print.

http://educared.org.ar/imaginaria/14/2/miscelanea-abalos.htm. Accessed November 11, 2004. Web.

Huerga, Feliciano. *Jorge W. Ábalos.* Buenos Aires: Editorial de la Universidad de Buenos Aires, 1981. Print.

Kordon, Bernardo. "Alias Gardelito." *Alias Gardelito. Un horizonte de cemento. Kid Ñandubay.* Buenos Aires: Editorial Galerna, 1981. 77–160. Print.

Martínez Payva, Claudio. *Ya tiene comisario el pueblo (nuevo libro). El lazo.* Buenos Aires: Editorial Astal, 1968. Print.

Medina, Mariano. "Jorge Luis Ábalos: una historia con y sin víboras." *Imaginaria; revista quincenal sobre literatura infantil y juvenil* 142 (November 24, 2004). November 11, 2008. http://imaginaria.com.ar./14/2lecturas-abalos.htm. Web.

Roa Bastos, Augusto. *Mis reflexiones sobre el guión cinematográfico y el guión de* Hijo de hombre. Asunsión: RP Ediciones, Fundación Cinemateca y Archivo Visual del Paraguay, 1993. Print.

———. *Hijo de hombre.* Buenos Aires: Losada, 1961. Print.

Roa Bastos, Augusto. Son of Man. Trans. Rachel Caffyn. New York: Monthly Review Press, 1988.

———. *El trueno entre las hojas.* Buenos Aires: Editorial Losada, 1953. Print.

Rojo, Violeta. "Eisenstein, Pasolini y Roa Bastos: realidad, ficción y tiempo en el cine y en la literatura." *Escritura* 15.30 (1990): 389–99. Print.

Wikipedia. "Shunko." November 18, 2008. http://es.wikipedia.org/wiki/Shunko. Web.

FILMOGRAPHY

Alias Gardelito. Dir. Lautaro Marúa. Perf. Alberto Argibay, Walter Vidarte, Tônia Carrera, Lautaro Murúa. Leo Kanaf para Río Negro, 1961. Videocassette.

La boda. Dir. Lucas Demare. Perf. Manuel Alexandre, Mercedes Barranco, Conchita Bautista, Graciela Borges, Susana Campos, José Canalejas. Producciones Huincul; Internacional, 1964. Videocassette.

Castigo al traidor. Dir. Manuel Antin. Perf. Sergio Renán, Marcela López Rey, Jorge Barreio, Eva Donge, Miguel Ligero, Aldo Mayo, Enrique Thibaut.Manuel Antín para Clase, 1966. Videocassette.

El demonio en la sangre. Dir. René Múgica. Perf. Rosita Quintana, Ubaldo Martínez, Ernesto Bianco, Arturo García Buhr, Wolf Ruvinskis, Lydia Lamaison, Graciela Dufau. Sergio Kodan para SADFO, 1964. Videocassette.

La Madre María. Dir. Lucas Demare. Perf. Tita Merello, José Slavin, Hugo Arana, Patricia Castell, María José Demare, Alejandra Da Passano, Adrian Ghio, Tina Serrano, Fernando Labat. Capricornio, 1974. Videocassette.

El portón de los sueños; vida y obra de Augusto Roa Bastos. Dir. Hugo Gamarra. Perf. Augusto Roa Bastos, Agustín Núñez, Gloria Muñoz, Hugo Gamarra. Ara Films Production, 1988. Videocassette.

Sabaleros. Dir. Armando Bo. Perf. Isabel Sarli, Armando Bo, Héctor Armendáriz.Araucania Films, 1958. Videocassette.

La sangre y la semilla. Dir. Alberto Dubois. Perf. Olga Zubarry, Romualdo Quiroga, Mercedes Jane, Roque Centurión Miranda, Celia Elís, Carlos Gómez, José Guuisone.Benjamín Bogado para BB, 1959. Videocassette.

La sed. Dir. Lucas Demare. Perf. Francisco Rabal, Vicente Ariño, Susy Catell, Lucas Demare, Carlos Dorrego, Carlos Estrada, Dorrite Ferrer.ASF y Suevia Films, 1961. Videocassette. Also known as *Hijo de hombe; choferes del Chaco*.

Shunko. Dir. Lautaro Murúa. Perf. Lautaro Murúa, Carlos Garay, Raúl del Valle, Ángel Greco, Oscar Llompart. Leo Kanaf, 1960. Videocassette.

Soluna. Dir. Marcos Madanes. Perf. Luis Medina Castro, Dora Baret, Mikaela, David Llewelyn, Lola Palombo, Guerino Marchesi, Diablada de Ouro. Imago Producciones, 1969. Videocassette.*El terrorista*. Dir. Daniel Cherniavsky. Perf. Emilio Alfaro, Jorge Cavanet, Oscar Ferrigno, María Rosa Gallo, Beto Gianola, Jacinto Herrera, Virginia Lago, Alberto Lares, Oscar Llompart, Horacio Nicolai./Siglo XX, 1962. Videocassette.

El trueno entre las hojas. Dir. Armando Bo. Perf. Isabel Sarli, Armando Bo, Manuel Arguello.Nicolás Bo para Film AM, 1956. Videocassette.*El último paso*. Dir. Daniel Cherniavsky. Perf. Norma Aleandro, José De Angelis, Inda Ledesma, Ubaldo Martínez.Siglo XX, 1962. Videocassette.

Ya tiene comisario el pueblo. Dir. Enrique Carreras. Perf. Niní Marshall, Ubaldo Martínez, Rafael Carret, Tristán, Ramona Galarza, Mario Lozano. ASF, 1967. Videocassette.

CHAPTER 4

POSTMODERNISM AND ITS SIGNS IN "JUEGOS NOCTURNOS" BY AUGUSTO ROA BASTOS

Fernando Burgos

This chapter examines the postmodern components of Roa Bastos's short stories, specifically concentrating on "Juegos nocturnos" ("Nocturnal Games"), which I affirm is a key to his literary production within the short story genre. I also discuss postmodernism itself in order to justify my reasons for inscribing Roa's texts within this aesthetics. "Juegos nocturnos" is not, of course, the only short story by Roa that assumes this artistic perspective. At the end of this study, I will make brief comments about the texts "Contar un cuento" ("To Tell a Story") and "Bajo el Puente" ("Under the Bridge"). These two stories share a proclivity toward the metaphysical as an axis of truth. The disillusionment or lack of confidence in writing expressed in the first story, and the poetic treatment of a metaphysics of time in the second, reinforce the thesis that many of Roa's short stories, especially those published after *El trueno entre las hojas* (*Thunder Among the Leaves*), were written primarily under the optics of postmodernism.[1]

This chapter first contextualizes the theoretical perspective of postmodernism used in "Juegos nocturnos," and then bases its subsequent analysis of Roa Bastos's story on this aesthetic modality. I do not establish an absolute correspondence with one or more postmodern philosophers, or privilege one theory over another, but rather adumbrate the principal points of postmodernism drawn from such explorations, in particular from the works of Deleuze, Fokkema, Hassan, Jameson, and Lyotard. I further show how this comprehension of postmodernism impacts my approach to Roa Bastos's short stories. My understanding of postmodernism has been equally guided by my own reflections and intuitions about the creative universe of Latin American literature generated through the reading of such writers as Roa Bastos, Borges, Lezama Lima, Guimarães Rosa, Cortázar, Sarduy, Eltit, Garmendia (Julio and Salvador), Cabrera Infante, Valenzuela, Benítez Rojo, Levrero, Elizondo, Peri Rossi, and Jaramillo Levi.

The questions of how postmodernism arose and the nature of its identity cannot be separated from those elements of modernism that led to its birth and development. Even for those theoreticians such as Fredric Jameson who delimit postmodernism to a specific historical period, this circumscription is only operative in terms of the contrast that can be established between the respective developments of modernism and postmodernism. Jameson connects postmodernism to a historical period starting after the Second World War, and whose initial effects were felt at the beginning of the 1960s, coinciding with the birth of the concepts of "postindustrial society" and "multinational capitalism": "I believe that the emergence of postmodernism is closely related to the emergence of this new moment of late, consumer or multinational capitalism. I believe also that its formal features in many ways express the deeper logic of that particular social system"(Jameson 20).

Among the relevant characteristics that Jameson identifies as essential to the aesthetic course of postmodernism are the following: (1) the use of pastiche over parody; (2) the complete disappearance of the myth of personal identity (the death of the subject); (3) the advent of a pop cultural production that through pastiche, plagiarism, and other forms creates a stereotypical nostalgia for the past—especially in the film of nostalgia—and thus abandons a true confrontation with the historical past; (4) the creation of a hyperspace in the city—in which the country environment has already lost its contrastive face—incapable of expanding in an organic and sensorial manner faced with this new postmodern space; (5) the focus on postmodern machines, practically apocalyptic in nature, as in the case of war machines, that have very little to do with the admiration for modern machines and the advances of civilization that are an expression of progress; and (6) the cessation of the subversive character of objects of art, in the context of a consumer society. Instead, such objects are immediately absorbed by the flow of consumer goods. Moreover, the taboo and subversive character of modern art becomes integrated into the postmodern canon, with its taste for assimilation that implies the loss of the entire notion of the antisocial (Jameson 3).

When Jameson situates the sociocultural and artistic event of post-modernism within a clear framework of historical periodization, he is affirming that postmodernism is not just a style that appears and reappears in the wide horizon of the development of modernity, whether we situate modernity in the Renaissance or in the first decades of the twentieth century: "[Postmodernism] is not just another word for the description of a particular style. It is also, at least in my use, a periodizing concept whose function is to correlate the emergence of new formal features in culture with the emergence of a new type of social life and a new economic order—what is often euphemistically called modernization, post-industrial or consumer society, the society of the media or the spectacle, or multinational capitalism" (Jameson 18).The genesis and framework of the action of postmodernism are very clearly defined for Jameson, as evidenced by the preceding quotation. However, not only should Jameson identify references in modern art that offer a point of comparison—divergence and disparity—with postmodernism, but he should also acknowledge that the differences do not so much reside in the question of content, but rather in the specific manner in which this content has been packaged, captured, or simply demarginalized from its former position: "Radical breaks between periods do not generally involve complete changes of content but rather the restructuring of a certain number of elements already given: features that in an earlier period or system were subordinate now become dominant, and features that had been dominant again become secondary. In this sense, everything we have described here can be found in earlier periods and most notably within modernism proper" (Jameson 18).

The best attempt at periodization of postmodernism is thus made relative by this giant spatial constellation called modernity. This certainly does not at all discard the outstanding contribution of Jameson to the slippery attempt to approach—we do not even speak of defining—the central principles of the sociocultural phenomenon that has come to be known as postmodernism. In terms of the galactic vision, expanded over the course of modernity, we may take, as an example, the globalizing mode with which Berman approaches modern sensibility. For Berman, being modern "is to experience personal and social life as a maelstrom, to find one's world and oneself in perpetual disintegration and renewal, trouble and anguish, ambiguity and contradiction: to be part of a universe in which all that is solid melts into air" (Berman 345). Berman tangentially addresses the question of postmodernity by criticizing the fact that established cultural media could study figures like Melville, Poe, Sterne, and other writers as postmodern. This, in his interpretation, would lend a certain confusion to artistic developments and proposals that foolishly tend to eliminate the artistic, cultural, modern space: "Others have embraced a mystique of post-modernism, which strives to cultivate ignorance of modern history and culture, and speaks as if all human feeling, expressiveness, play, sexuality and community have only just been invented—by the post-modernist—and were unknown, even inconceivable, before last week" (33). Clearly, Berman supports this ample vision of the modern experience through the concept of the dizzying transformation of the individual, society, and methods of cultural production during the modern period. The effects of modernization were completely and passionately unleashed at the international level in the twentieth century, but its first stage—in this extended historical course of modernity—can be traced from the beginnings of the sixteenth century. Nothing remains the same in this vortex of change imposed by modernity. The modern tradition undergoes distinct, recognizable phases according to principles of innovation, discovery, wonderment, and creativity in its dismemberment and recreation of cultural forms.

Lyotard cites Proust as an example of modern writing, and Joyce as an example of postmodern writing. According to Lyotard, each complies with the modern axiom of artistically giving expression to the ineffable: the interiority of time in Proust, the event itself of writing in Joyce. However, the French writer maintains narrative unity, while the Irish writer abandons such preoccupation with unity, form, and artistic standards. Thus, Lyotard's assertion that postmodernity cannot be placed at the end of modernity, and that a modern project should first be postmodern, attributes an inherently subversive character (antischool and antireception) to art as a completely free production: "The Postmodern would be that . . . which denies itself the solace of good forms, the consensus of taste which would make it possible to share collectively the nostalgia for the unattainable; that which searches for new presentations, not in order to enjoy them but in order to impart a stronger sense of the unpresentable."[2] We can then appreciate how, even in Berman's refutation of postmodernism, the postmodern space is created in its own vortex of transformations that Berman perceives in the vast course of modernity. Also, in the antithetical positions of Jameson and Lyotard, the common denominator between the two turns out to be the realization that the advent of postmodernism cannot be understood without modernity, since the recognition of both spaces as sociocultural conditions and aesthetic practices presupposes a series of dialectical relationships between the discourses that inform and signify them.[3]

Borges, Cortázar, Fuentes, and García Márquez are the four Spanish American writers cited by Douwe Fokkema as examples of authors whose works exhibit the postmodern code. In particular, Fokkema attributes to the first of these writers a decisive impact as far as the establishment of the term on a critical level and on influencing European literature are concerned. I will not discuss here if these writers are a representative sample of postmodernism in Latin American literature or which of their works would be most distinctive in this regard. Fokkema's study interests me in particular for its assignation of "impossibilities" to the realization of postmodernism. Such impossibilities do not stem from the fact that postmodernism cannot be put into practice aesthetically, but from its declared dependence on the imagination, which assails all types of barriers and codes from the sociopolitical to the cultural and institutional, creating linguistic universes and artistic visions of challenging and also impossible (at least in its historical actuality) decodification: "Why did I speak of Postmodernist impossibilities? The Modernist wrote about conceivable, possible worlds; the Postmodernist writes about conceivable, at least thinkable, but impossible worlds, worlds that—so reason tells us—can exist only in our imagination" (Fokkema 54). Moreover, this citation shows that Fokkema, like Hassan—although without the necessity of seeing one modality as the intensifier of the other—also relies on the comparison between modernism and postmodernism with the goal of clarifying the most transcendental directions of postmodernism. One such direction that appears central to such differentiation shares a certain similarity with what Deleuze and Guattari call the rhizomatic, in the sense of stemming from different points without respect for a determined hierarchy, classification, or organization: "Whereas Modernist texts relied on the selection of hypothetical constructions, the socio-code of Postmodernism is based on a preference for nonselection or quasi-nonselection, on a rejection of discriminating hierarchies, and a refusal to distinguish between truth and fiction, past and present, relevant and irrelevant. Yet, as a code it has contributed to texts that as a result of their discussions of basic philosophical problems, such as the nature of causality, or morality, or evolution, or time, or infinity, are highly relevant to contemporary thought" (Fokkema 42). Among the significant characteristics that Fokkema delineates with respect to postmodernism are the malleable relationship between author and text—in the sense that the text can take on its own existence and the author thus ceases to emphasize specific directions, connections, or ends of the text—increasing the text's discontinuity and fragmentation. Other textual aspects that Fokkema distinguishes as characteristic of postmodernism are: (1) the duplicity of writing and multiplicity of signs in a literary work; (2) the text conceived as a palimpsest that collects the traces of numerous writings; and (3) the emphasis on the construction itself of the text—on its fictitious assembly rather than on the story that is told.[4]

In my perspective, upon studying Roa Bastos's short stories through the optics of postmodernism, I understand that the postmodern artistic course is a new artistic avenue within the spatialized trajectory of modernity. In some cases, postmodernism is a new aesthetic source— the reaction to modern forms that tend to become fossilized—while in other cases, postmodernism represents the artistic surrender to the most extreme developments of modernity. Postmodernism can be an intensifying force of modernism, or simply a marginalized reaction to a perceived placing of modernism within an established aesthetic system that has thus lost the natural subversive inclination of the modernist sensibility. In either of these situations, postmodernism is not an artistic occurrence that is positioned after modernism, but on the contrary, cohabits with it. Their coexistence should not be alarming if one takes into account the foundational moments of modernity. Clearly, it seems to us that it is not necessary to wait for postmodernism until the final stage of capitalism or the manifestations of the most daring technological innovations, as Jameson claims. Ihab Hassan states, "Whether we tend to revalue Modernism in terms of Postmodernism (Poirier) or to reverse that procedure (Kermode), we will end by doing something of both since relations, analogies, enable our thought. Modernism does not suddenly cease so that Postmodernism may begin, they now coexist. New lines emerge from the past because our eyes every morning open anew" (Hassan 53). However, the relationship between modernism and postmodernism does not suggest that the latter is suddenly subordinated to the former without being able to completely liberate itself from the modernist tradition to undertake new and even more extreme artistic visions, which it in fact amply succeeds in doing. The association between modernism and postmodernism indicates only the fact that postmodernism is a process with nonhierarchical relationships from which it unfolds itself freely, escaping limits of periodization. Moreover, postmodernism is completely agitated by the uneasy voices that arose in the first artistic manifestations of modernity.

Postmodernism—even when it incorporates the tradition of modernity—implies a process of differentiation. It promotes a multipolar conglomeration from which it unleashes elements of artistic configuration, losing interest in pre-postmodern art's compulsion for finding a coherent interpretative universe and a visible vision of the world. In other words, postmodernism fails to make the case for its aesthetics of creation, although such an aesthetics may be potentially implied in its creative process. The reason behind postmodernism's failure to promote its own aesthetic theory is that creation itself becomes questionable because it presents itself as a congruent production, as the concatenation of ideas, as the pedestal from which an exquisite piece of knowledge, the visions of a prophet, or the material of incontestable reasoning emanate. In Spanish literature, from *El Quijote* on forward, modernity arises from that glance that looks back toward its own work. In other words, as Paz very lucidly indicates, the spirit of modernity resides in its capacity to criticize itself. In postmodern literature, this critical contemplation is converted into doubt. First doubt arises, and then doubt about that doubt. There is vacillation about the steps of creation and about whether this internal, self-contemplative auscultation is efficient and conducive to some type of resolution. This perceived complexity of postmodern works often resides in the works' resistance to interpretation or in the fact that interpretations of these works can proliferate, thus causing an unpleasant sensation in those who envision art as a decipherable symbolic totality or, even worse, as a linguistic entity-product of communication. There is also a distrust that it is possible to arrive at an equation between critical introspection and aesthetic realization. Consequently, a significant corpus of postmodern production leans toward the most varied forms of existentialism, reaching nihilistic positions. It also directs itself to questions relating to a metaphysics of time and its relationships with language—expressive impotence—and death. Hence, that postmodern critical contemplation to which I refer can, at times, manifest itself in silence in the forms of narrative mutism, blank spaces in artistic representation, absence of plots, or disdain for the anecdotic. Contrarily, it can realize itself in the proliferation of repetitive and chaotic narrative voices, or the desire of a voice to submerge itself in its own orphanhood (disauthorship and disauthorization), psychic displacement, subconscious and oneiric creases. Yurkievich emphasizes the authentic celebration of the free will of postmodernism: "Descree de cualquier ortodoxia, depone toda sistemática renuncia a preceptivas canónicas; quiere individuar la obra, acentuar lo personal y lo fantasioso, por eso reivindica una libertad imbuida de subjetividad" ("It disbelieves any orthodoxy, deposes all systematic renouncing of canonical precepts; it wants to individualize the work, accentuate that which is personal and conceited, that is why it vindicates a liberty imbued with subjectivity"; Yurkievich 12). Postmodernism does not place itself against interpretation (Sontag) as much as beyond interpretation. This—if necessary—is a factor of reception, a question that the launchers of postmodern art dislodge from the plane of their preoccupations. It is not so much a question of indifference toward the exercise of reading an aesthetic production, as the confirmation that this potential reading is an integral part of the doubts that assault one upon writing. If interpretation is possible, it is in the body of writing, in its interstices instead of occurring outside of writing. Meanings attract each other as if they were crowded clusters, creating a powerful force of attraction in their crossing and accumulation as well as in their dispersion. This postmodern operation captures residual meanings and incorporates them in a prominent way, or simply absorbs them like cosmic gravitation, as if it were the infinite whirlpool of a supermassive black hole.

These reflections on postmodernism are necessary in order to attempt an elucidation of Roa Bastos's work that creates a *zone* of reception according to the singular creative texture of the Paraguayan writers' *oeuvre*, understanding that one of the characteristics that puts Roa Bastos's aesthetics into perspective is the rhizomatic nature—in the Deleuzian sense—of the postmodern condition of his work. Roa Bastos's assumption of postmodernism results in the invention of an aesthetics that does not specify a departure or arrival point, or respond to a centralized hierarchy of principles, or manifestos that orient his works' processes. He starts from whatever point he can and extends himself to whatever point possible. There is no negativity or excuse surrounding the uneven growth of his works: "Unlike trees or their roots, the rhizome connects any point to any other point and its traits are not necessarily linked to traits of the same nature; it brings into play very different regimes of signs and even non-sign states. The rhizome is reducible neither to the One nor the multiple . . . It is composed not of units but of dimensions, or rather directions in motion. It has neither beginning nor end, but always a middle (milieu) from which it grows and which it overspills (Deleuze and Guattari 21). The comprehension of the rhizome as an incessant activity of growth in diverse and uncontrollable directions, and in permanent movement, not only configures a provocative metaphor for understanding postmodernism, but also an extraordinarily productive space for the exegesis of Roa Bastos's work.[5]

I suggest an approximation to Roa Bastos's short stories based on the hybrid proclivity of postmodernism, on the fact that its plurality is the reflection of its origins and foundations, which also explains its multipolar functionality. This approach is also founded on the fact that postmodernism reinvents the transformative aesthetics of modernism, sometimes radicalizing ruptures with modernity and other times seeking to distance itself from everything that seems to have been converted into precept, even when such precepts are presented as modern. Thus, I do not consider postmodernism to be a historical phenomenon that occurred after modernity, but rather the necessary vanguard agitation for renovation that nurtures the very notion of change to which modernism subscribes. That is why I defend the idea that in the case of Spanish American narrative, authors who write during time periods as distant as Macedonio Fernández, Juan Emar, and Vicente Huidobro (vanguard contemporaries), on the one hand, and Severo Sarduy, Enrique Jaramillo Levi, and Roberto Bolaño, on the other (who wrote from the 1970s into the twenty-first century), can be studied within a postmodern perspective. I am just citing one example in "Juegos nocturnos," but there are certainly many others in the literary development of the twentieth century and beginning of the twenty-first century in Latin America. In the case of "Juegos nocturnos," I am specifically referring to the story's ability to achieve a form of literary silence and to the challenge of expressing its artistic vision of time through philosophical concepts such as that of duration. One must thus accept the tremendous impact the story has as a different narrative mode. "Juegos nocturnos" is a fine literary production that presupposes a particular metaphysical vision of time. I am not advocating, thus, for an integral and homogenous postmodernism that results in the articulation of a single, defined, and constituted aesthetics, but rather for the uneven sprouting of postmodern formations that frequently barely insinuate themselves. By making itself synonymous with heterogeneity and relativity, postmodernism creates an affinity with any aesthetics in formation, transforming the idea of artistic execution into an experiment.

One of the most radical encounters between Roa Bastos and the principles that configure postmodernism in the terms I have just described is the story "Juegos nocturnos," included in the collection *Moriencia* in 1969. David W. Foster has very accurately referred to the structural complexity of this story as well as to the surreal level of individual consciousness that one can detect throughout the narration, especially in the narrative trajectory of the main character who expresses himself through a fluid stream-of-consciousness (79–83). There is also an extraordinary wealth of artistic perspectives in the text, which suggests that Roa Bastos was sensitive to diverse aesthetic positions in his search for his own literary direction. This confers a *sui generis* postmodern realization of the text in which the perplexity experienced by the act of reading it contrasts with the deliberate perfection of its narrative strategy. Such ingenuity invokes a call to hermeneutics, which makes the scarce critical attention paid to this story even more surprising. It is possible that an isolated perception of its complexity might serve as a deterrent for such a focus, although the challenge of a complex work of art represents one of the greatest stimuli for enjoyment within critical activity. On the other hand, it is unquestionable that complexity *per se* is not what determines the postmodern condition of a work. Admittedly, it is probable that this perceived complexity might have to do with the unfamiliarity of the new aesthetic territory opened up by a work that takes new paths, especially in the case of the postmodern period, in which directions are not embedded in a recognizable or familiar principle, as Lyotard indicates: "A postmodern artist or writer is in the position of a philosopher: the text he writes, the work he produces are not in principle governed by pre-established rules, and they cannot be judged according to a determined judgment, by applying familiar categories to the text or to the work. Those rules and categories are what the work of art itself is looking for. The artist and the writer, then, are working without rules in order to formulate the rules of what will have been done" (Lyotard 81).

The first temptation when analyzing "Juegos nocturnos," particularly taking into account its title—the persistent image of a man in bed, its high level of narrative disassociation, and its generally fragmentary style—is to envision the story as oneiric discourse. Although limited, such a perspective is not erroneous. The fact that the main character only manages to fall asleep toward the end of the story points more toward the insistence of a linear reading than the absence of dreams in the text. The oneiric and the desire for, and production of, narrative ambiguity are present in latent form. This, of course, is not the only possible interpretation of the text. This is the point at which the postmodern pulsation enters "Juegos nocturnos." Roa subverts this initial expectation for textual analysis, creating a complex and inventive interactive network of artistic planes. The Paraguayan writer offers a guideline with respect to one of many modes of exploring, enriching and renovating the modern tradition of the short story in Latin America. On the one hand, this network to which I refer will connect the interior treatment of time as a contraction of the past converted into present to a zone of narrative silence. On the other, it will artistically concretize duration as a multitude of experiences condensed into one within a nihilistic and existentialist background that will reveal a complete metaphysics of time and being.[6]

On the threshold of a hyperreal space, in which the conscious and subconscious states are practically indistinguishable, one glimpses the dramatization of a deep oneirism in "Juegos nocturnos." I do not mean to say that there is a nightmarish dream, but rather the fall into a deterritorialized space from which arises a specter of aimless movements, gestures, and insinuations. This space without territory is, in reality, time, which, following Bergson's perspective, cannot be captured as space because, in that case, its divisibility would make the experience of duration of time impossible. In other words, the heterogeneous register of the past, for example, can be assimilated to an individual's interior psychological experience of that same past, which can be perceived as an authentic experience and not merely as the sum of the occurred events. The experience of past duration in "Juegos nocturnos" is not a homogenous horizontal line constituted by a determined number of points in space but a confluence of the heterogeneous distribution of these points. The past is interiorized as if it were a living organism fused with the present.[7] Interpreting the Bergsonian dialectic of the past and the present, Deleuze makes a significant affirmation in this regard:

> Las grandes tesis de Bergson sobre el tiempo se presentan del siguiente modo: el pasado coexiste con el presente que él ha sido; el pasado se conserva en sí como pasado en general (no cronológico); el tiempo se desdobla a cada instante en presente y pasado, presente que pasa y pasado que se conserva. Con frecuencia se redujo el bergonismo a la idea siguiente: la duración sería subjetiva y constituiría nuestra vida interior. Y sin duda era preciso que Bergson se expresara así, al menos al comienzo. Pero poco a poco irá diciendo otra cosa: la sola subjetividad es el tiempo, el tiempo no cronológico captado en su fundación, e interiores al tiempo somos nosotros, no al revés.
>
> Bergson's great theses about time are presented in the following way: the past coexists with the present that it has been; the past is preserved in itself as the past in general (not chronological); time unfolds at every instant in present and past, present that passes and past that is conserved. Frequently, the Bergsonian idea was reduced to the following: duration would be subjective and would constitute our interior life. And without a doubt it was necessary that Bergson express himself thus, at least in the beginning. But little by little he will say something else: the only subjectivity is time, nonchronological time captured at its foundation, and we are within time, not the other way around. (My translation)[8]

The unavoidable sensation, and yet simultaneous uncertainty, that in "Juegos nocturnos" time has retreated toward the inaccessible dimension of psychic meanderings or unexpected oneirism; the stumbling voice completely disinterested in guiding narrativity, and the metaphysical desire for temporal annulment, all destroy the idea of representation precisely because what one is looking for is not to represent, but rather to reveal in an expressionistic way, sensations that cannot be measured by the succession of time intervals. If such a succession were to occur, it would signal the presence of a chronological temporality. In this text, measurable time disappears since this time lacks quality with regard to psychic expression, whether such psychic expression manifests itself in conscious or semiconscious wakefulness, or in the resulting reality of dream, or in the activation of the subconscious. When Bergson posits spatial motion with sensations that occur in consciousness as essential alternatives for human beings with respect to time, he insists upon the indivisible nature of sensations: "Sensations, essentially indivisible, escape measurement; movements, always divisible, are distinguished by calculable differences of direction and velocity."[9]

Roa Bastos considers artistic expression to be exquisitely close to that of painting, and this allows him to make dynamic, in various settings, the flow of sensations of a figure who basically lies in his bed. His futile attempts to light a cigar, sit up in bed, read, stand up, move to another room, and turn a fan on and off inevitably return him to his horizontal position—of a stretched-out silhouette upon whose head a circle of light from the bedside lamp falls. However, this shining light does not alter the darkness of the environment, a space that, at this point, has clearly become the unfolding of a consciousness instead of a recognizable territory (such as the house or the room). Nor does it provide the palpable presence of an identifiable being like the character within such bounds of literary convention as the substance of his history, or an anecdotal progression. That is precisely why I prefer the term *figure* (also used in the story) instead of *protagonist*, since in the case of the latter, interest would center on the course of an existence measured or counted by the succession of time intervals, which would lead us to chronological time—clearly the dimension rejected by this story. It is also necessary to observe, in this respect, that although the story opens and closes with the term "man," in order to refer to the principal character—upon whom a name is never conferred—it is in the text itself that the terms "figure" and "silhouette" appear in view of the gradual dissolution of the man's physical materiality as well as his assimilation into the vaporous and malleable character of time. That is, the figure at a certain point integrates itself within that flow of temporal images. The reading of the crumbling of this psychic shadow who is lying on the bed, together with an uninterrupted "círculo de luz subiendo y bajando sobre el pecho" ("a circle of light rising and falling above his chest"; *Moriencia* 62), thus experiences a transformation from the preoccupation with the history of a man and the expectation of its representation to the discontinuous wandering of an evocative consciousness.

This atmosphere possessing the texture of an expressionistic painting—based on the strokes of the sensations of a consciousness and not the events that occur to a determined protagonist—portrays the stillness of a man in a bed with his resulting subconscious states, either referring to the reading of a specific work, or a oneiric voyage, or of semi-immobility. Such a state is close to that of sleepwalking, and is hardly distinguishable from his persistent condition of adherence and subjection to horizontality from which the subterraneous processes emerge that inform the psychic event. This flow of consciousness gives rise to Bergsonian resonances with respect to the concept of *duration*, especially applicable in the story to the voyages of the memory relating to fragments of conversations, to references to the man's friends, and to the memory of the relationship that he had with an English woman: "The duration lived by our consciousness is a duration with its own determined rhythm, a duration very different from the time of the physicist, which can store up, in a give interval, as great a number of phenomena as we please" (Bergson, *Matter*, 272).This plural quality of the rhythms of duration demonstrates, as Deleuze has indicated in his essay on Bergson, the absolute character that duration achieves.[10] The displacements of the consciousness of this figure—"monumental silhouette," as he is called in the story—do not refer to the apprehension of a uniform time ("homogeneous" in Bergson's terminology) in which events progress by time intervals without a condensation or tension that captures the heterogeneity of that experience in terms of its duration (in other words, of an interiorized and indivisible revelation of time).

The motions of psychic flow of this figure are scattered throughout the entire story from the beginning to the end, interrupting, from time to time, the narrative course of other stories or referents such as that of reading, for example. Moreover, these movements depict a clear situational framework that marks their entrance: "No—dijo el hombre sin sacar los ojos de las páginas del libro, ni el húmedo cigarro de la boca" ("No—said the man without taking his eyes off the pages of the book, nor the humid cigar in his mouth"; *Moriencia* 55). Later on, as a coda of the text, the story repeats: "No—dijo el hombre, sentado en la cama, restregándose los ojos" ("No—said the man, seated on the bed, rubbing his eyes"; *Moriencia* 62). Both invocations of "no" suggest the placement of watchtowers of referents, as if it were necessary to make explicit that what occurs in that intermediate narrative space involves some type of relationship with the oscillations of a consciousness, whether this is the eventuality of the protagonist's disorientation, the absorption in his reading or in a deep sleep, the remembering of the past, or any other exterior or interior state that parallels, or is confused with, his state of sleeping. These "nos" of entering and leaving also create the illusion of a narrative structure of perfect coherence in which the former would permit the entrance into dream, and the latter, the exit from the same. However, in reality, the first "no" implies a state of lethargy characterizing the man in his bed and his brief attempts, already described, to realize a minimal activity markedly related to objects around him rather than to other human beings. The second "no," instead of waking him from a dream, induces him to it, ending with the sporadic and feeble attempts at activity, casting him back into the bed: "Hizo girar los ojos turbios de sueño a su alrededor, intentando un impulso de levantarse, pero se desmoronó de nuevo. Después se agachó, oprimió la perilla del ventilador, parpadeó dos o tres veces hasta oír que el zumbido encerrado en la caja llenaba la habitación y se quedó dormido con el círculo de luz subiendo y bajando sobre el pecho" ("He made his eyes cloudy with sleep look around him, attempting an impulse to get up, but he collapsed again. Afterward, he bent down, pressed the knob of the fan, blinked two or three times until he heard that the buzz enclosed in the box was filling the room and he fell asleep with the circle of light rising and falling on his chest"; *Moriencia* 62).

We do not know what transpires before the first "no" or what happens after the second "no." Before the first, we have nothing—the absence of narration, the disembodiment of all fictitious trace. After the second, we witness the end of the fictitious with the consequent disappearance of the figure, and, in the best of cases, what we have in the remnants of textual permanence is the mystery that dreams allot to us, which, for this figure, is also synonymous with nothingness: "Los dos entran ahí o se están a los arrumacos y a las caricias, mientras *yo me hundo en la nada del sueño*" ("The two enter there or are being affectionate and caressing each other, while I sink into the nothingness of sleep"; *Moriencia* 55). On the other hand, as symbols, these negations—that signal a specific narrative location—reveal an existential function with respect to this silhouette's vision of the world. His reclined position, horizontal like a persistent image of the text, rules the universe constituting his very existence and desires: the nothingness of sleep. Even when this figure succeeds in sitting up momentarily, his final destiny is to return to his horizontality, to the oneiric fall. He does not wish to leave this zone unless it is in a hypothetical manner of a postponed obligation that probably will never happen, as the use of the conditional tense suggests: "Tendría que levantarme, caminar un poco, probar algún bocado, antes de que ellos lleguen" ("I would have to get up, walk a little, eat something, before they arrive"; *Moriencia* 55). While the first "no" follows that uncertain "would have to" (unrealizable, in essence), and the miragelike probabilities of "Tal vez sí, tal vez no; todo es y no es" ("Perhaps yes, perhaps no; everything is and is not"; *Moriencia* 55), the second "no" is followed by a definite refutation of what is known or remembered: "No sé . . . dijo luchando por recordar algo" ("I don't know . . . he said struggling to remember something"; *Moriencia* 62). The doubt and refutation of one and another "no" coincide in their notion of incredulity, which presents no other alternative than the state of return or reintegration into bed, drawing itself once again within this picture of a horizontal line—corresponding to the idea of duration (not of time) in the middle of which transmigrate sensations of reading (formative and discursive process of humans); of sentimental connection (the interpenetration of time and memory and the recuperation of the past as present); of scattered conversations with friends (the social networks in their absurd functioning); human psyche and biology (the voyeuristic inclination of desire that projects contemplating the sexual relationship that a couple is going to have near his house); and the sexuality of the two young people mediated by violence (the physical abuse of the young girl). This last instance—the wait and arrival of the couple—can be linked to the focal points of the story corresponding to the fluctuations transpired between wakefulness—semiconscious activity, in the case of this character—and sleep. That is, that the desire for the voyeuristic act and its interruption by violence do not seem to relate so much to the time of reverberation of memory but rather to a distinguishable sensation of stimulation.

It is important to stress that none of these instances is *told*. The text is not the narration of a man on the threshold of dreams who is going to tell five stories in order to finally fall asleep. Such a synthesis exposes, at best, the absurd reductionism of a reading preoccupied with identifying content in literature, and, at worst, perceiving events as if the literary space could not exist outside of determined systematizations of rational inference. We should acknowledge that the inherent limitation of every critical reading—from intellectual formation (number, absorption, and impact of all kinds of philosophical, historical, sociological, anthropological, artistic, and scientific readings) to the comprehension of the nature of art (an attitude more in consonance with the humility of the *silences* that the artist has faced)—begins with the transformation of one's own reading in an attempt—albeit failed—to approach the sounds of those *silences*. Before organizing contents and interpreting them as if each one of these units responded to a certain problematic exposed in the work, it would be preferable to reconsider what Blanchot affirms about the artist: "The poet is one who, through his sacrifice, keeps the question open in his work. At every time he lives the time of distress, and his time is always the empty time when what he must live is the double infidelity: that of men, that of the gods—and also the double absence of the gods who are not longer and who are not yet" (Blanchot, *The Space of Literature*, 247). On the other hand, there is the theme of voyeurism associated with waiting for the couple who is going to have a sexual relationship: "Lo único que podemos inventar son nuestros vicios" ("The only thing that we can invent is our vices"; *Moriencia* 55). There is also the issue of a wasteful consumer society with scars of poverty related to the comments of the book that the man is reading, encompassing an important section of this psychic wandering, which leads us to question the reasons why they occupy that space and the possible connection between these topics. In his introduction to *Anti-Oedipus: Capitalism and Schizophrenia*, Mark Seem discusses some central tenets of Deleuze's and Guattari's thesis. One of them seems significant to me for the comprehension of this apparent thematic dissimilitude, which really is not such if one takes into account that, in both cases, it is a question of flows, the libidinal, and that of the circulation of money, which Seem anticipates. In the case of Deleuze and Guattari, these concepts are not separately visualized, as occurs in other thinkers who reflect upon the synthesis of thought between Freud and Marx and the importance of their analysis in contemporary society: "Deleuze and Guattari, on the other hand, postulate one and the same economy, the economy of flows. The flows and productions of desire will simply be viewed as the unconscious of the social productions. Behind every investment of time and interest and capital, an investment of desire, and vice versa" (Deleuze and Guattari xviii).

Conjecturing about "Juegos nocturnos," with respect to what happens and what is told, is a question that, in reality, does not interest me not only because, in essence, nothing is told or happens in this story, but also because such a desire coincides with a traditional, content-based reading. We interrogate, preferentially, one possibility of those *games*: between the focal points of two "nos"—constitutive of an existentialist position of both a skeptical and nihilistic nature, the meaninglessness of all actions precipitates the ulterior descent into the nothingness of sleep. Here the material of a memory is activated in which at least two clear past moments stand out—like a recuperative option—and these moments are registered and confused in the present. I am not referring to clearly discernable temporalities, but rather to an experience of duration in which the arrow of *time* travels from the past to the present: "The truth is that memory does not consist in a regression from the present to the past, but, on the contrary, in a progress from the past to the present" (Bergson, *Matter*, 319). This demonstrates that the total mixture of temporal planes in the story makes the divided notion of times disappear. Foster believes that it is possible to circumscribe the narrative lapse in the story: "The narrative time of the story extends over a brief stretch of the past, during a late hour of the evening in which—the man—is reading Harrington's book, his window open to the sounds of a neighborhood dance; he is also awaiting the arrival of the two lovers, his 'clients'"(Foster 81). This demarcation, however, projects a fixation with the idea of finding a measurement—expressed as time—for the "semiconscious" state of the man, and classifying what happens in the middle (until finally this human shadow falls asleep) as what cannot be temporally measured, that is, the stream of consciousness of the being who journeys through the story. Technically, the reader can detect the events that occur between the two "nos," that is, between the moment in which the man lays down to read and when he falls asleep, which will include the reading of the book by Harrington and his comments; the wait for the arrival at his house of the two young people who are going to have a sexual encounter; the arrival of these young people, in which the girl is physically abused; the intercalated conversations with friends, among whom Pepe, Martín, MacGregor, and Julia's husband are mentioned; and the man's relationship with Carolina, the widow who enjoys Edward Elgar's music. Artistically, however, the fusion of all these lapses is what sustains the creation of a single psychic flow.

The distinction between these various instances thus creates an aesthetic simulacrum in which, in appearance, two narrative courses coexist: that of the figure stretched out on the bed that finally falls asleep and that of the two settings previously described. However, the mutual tangling of all of these courses integrates the nocturnal games of a consciousness whose horizontal position is presented in the form of "una inmovilidad de *flotación* en la que el hombre parece encallado" ("an immobility of flotation in which the man appears to run aground"; *Moriencia* 56). The "immobility of flotation" represents a key metaphorical enunciation in the text because it situates the state of a consciousness experiencing sensations of duration produced without divisions. The fragmented and discontinuous mode occurs in the perception of the reading, which corresponds to the attempt to rationalize what is not possible and find *contents* in the stories of the aforementioned settings. The text is an aesthetic proposal that does not have anything to do with telling, but rather with traveling within the durative processes of a consciousness, which explains what we perceive as temporal transfers or stories that appear unfinished, breaks in the narrative flow, and dispersion of memories: "To perceive means to immobilize," Bergson says (Bergson, *Matter*, 275). That is, memory, instead of expanding events that occurred in the past in a scattered fashion, restores their occurrence in a moment that was present, thus joining together the sensations that make possible the experience of duration and recuperation. In other words, the contraction or condensation that can induce this type of immobilization is what makes possible the personal experience or presence of the past as present. This past, we should clarify, was already constituted in the moment in which it was its turn to be present, instance in which it was not visualized as past but rather as the possible register of the future. This temporal dialectic is discussed by Deleuze when he studies Mankiewicz's films: "Jamás podría la memoria evocar y contra el pasado si no se hubiera constituido ya en el momento en que el pasado era todavía presente, y por tanto con una finalidad futura. Precisamente por eso es una conducta: sólo en el presente nos construimos una memoria y lo hacemos para servirnos de ella en el futuro, cuando el presente sea pasado" ("The memory could never evoke against the past if it had not already constituted the moment in which the past was still present, and therefore with a future finality. Precisely for that reason, it is a conduct: only in the present do we construct a memory and do it in order to make use of it in the future, when the present is past"; Deleuze, *La imagen*, 77). This allows us to understand that in "Juegos nocturnos," the two registers clearly associated with the past—the conversation with the man's friends and his relationship with the widowed Englishwoman—are inserted in an amalgamated way into the supposed present of the reading of Harrington's book. In fact, between the last comment of this book and the story of the English woman, there is no transition at all.

In a postmodern realization of the text, divisible physical and spatial time have disappeared in order to create a crowded vision of presents—from presents that belong to perceptible experience and those that are restorations of the past. However, the conglomeration of presents (this time all reunited, the present presents and the past presents) prepares for the future reconstruction of the present as past, which, in this last case, would devolve from the scope of the protagonist to be textualized as the faculty of reading. This experience, as we have affirmed throughout this chapter, is best apprehended in Bergsonian terms, understanding that the compact grouping of presents is not the sum of various times or intervals of times, but rather a flow of sensations interiorized as duration. Bergson states in this regard:

> Es precisamente esta continuidad indivisible de cambio lo que constituye la duración verdadera . . . la duración real es lo que siempre se ha llamado tiempo, pero el tiempo percibido como indivisible. No estoy en desacuerdo con que el tiempo implica sucesión. Pero que la sucesión se presente en primer lugar a nuestra conciencia como la distinción de un 'antes' y un 'después' yuxtapuestos, eso yo no podría aceptarlo. Cuando escuchamos una melodía, tenemos la impresión más pura de sucesión que podemos tener—una impresión tan alejada como es posible de la simultaneidad—y sin embargo es la continuidad misma de la melodía y la imposibilidad de descomponerla lo que causa en nosotros esa impresión. (Bergson, *Memoria*, 27)
>
> It is precisely this indivisible continuity of change that constitutes true duration . . . disagreement with the fact that time implies succession. But that this succession presents itself in the first place to our consciousness as the distinction between a juxtaposed "before" and "after," I cannot accept. When we listen to a melody, we have the purest impression of succession that we can have—an impression as distant as possible from simultaneity—and nonetheless it is the continuity itself of the melody and the impossibility of decomposing it that creates this impression in us.

It is for that reason that decomposing "Juegos nocturnos" into the previously signaled intervals functions only on the plane of metareading, like a disquisition on the resources of narrative techniques in the short story.

Aesthetically, what our reading captures is the dizzying surge of a psychic flow that does not have time, and for which—now on a metaphysical level—the concretions of the past and the future disappear, since before them only remains the profound interiorized experience of presents through a consciousness going in the direction of nothingness. Neither the fervent commentaries on Harrington's book, nor the story of the English woman, nor the reverberations of social interactions with friends, nor the wait for the lovers, their arrival, quarrel, and unleashing of violence, have transcendence. The narrative subject will finally enter the world of dreams conceived by him as the course of nothingness. This is another postmodern manifestation: the true narrative subjects are the trajectory of a time without time and the life of a being—dissolved from a man into a figure and silhouette—who faces the final submergence into nothingness. It is from this point—once understood, this relation of relativity to the possibility or impossibility of representation of being and time and being and nothingness—that one can also attempt a reading in which the totality of the five aforementioned settings, including the fusion of intermediate presents and presents that are restitutions of the past—would be no longer considered a psychic flow but rather an oneiric experience. In this case, following Deleuze's comprehension of Bergson's thought, this subject also would be affected by the entire universe that surrounds him together with his reconnection to a shifting past: "La teoría bergsoniana del sueño demuestra que el durmiente no está cerrado en absoluto a las sensaciones del mundo exterior e interior. Sin embargo, él las pone en relación no ya con imágenes-recuerdo particulares sino con capas de pasado fluidas y maleables que se contentan con un ajuste muy amplio o flotante" ("Bergson's theory of sleep demonstrates that the sleep is not at all closed to the sensations of the exterior and interior world. However, he relates them not only to particular images-memories but also to fluid and malleable layers of the past that are satisfied with a very wide and floating adjustment"; Deleuze, *Bergsonism*, 32). This adjustment indicated by Deleuze would correspond in the case of Roa's story to a perceived image of the narrative subject's flotation. I have already noted that this narrative figure also sits down, walks, stretches out his hand, and scratches his neck, among other physical movements. Thus, when I say image, I am referring to a recomposition and perception about how the narrative figure impacts us. Thus, this final absorbing metaphor inherent in all great artistic works reveals the picture of a consciousness represented in the fabric of writing like that of a floating, horizontal line, constructed by presents or vanished times, without movements, which raises the expectation of dreams pointing toward a hopeless destiny bound for the direction of nothingness.

In examining "Juegos nocturnos," the reader can appreciate that the postmodern condition of this text does not seek the production of messages that can be decodified in an *interpretation* converted into *the interpretation*. "Juegos nocturnos" and other stories by Roa

Bastos are, rather, texts that gyrate around a flow of nonmethodical pulsations, in the middle of what Deleuze calls "region of intensities."

I will now further illustrate this affirmation with some concise observations about the potential avenues of exegesis of the stories "Contar un cuento" (To Tell a Story) and "Bajo el Puente" ("Under the Bridge"). By proposing a hermeneutics that implies a shifting conception of the postmodern, I will attempt to capture the ways in which these two stories by Roa Bastos are transformed into bodies and textual extensions that pursue directions with total dispensation for the establishment of an agenda—the gestation of an ideology and that of its stagnation—or the desire to arrive at a determined meaning or series of meanings. These are texts that reject the temptation to systematize their artistic vibrations.

"Contar un cuento"—from *El baldío* (1966)—conjectures about writing as abstraction, as well as the existence of the short story genre in which writing is conceived as constant invention and deception. However, the story told is not only the artifice of the experience of writing, a metafiction of its psychic and paraliterary reverberation, but also a dismounting of the layers of reality, an exercise through which only the movement of an interminable narration is achieved. We will concentrate on two problems suggested by the text. The first concerns a scrutiny of the status of reality: what is reality in truth, where is it situated, what is its composition, substance, or pure projection? The text employs the image of the onion, whose continuous removal of one layer after another leads to nothingness. The apparent deception of removing these layers, leading to emptiness, is transformed, however, into an epiphany in the end because it is an obligatory blow that awakens one to the absolute necessity of this process to the formation of a consciousness: "esa nada es todo, o por lo menos un tufo picante que nos hace lagrimear los ojos" ("that nothing is everything, or at least a piquant odor that makes our eyes tear"; *Moriencia* 64). Reaching the nucleus of reality thus presupposes separating it from its substance, bringing to bear upon it a productive nihilism in terms of which dissimulation and tricks can be unmasked only with great difficulty. It is necessary to remove everything, to retrace each of the gaps with which the notion of reality has been socially and historically constructed: "Para mí la realidad es lo que queda cuando ha desaparecido toda la realidad" ("For me, reality is what remains when all of reality has disappeared"; (*Moriencia* 63–64).

The second question reminds us of Blanchot's formulation: "Admitamos que la literatura empieza en el momento que la literatura es pregunta. Esta pregunta no se confunde con las dudas o los escrúpulos del escritor" ("Let us concede that literature begins at the moment in which it is a question. This question, however, should not be confused with the writer's doubts or scruples"; Blanchot, *De Kafka*, 9). "Contar un cuento" presents a narrator who is perceived as adipose matter rather than a fat person whose repertoire of storytelling is similar to the interminable stories of Scheherazade, except that, in his case, the indefinite telling does not save him but leads to his own death after having dreamed of the space in which he would die. Thus, just as in "Juegos nocturnos," this story offers the presence of another character on the path to dissolution like "flabby unreality" first, and like total volatilization later on. Where, then, does this conversion of literature into a question lead us? Roa suggests the necessity of interminable narrative repetition (or finite with the death of narrative material) in order to achieve an absolutely new, renovated language: "Habría que encontrar un nuevo lenguaje, y mejor todavía un lenguaje de silencio" ("One should find a new language, and better yet, a language of silence"; *Moriencia* 64). At this point, both problems converge, since the notion of reality is presented as a project of discovery in which it is necessary to remove one layer after another in order to finally descend into a nothingness permitting the awakening of a consciousness that can grasp deception. Such an achievement cannot be realized by means of a language that is inscribed in that illusory reality because such language allows for the simulation in which we live. This new adopted language will then be silence, connected now to the necessity that the endlessly narrated material should die. Literature as narration and communication is going to die. From its death, the language of silence will be born. Thus, the last story is the one in which the storyteller (the fatty material) is revealed as pure fiction, and fiction ends there, in that last layer: "Contó varios cuentos. Quizás fueran uno solo, como siempre desdoblado en hechos contradictorios, desgajado capa tras capa y emitiendo su picante y fantástico sabor" ("He told various stories. Perhaps they were only one, as usual unfolded into contradictory facts, separated layer by layer, and emitting their piquant and fantastic flavor"; *Moriencia* 67). In the final prophecy of space where his death will occur, next to him, will also be his disturbed readers-disciples, those bewitched by the cyclical telling. It is the instance of absences, of silence and of nothing happening, but the epiphany of this experience can be surprising. In this regard Lyotard states: "The possibility of nothing happening is often associated with a feeling of anxiety, a term with strong connotations in modern philosophies of existence and of the unconscious. It gives to waiting, if we really mean waiting, a predominately negative value. But suspense can also be accompanied by pleasure, for instance pleasure in welcoming the unknown, and even by joy" (Lyotard, *The Inhuman*, 92). Lyotard continues his analysis of the meaning of the contradictory sentiments experienced when one is faced with the fact that nothing happens. He illustrates how this situation gave rise to the birth of the sublime together with the triumph of modernity in the seventeenth and eighteenth centuries (Lyotard, *The Inhuman*, 92). The ineffable condition of the sublime, and the diverse capacities for expression that it generates, are perfectly welcomed by the artistic movements of the vanguard. These tendencies belong to that postmodern desire to transform oneself in the moment in which stability is installed. Upon telling a story, Roa has to decompose its mechanisms and kill the narrator, consequently destroying the author and his production. Another epiphany is the resulting consequence. There is nothing behind the layer of an onion except more layers of onion. There is nothing behind the scenes of the story except the reverberations of fiction. Silence makes its presence felt and imposes itself. The arrival of silence does not represent a negative experience, but is instead a dislocated sign of warning and enrichment regarding the challenges of a creation whose prime material is precisely silence, a nonlucrative instance of time, which it is not necessary to measure but simply to feel "resonating the fragility of its lines," as the composer and violinist Malcolm Goldstein would say.

The reference in Roa's story to the lion full of lilies by da Vinci—the mechanical lion that Leonardo constructed causing admiration in the court of Luis XII—is also related to this idea of looking within, seeing what that fiction permits. What is symbolic in Leonardo's lion, apart from its humanistic message, is not the lilies that obviously activate the mechanical movement of the lion, but the tricks of invention it implies. These tricks are metaphysical in Roa: in the death of literature resides its birth. Roa's admiration for Da Vinci is declared: "Cuando hacia 1968 comencé a compilar *Yo el Supremo*, encontré el cuento esfumado ("Lucha hasta el alba") entre las páginas del Tratado de la pintura, de Leonardo da Vinci, libro que yo aprecio particularmente y que me enseñó a ver el sentido del mundo como un vasto jeroglífico en movimiento pero cuyos signos son también indescifrables" ("When around 1968 I began to compile *I The Supreme*, I found the disappeared story [Fight until Dawn] among the pages of a Treatise on Leonardo da Vinci's painting, a book I particularly appreciate and that taught me to see the meaning of the world as a vast hieroglyphic in movement, but whose signs are also indecipherable"; *Antología personal* 185). In Roa's thought, one can appreciate the enormous humility with which he undertook his literary projects. Each time that one of his texts searches deeper into that space of signs whose power, for Roa, is found in its own ineffable character, his texts reveal themselves to be true artistic attempts rather than definitive proposals.

The treatment of time in "Bajo el Puente"—a text that is included in *Madera quemada* (Burnt Wood; 1967)—refers directly to the question of duration, already presented from a postmodern perspective of existential, poetic, and metaphysical discourses. Such discourses have been present in Roa Bastos's short stories in texts as early as "La excavación" ("The Excavation")—from *El trueno entre las hojas* (1953)—and "El baldío" ("The Vacant Lot"), included in the collection by the same title, which appeared in 1966.[11] "Bajo el Puente" is the story of a schoolteacher in a desolate village who is found dead one day underneath the bridge. It is narrated by one of the teacher's students, who, as an adult, evokes his relationship with that teacher. The geographical spaces identified in the texts are Itacuruví, the village where the action transpires, and Villarrica del Espíritu Santo, a place where "se oía el tronar del cañón y el matraqueo de las ametralladoras" ("one could hear the cannon thunder and the din of the machine guns"; *Madera quemada* 53). This last event explains the arrival of a military train in the town, although it is clearly indicated that the soldiers did not fight in the village. The presence of the soldiers does not constitute a summary of historical events, but rather is a significant reference of contextualization, very much in line with the sophisticated and allusive nature of Roa Bastos's narrative. The importance of this episode to the story resides in the visit that a commander makes to the teacher's school while the teacher is conducting a class. During this visit, the narrative counterpoises the positivistic discourse of the commander, his trite rhetoric to the young people as "hope of the nation" (*Madera quemada* 54), and his look focused on the future, with the immobility, indifference, and irony of the teacher, whose only interest is to ask for a replacement in the rare instances in which someone from outside arrives at Itacuruví. It clearly represents a contrast in attitudes in regard to time.

The commander's time is measured in progression. The teacher's time is the circulation of a mythic and poetic flow that allows for a rebirth of the distant past, and thus an encounter with the desires of the present that have never been fulfilled and that will never be postulated as the future. The life of the teacher is a passage minimized in every sense, starting from the description of his aged body: "Todo él se iba achicando. Apretado, atorado en un agujero, pujando por salir. Pujaba y se atoraba. Solo, en el profundo agujero" ("All of him was shrinking. Squeezed, choked in a hole, pushing to leave. He pushed and he got stuck. Alone, in the deep hole"; *Madera quemada*, 58–59), and ending with his perception of reality in general and especially faced with the grandiloquence of projects that in his entire life as a teacher he failed to see realized. For example, when the commander promises to build a school, the teacher limits himself to saying: "Lo poco basta. Lo mucho se gasta" ("A little bit is enough. A lot gets wasted"; *Madera quemada* 55). The teacher's own house, located on the edge of the mountain, is finally invaded by nature, and even the immobile time that surrounds the teacher's existence seems to disappear. A dominating sense of regression in the text not only eliminates the possibility of futures, but also the formation of presents: "El mismo se había puesto un plazo, vamos a decir, no hacia delante sino al revés . . . Mañana no era un día para él ("He himself had imposed a time limit, let's say, not in the future, but backward . . . Tomorrow was not a day for him"; *Madera quemada* 51–52). It becomes more necessary, each time, to return to the past, but not to a past perceived as reminiscence of the present converted recently into past, but instead to a moment in which death and birth are paradoxically united, since the waters underneath the bridge do not reflect the dead body of the old teacher, but that of a newborn: "De golpe había volado hacia atrás, hacia el principio" ("Suddenly he had flown backward, toward the beginning"; *Madera quemada* 59).

In this new body, many people live together who are the same and there are many temporalities that are the same. It is the body of the teacher, that of the replacement that the teacher asked for, that of the stranger that he announced, and that of the narrator himself in his cyclical existence of replacement. In this mixture of times that return, the little boy who attended the teacher's classes becomes an adult and narrator of the story. In the intentionally unstable narrative present, he is the same age that the teacher was when he died under the bridge (more than sixty years old). On the one hand, the death of the teacher announces the character's own transformation. It is the metaphysical redemption of a desolate life. On the other hand, the transformation of the little boy into the teacher represents a psychological extension of the excellent relationship that he had with his teacher, although the teacher sometimes also exacted punishments: "El castigo más temido: el palo pelado alto, y el culpable ahorquetado en la punta, achicharrándose al sol" ("The most feared punishment: the tall, stripped stick, and the guilty one hung on the end, sizzling in the sun"; *Madera quemada* 50). The teacher, in contrast with the boy's father, does not humiliate the boy, but teaches him. The teacher also understands the boy, and even cures his injured eyes when the boy leaves his house because of his father's humiliating behavior. The relationship between the boy and his father (*el taitá*) is completely traumatic. The father, as a part of his punishment-joke because the boy fell asleep, makes him lower his trousers, threatening castration with a knife that he used to castrate animals: "Desde entonces me dura el susto. Una especie de vacío en esa parte del cuerpo" ("Since then I am afraid. A kind of emptiness in that part of the body"; *Madera quemada* 57). It is a maltreatment that leads the boy to hurt himself, fleeing to the mountain and exposing his eyes to the sun until they were damaged. From the trauma of abuse and his self-inflictment of pain, the boy ends up completely transformed—he will see with profundity. The teacher also changes: "Después se me destapó adentro otra Mirada, y en los ojos entraban más cosas que antes. De una manera diferente. Ver era desear y desear era recordar. Volví a la escuela. El maestro también distinto: el mismo, pero una persona diferente" ("After, I discovered another look within me, and more things than before entered my eyes. In a different way. Seeing was desiring and desiring was remembering. I returned to school. The teacher was also different: he himself, but a different person"; *Madera quemada* 57). The teacher also inflicts damage upon himself, his own death—underneath the bridge—in order to return in another way. From the incident, which affects the boy and the teacher, results a vision that allows for a different comprehension of existence in which the capture of its ineffable expression cohabits with the poetic appropriation of language. A simultaneous experience of time also emanates from this, in which time does not coincide with its homogenous visualization as if it were a space, but rather with the concept of duration as expressed by Bergson: "It is true that, when we make time a homogenous medium in which conscious states unfold themselves, we take it to be given all at once, which amounts to saying that we abstract it from duration. This simple consideration ought to warn us that we are thus unwittingly falling back upon space, and really giving up time" (Bergson, *Time and Free Will*, 98).

The metaphysical immateriality and the existentialist surface of this story occur only in the interior personal experience of time. However, such time loses its transparent notion of category and measurement in order to outline itself as a horizon of poetic fluency whose intensity increases with the fragmentation of temporal experience. The futures cannot be registered and the pasts become too unmemorable in order to sustain themselves, which is why they insert themselves behind the curtain of time, and the presents accumulate without ever disappearing as a mode of escape from the pain of the past. Time is metaphysical, and the stream-of-consciousness narrative lines require this multipolar connection with poetry in the form of a vision that captures the signs of the universe convoking the mythopoetical origin of all language.

NOTES

1. I do not entirely abandon a discussion of postmodernism in *El trueno entre las hojas*. There are a number of stories in this collection that can be studied within that postmodern perspective.

2. Lyotard, *The Postmodern Condition* 81. In the chapter "Rewriting Modernity," included in *The Inhuman*, Lyotard adds even more ideas that support his dialectical reflection on the relationships between modernity and postmodernity, especially the tremendous force contained in modernity that allows itself to be transformed into something other than the desire for modernity: "Rather we have to say that the postmodern is always implied in the modern because of the fact that modernity, modern temporality, comprises in itself an impulsion to exceed itself into a state other than itself . . . Modernity is constitutionally and ceaselessly pregnant with its postmodernity" (25).

3. In the first edition of *Faces of Modernity* in 1977, Calinescu discusses the then "recent" use of the term postmodernism as a subcategory of the vanguard. This position is revised in the second edition from 1987 in which the title of the book is changed to *Five Faces of Modernity*, and in which postmodernism is seen as one more phase of modernism even when Calinescu proceeds with caution with respect to an ultimate and closed definition of postmodernism: "My own theory or, better, understanding of postmodernism remains largely metaphorical and can be best stated in terms of the physiognomical "family of resemblances" to which I have referred earlier. Postmodernism is a face of modernism. It reveals some striking likenesses with modernism (whose name it continues to carry within its own), particularly in its opposition to the principle of authority, an opposition that now extends to both the utopian reason and the utopian unreason that some modernists worshipped" (Calinescu 312).

4. Regarding this characterization of postmodernism, see Fokkema's chapter, "Postmodernist Impossibilities: Literary Conventions in Borges, Barthelme, Robbe-Grillet, Hermans, and others," 37–56.

5. *Yo el Supremo*, undoubtedly, can be studied within this perspective. For his short stories, aside from the texts discussed in this essay, there are various other stories ascribed to the proposed postmodern characterization. In the genre of short story, however, there is a great difference between his first collection, *El trueno entre hojas*, and *El baldío* as well as other new stories that he wrote for the collection *Moriencia*.

6. For the concept of duration and its relationships with matter, time, and memory, I base this work on three texts by Bergson, noted in the bibliography: *Matter and Memory*, *Time and Free Will*, and *Memoria y vida*. This last work is a recompilation of texts by Bergson selected by Gilles Deleuze. It includes a preface by Angel Rivero (7–11). There is no introduction by Deleuze. The original French version is *Bergson. Memoire et vie (Textes Choisis peur Gilles Deleuze)* [France: Presses Universitaires de

France, 1975]. The first edition dates back to 1957, and also does not include an introduction by Deleuze.

7. The enormous influence that Bergson's thought exercised in the first few decades of the twentieth century gradually receded. After the end of the Second World War, this first plane occupied by his writings was merely an echo. This explains, in part, the association of Bergson's thought with modernism and not with postmodernism. However, the reevaluation of Bergson by Deleuze in *Bergsonism* and *La imagen-tiempo* (works also included in the bibliography) puts the fact that Bergson's ideas go beyond an exclusive filiation with the expositions of modernism into perspective. Deleuze refers to the "rediscovery" of Bergson in terms of the French philosopher's own philosophical directions: "To rediscover Bergson is to follow or carry forward his approach in these three directions referring to: 1) the necessity to see the Bergsonian idea of intuition of a method; 2) the fact that all science requires a metaphysics; 3) how the concept of duration should be understood, which, as a type of multiplicity, carries a distinction between continuous and discontinuous multiplicity, one spatial and the other temporal, one virtual and the other real, connecting, as Deleuze himself indicates, with Einstein's thought" (*Bergsonism* 117). Similarly, Deleuze considers that "a return to Bergson" does not only mean a renewed admiration for a great philosopher, but a renewal or extension of his project today in relation to the transformations of life and society, in parallel with the transformation of science" (*Bergsonism* 115).

8. Deleuze, *La imagen-tiempo* 115. Please note that all English translations in the text are mine.

9. Bergson, *Matter and Memory* 267. In the chapter dedicated to Bergson in *Founders of Constructive Postmodern Philosophy*, Gunter indicates that one of the aspects in which the author of *Matter and Memory* places himself beyond modern ideas would be the following: "One of Bergson's most fundamental departures from modernist thought is his extension to matter of the basic characteristics of psychological duration. The extent to which his bold move presaged the discoveries of classical quantum physics, nearly thirty years later, is astonishing, although it is not yet widely recognized" (137). Moreover, Gunter argues, Bergson's postmodern thought can be seen in his viewpoints relative to questions that in today's postmodern society are discussed, for example, feminism, ecology, and wars: "There is further insight to be gained from this. The problems of the abolition of war, of environmental degradation, and of feminism are precisely postmodern problems. Bergson was the first to see—or at any rate the first to say explicitly—that these problems are bound together by a common effort to overcome the closed society, paternalism, and 'natural religion.' He was also the first to see that no one of them can be solved apart from the others" (158).

10. Bergson does indeed speak of a plurality of rhythms of duration, but in this context he makes it clear—in relation to durations that are more

or less slow or fast—that "each duration is an absolute, and that each rhythm is itself a duration" (*Bergsonism* 76).

11. In my article "Historia e intrahistoria en la cuentística de Augusto Roa Bastos," included in *Augusto Roa Bastos* (111–23), I discuss the existentialist dimension of the stories "La excavación" and "El baldío."

Works Cited

Bergson, Henri. *Matter and Memory*. Mineola, NY: Dover, 2004. Print.

———. *Memoria y vida. Textos escogidos por Gilles Deleuze*. Madrid: Alianza Editorial, 2004. Print.

———. *Time and Free Will: An Essay on the Immediate Data of Consciousness*. New York: Harper Torchbooks, 1960. Print.

Berman, Marshall. *All that is Solid Melts into Air: The Experience of Modernity*. New York: Simon and Schuster, 1982. Print.

Blanchot, Maurice. *The Space of Literature*. Lincoln: University of Nebraska Press, 1982. Print.

———. *De Kafka a Kafka*. México: Fondo de Cultura Económica, 1991. Print.

Burgos, Fernando, ed. *Las voces del karaí: estudios sobre Augusto Roa Bastos*. Madrid: Edelsa. Edi-6, 1988. Print.

Calinescu, Matei. *Five Faces of Modernity: Modernism. Avant-Garde. Decadence. Kitsch. Postmodernism*. Durham, NC: Duke University Press, 1987. Print.

Deleuze, Gilles, and Félix Guattari. *A Thousand Plateaus: Capitalism and Schizophrenia*. Minneapolis: University of Minnesota Press, 2007. Print.

———. *Anti-Oedipus: Capitalism and Schizophrenia*. Minneapolis: University of Minnesota Press, 2005. Print.

Deleuze, Gilles. *Bergsonism*. New York: Zone Books, 1991. Print.

———. *La imagen-tiempo. Estudios sobre cine 2*. Barcelona: Paidós, 1986. Print.

Fokkema, Douwe W. *Literary History, Modernism, and Postmodernism*. Amsterdam: John Benjamins Publishing Company, 1984. Print.

Foster, David William. *Augusto Roa Bastos*. Boston: Twayne Publishers, 1978. Print.

Giacoman, Helmy F., ed. *Homenaje a Augusto Roa Bastos: variaciones interpretativas en torno a su obra*. Long Island City, NY: Las Americas, 1973. Print.

Gunter, P. A. Y. "Henri Bergson." *Founders of Constructive Postmodern Philosophy : Peirce, James, Bergson, Whitehead, and Hartshorne*. Ed. in David Ray Griffin, et al. Albany: State University of New York Press, 1993. 133–63. Print.

Hassan, Ihab. *Paracriticisms: Seven Speculations of the Times*. Urbana: University of Illinois Press, 1975. Print.

Jameson, Fredric. *The Cultural Turn: Selected Writings on the Postmodern, 1983–1998*. London: Verso, 1998. Print.

Lyotard, Jean-François. *The Postmodern Condition: A Report on Knowledge*. Minneapolis: University of Minnesota Press, 2007. Print.

———. *The Inhuman. Reflections on Time*. Stanford, CA: Stanford University Press, 1991. Print.

Paz, Octavio. *Los hijos del limo: del romanticismo a la vanguardia*. Barcelona: Seix Barral, 1974. Print.

Roa Bastos, Augusto. *Antología personal*. 2nd ed. México: Editorial Nueva Imagen, 1981. Print.

———. *El baldío*. Buenos Aires: Losada, 1966. Print.

———. *Madera quemada*. 2nd ed. Santiago, Chile: Editorial Universitaria, 1972. Print.

———. *Metaforismos*. Buenos Aires: Seix Barral, 1996. Print.

———. *Moriencia*. Caracas, Venezuela: Monte Ávila, 1969. Print.

Sontag, Susan. *Against Interpretation, and Other Essays*. New York: Farrar, Straus & Giroux, 1966. Print.

Yurkievich, Saúl. *La movediza modernidad*. Madrid: Taurus, 1996. Print.

C H A P T E R   5

Rhizomatic Writing in Augusto Roa Bastos's Short Stories

Fatima R. Nogueira
Trans. Hortensia Groth

"If I were asked to describe my literature, I would say it is an escape to the future."

—Augusto Roa Bastos

Augusto Roa Bastos's narrative bases itself upon a patent transtextuality as well as a marked propensity to continuously modify (reorganize, redistribute, and revise) the texts that form it.[1] These elements are supported by the "poetics of variations," outlined in the "Author's Note" in the final version of *Hijo de Hombre* (*Son of Man*). This poetics highlights the uninterrupted modification and communication with other texts that is an integral part of the composition of a literary work.[2] Both features—modification and communication with other texts—accentuate the Paraguayan writer's search to achieve a text that moves constantly, resisting any type of closure, including that of the printed letter.[3] The immediate consequences of this gestational conception of the text are the work's inconclusiveness and an intentional disruption of genre.[4]

In this chapter, I focus on the transtextual (intratextual and intertextual) movement of the following short stories by Roa Bastos: "Contar un cuento" ("To Tell a Tale"), "Ajuste de cuentas" ("Settling Accounts"), "Él y el otro" ("He and the Other"), "El aserradero" ("The Sawmill"), and "Juegos nocturnos" ("Nocturnal Games"). This transtextuality is produced by the mobility between texts as much as by the multiplicity of narrations within one story, creating a relationship of rupture and of continuity between them. In other words, the transtextual rapport between the stories here analyzed establishes, through a series of segments as well as of characters transferred from one story to another, a fragmentary and, at the same time, complementary relationship. This relationship is possible because a process of displacement completes or alters a previous text to which the second text refers.

This study aims to clarify Roa's ability to reinvent the concept of transtextuality, and to contextualize his particular aesthetics, which guide the narrative complexity of his short stories. I establish a correlation between these stories and the rhizomatic system formulated by Deleuze and Guattari in *A Thousand Plateaus*. This analogy is based on the existence of certain common features that include four main principles: those of multiplicities, connection, heterogeneity, and cartography. The first of these principles refers to the desire to flatten all the multiplicities to a sole plane of exteriority, which indicates a proportional relation between fragmentation and totality. That is, the writer attempts to create the ideal book in which a single page agglutinates "lived events, historical determinations, concepts, individuals, groups, [and] social formations" (Deleuze and Guattari 9).

The second principle concerns itself with the rhizome's capacity to break itself at any of its points and to connect with any other, establishing, in this way, "connections between semiotic chains, organizations of power, and circumstances relative to the arts, sciences, and social struggles" (Deleuze and Guattari 7). According to this principle, this infinite power to form associations is mainly due to the fact that rhizomatic writing tries to deterritorialize itself through abstract lines of flight,[5] directed at a midpoint.[6] Such permeability allows the creation of new rhizomes.[7] Roa Bastos's writing, as the expansion promoted by the rhizomes, seems to be able to break itself at any point in order to insert, through lines of flight, a story within another story. This causes a constant rupture, destabilization, and decentering of the narrative axes, and suggests new significations.

I also consider here an essential literary element that is found in Roa Bastos's work: the creation of lines of flight that form other groupings to reterritorialize themselves in new combinations that point to the relevance of cultural, philosophical, and psychological contexts. These sociocultural associations, in turn, always signal the fundamental issue of the literary work's texture, and shape the different planes of exteriority that develop in nonparallel ways. There are matters of identity and difference, the fallacy of the conscious subject, the problem of alienation, and theories of multiplicity, as well as issues of reality and fiction, the relationship between literature and other forms of art, and oral versus written expression. The artifice of words and the role of the artist in a changing social context are also discussed. Lines arise between literature and its sociocultural referent that do not cease leaping from one plane to another. Hence, it may be inferred that in Augusto Roa Bastos's narrative production (even in those works whose most outstanding feature seems to relate to literature's sociopolitical nature), the obsessive theme would be the making of the literary text and, consequently, language. Roa achieves a decentering of other dimensions and registers that are also present in his writing.

The stories "He and the Other" and "To Tell a Tale" appear for the first time in *El baldío* (*The Vacant Lot*), and are republished together in the volume *Moriencia* (*Slaughter*) in the section that includes "Nocturnal Games." This same distribution recurs in the second publication of *The Vacant Lot* (1972), signaling an attempt to form a trilogy anchored in the figure of the fat man as the protagonist and narrator. According to the rhizomatic condition of Roabastian writing, I will analyze the behavior of these lines of flight following the variations that fashion the character of the fat man in "Nocturnal Games," "To Tell a Tale," and "He and the Other." I will also consider the relationships that these stories establish with "Settling Accounts" and "The Sawmill," with regard to either narrative rupture or narrative continuity.

Evidently, this combination of stories represents one of several possibilities or attempts to map the *sui generis* displacement of the narration's culmination toward the interstices of rhizomatic writing. Such interstices are a privileged place for deterritoralization and for ruptures that force a constant movement of readaptation of all the elements involved in the act of narrating.

The fat man appears as a secondary character in "Settling Accounts," and also in the third chapter of *Son of Man*. These texts corroborate some of the fat man's features as represented in the stories where he plays a leading role. The novel pictures him as a young man, supplementing the concise information that the stories offer about him. These two works also reveal the fat man's place among the rural aristocracy and his membership in the Paraguayan community exiled in Buenos Aires. In this way, we become aware of the instability of his political position due to a succession of revolutions that displaced the group in power that alter the fat man's situation from supporter of the government in force to the position of opponent of the subsequent regime. Such instability leads us to assume that the fat man will go into exile (voluntarily or involuntarily) to Buenos Aires in the story's future narration. This conclusion comes from the fact that all the stories—with the exception of "To Tell a Tale," where the space is confined to one room, and "The Sawmill"—convey specific spatial indications, referring to the Argentine capital.

The character's identification with an affluent class suggested in *Son of Man* is compatible with his Western classical artistic and cultural formation, confirmed by his literary (Homer, Shakespeare, Cervantes, Dante, Goethe, Kafka) and musical (Bach, Beethoven, Mozart, Chopin, Brahms) knowledge evident in the stories. Reconstructing his most important features, we observe that three characteristics stand out from his description: his narrative talent, his passion for music, and his physical monumentality. His ability to tell stories is extensively explored in "To Tell a Tale," and it is possible to speculate about a link between this aptitude and his characterization as a musician, since it is suggested that he narrates as well as he plays the piano. Some clues about this particular feature of his narrative are already sketched in *Son of Man*: "Tres hombres flacos y uno con facha de estanciero. Este contaba a los otros la historia, deshilachándola, como si pasara los dedos al tanteo por una trama rota. No la sabía muy bien o la contaba a mal sabiendas, para marear a los otros" ("Three skinny men and another one looking like a ranch owner. The latter told the story to the others, unraveling it, as though he roughly felt with his fingers a broken weft. Either he did not know the story very well or he told it inaccurately in order to annoy the others"; 62). These clues reappear in the same form in "To Tell a Tale": "¿Hay algo más fantástico que el tacto de la madera en la yema de un dedo?" ("Is there something more fantastic than the feel of the wood on the fingertip?"; 255).[8]

This similarity between the act of narration and music echoes the words of Deleuze's and Guattari's theory and those of Roa Bastos's "poetics of variations." For Deleuze and Guattari, music identifies with the rhizome, since music makes possible that the lines of flight "like so many transformational multiplicities" (Deleuze and Guattari, 12) pass through it creating new rhizomes that originate new executions. The endeavor of moving musical form to the written text is carried out in Roa Bastos's short stories through repetitions, evolutions, and ruptures fused in a sort of a musical proliferation. However, since the written narration is not able to preserve an absolute coincidence with the rhythmical beat of music, the Paraguayan writer configures his text on the basis of oral qualities. Such an oral base is not only similar to the compassed rhythm of musical form, but also preserves the variations between different versions and diverse forms of telling the same story. Thus, the fact that the fat man narrates in the manner that he plays the piano suggests a splitting of his perception. On the one hand, there is the possibility that the character's way of narrating—since it is compared with musical form—is also carried out as a rhizome. On the other hand, the comparison of the storyteller's function to that of the musician, present in the fashioning of the character, can be verified by the emphasis on the description of his "manos . . . de pianista en relâche" ("relaxed hands of a piano player"; 198). In the essay "The Storyteller," Benjamin asserts that in oral narrative, "soul, eye, and hand are brought into connection. Interacting with one another they determine a practice. We are no longer familiar with this practice" (Benjamin 108). The interaction between these elements may be plainly observed in "To Tell a Tale," where the protagonist's hands do not cease to move as he narrates, in such a way that they become integrated into the narration. Those restless hands make a noise with their nails dramatizing the gesture of killing fleas, which represents nothingness. They also rest on the fat man's lips when he burps, representing the sourness of the onion, which is presented as a metaphor for the very act of narrating. The fat man's hands mark the rhythm of the narration, thus filling the interruptions and silences while they make the gin glass turn and wipe the sweat from his forehead. Finally, the fat man's hands signal forward in the moment of his death. In the same way, his eyes complement the narration refuting or introducing doubt about the veracity of his words—"Ahora mismo sus ojillos . . . desmentían . . . sus palabras" ("Right now his . . . little eyes belied his words"; 255)—or establishing between the narrator and his audience a complicity that will be verified at the end of the story. This is a moment of complete integration between the soul, the eyes, and the hands through death. The character's interrelation with the act of telling not only corroborates the oral nature of his narrative, but also confirms that the narrator, according to Benjamin, is "the man who could let the wick of his life be consumed completely by the gentle flame of his story" (Benjamin 109). Thus, we can verify that in "To Tell a Tale," what seemed like an impossible task (the fat man narrating his own death) is an inherent function of the act of telling.

The tacit agreement between the narrator and his audience may be observed in the final sentence of the story: "Los ojillos vidriosos se hallaban clavados en nosotros con una burlona sonrisa" ("The glazed little eyes were gazing at us with a mocking smile"; 259). Such complicity is part of a shared pragmatic experience that is the basis of oral transmission. This pragmatism is also connected to the utilization of inverted aphorisms present in "To Tell a Tale" (256): "Si en el país de los ciegos te falta un ojo, quítate el otro" ("If in the country of the blind men, you miss an eye, get rid of the other one") or "supo andar en la lluvia sin mojarse" ("he knew how to walk in the rain without getting wet"). "Nocturnal Games" repeats this proverb by underscoring certain factors of bourgeois society's composition, such as its rejection of any type of difference that might disturb the estab- lished order, and its ability to act in order to ascend to a higher social class. In this sense, the inversion of maxims accentuates the disruption of social values, and the subject's loss of consciousness within a world whose axis is worn out.

The narration of one's own death once again allows us to exam- ine the functioning of the rhizomatic system as multiplicity since this technique attempts to inscribe all the stories within a sole plane of exteriority, leading them toward a single end and beginning. This repetition evidently displaces the point of interest to the middle of the story. We know that in Roa Bastos's world vision, mediated by the Guarani tradition, the end and the origin unite to close a circle.[9] Thus, all the stories lead to death, which is the organizing principle of the experience transmitted by the storyteller. Experience, whether reconstructed through one's own memory or that of another, reaches its totality in death since that is the moment when a man's life acquires its full meaning. The protagonist's death, figuratively speaking, repre- sents the end of the story. His death encourages us to share the sum of his experience narrated by somebody else. It should be noted that the story's narrator only assumes his role entirely when he narrates the protagonist's death. At this moment, the narrative accelerates, digressions cease, and the two narrative voices that were articulated separately fuse. Thus, on the one hand, the death of the narrator- protagonist in "To Tell a Tale" generates the writing of the tale itself, while, on the other hand, this death makes possible the continuity of the narrator-protagonist's life in the memory perpetuated by the writ- ten text. The play between the beginning and the end creates a circle. This very circle achieves the fat man's solution of the enigmas he initially proposed through his consummation in the flame of his own narration. Thus, one perceives that the nothingness that is left "al que más sabe" (97)—"to [the one who knows the most]—and the "wholeness of the 'tufo picante'" (97) ("pungent odor") when slicing an onion, suggest that the essence of all reality is only revealed totally during death.

The key to the construction of the single text in "To Tell a Tale" may be formalized via the axiom that asserts that every story is fashioned by a diversity of other stories. Such a proposition is revealed through narrative construction and reiterated through the metaphor of peeling the onion elaborated at the beginning of the tale by means of two of the protagonist's allusions. This metaphor is disseminated throughout the text by two other references made by the narrator that gradually delimit it. Thus, we can see that the first mention of peeling the onion points to a reality "que queda cuando ha desaparecido toda la realidad" ("that is left when all reality has disappeared"; 197), including the nature of fiction itself. The second mention of the onion refers to the specificity of literary activity. The narration reflects upon the nature of the word by reiterating the relationship between the narrative act and death, and by referring to the inherent fragmentation of an art fashioned with words: "La palabra es la gran trampa . . . Yo mismo hablo y hablo . . . Para sacar nuevas capas a la cebolla" ("The word is the great trick . . . I, myself, I talk and talk . . . In order to take new layers out of the onion"; 255).

The delimitation of fiction to narrative art is explicit when the narrator mentions the metaphorical representation of the onion, referring to the specific way of telling of the fat man. This way of narrating deliberately assumes its rhizomatic nature, showing the constant lines of flight in a fragmented text: "El saltaba de un tema a otro sin transición . . . en medio de bruscas interrupciones, de largos e impenetrables silencios" ("He jumped from one subject to another without any transition . . . during abrupt interruptions, during long and impenetrable silences"; 257). However, such a fragmentation demonstrates the paradoxical ambition of constructing a single text through fragments: "Contó varios cuentos . . . Quizá fueran uno solo" ("He told several tales . . . Perhaps they were only one"; 259).

It should be observed that the allusion to the fact that a text is composed of fragments of other texts is exemplified in the story through the narrator's appropriation of the metaphor elaborated by the protagonist, and also through his *modus operandi*. In the first case, the textual reference to the metaphor of the onion vanishes into the narrator's elucidation of the narrative act that avoids its literal transcription, but still alludes to it, showing that the literary text is composed of a series of quotations from other texts. In the second case, the narrator fully assumes the protagonist's way of narrating by continuously interrupting the story with digressions about this style of recounting, and then by inserting an allusion to one of the fat man's romances—insinuation totally devoid of context—which thus becomes one of the many lines of flight that cross the story.

Another important topic in "To Tell a Tale" is the relationship between writing and oral expression. Walter Benjamin points out the linkage and also the separation between these two modalities, recognizing that "the short story, which has removed itself from oral tradition and no longer permits that slow piling one on top of the other of thin, transparent layers which constitutes the most appropriate picture of the way in which the perfect narrative is revealed through the layers of a variety of retellings" (Benjamin 93). The similarity between the metaphors about the oral tale created by Benjamin and by Roa Bastos (the transparent layers and the onion, respectively) is enriched by the variety of tones utilized in the story. In "To Tell a Tale," the importance of oral discourse is clear, not only because the fat man is the character who carries out most of the narration, but also because of the conflict between oral expression and writing that takes place between the protagonist and his audience: "Lo escuchamos impacientes y ávidos porque siempre podíamos aprovechar algo en nuestras colaboraciones para las revistas . . . teníamos que imaginar y reinventar lo que él imaginaba e inventaba" ("We listened to him impatiently and eagerly because we could always use something for our contributions to the journals . . . we had to imagine and to reinvent what he imagined and invented"; 258).

The opposition between the fat man and his audience, perhaps a group of aspiring writers or journalists, reflects the antagonism between oral and written discourse, indicating that writing derives from oral expression and simultaneously opposes it, principally because of the impossibility of reproducing oral discourse. The importance of oral discourse is also represented through a climate of informality created among elements that exchange and share a life experience. Written discourse, on the other hand, requires more precision and formality. These metaliterary reflections lend a metaphorical dimension to the character that supports writing or, more precisely, the as yet unwritten text, the text still in process of production. We can see that the fat man, as an oral producer of tales, has an inexhaustible repertoire connected somehow to his obesity, which is presented as unreal: "Tenía un aire de . . . fofa irrealidad" ("He had an aspect of . . . flabby unreality"; 256). In this case, the "flabby unreality" may be metaphorically interpreted as fiction itself. That is, this huge fictitious character overflows into unlimited creations that become inscribed on his body. As for his material aspect, this body represents the single text that, due to its flexibility, permits a porosity through which lines of flight arise.

In addition to this material symbolism, his enormity connotes the utopian idea that all texts may be inscribed on a single page, for they are creations that permit a twofold movement of prolongation and suspension. In the first case, one story flees toward another, while in the second, the remaining components readapt after the escape of some elements. Hence, the reader comprehends the emphasis placed on the protagonist's respiratory movement. His panting inflates, deflates, and deforms his body. This emphasis appears again in "Nocturnal Games." If this character represents Roa Bastos's preoccupation with writing in opposition to oral expression, the constant panting of his irregular respiration represents the yearning for a writing that, in consonance with the author's "poetics of variations," is presented as mobile, voluble, and therefore indecipherable.

Once these movements of rupture open a hole in the text, it is possible to go on to another story related to "Nocturnal Games." Adelfo Aldana proposes that a text splits into a variety of texts as a man splits into another man,[10] an idea suggested by the physical description of the fat man: "Encerrados en la masa del tejido adiposo parecía haber dos hombres que no querían saber nada entre sí . . . La ronca y monótona voz servía sin embargo a uno y a otro, por igual, sin favoritismos" ("Contained in the mass of the adipose tissue, there seemed to be two men who didn't want to know anything about each other . . . However, the hoarse and monotonous voice served both equally without any favoritism"; 256). The transcribed quotation displaces the metaphorical representation of the character's monumentality from the body of writing to a complete identification with the literary object's gestational process, as well as with the speaker's role of producer of utterances. Such a practice is summed up in the fact that the character's voice resounds among the multiplicity of voices surrounding the object. Therefore, the character acts as a receptacle for other voices that reverberate in his discourse, illustrating the Bakhtinian view that asserts that every discourse is dialogic: "In all its paths to the object, in all the directions the discourse meets the other's discourse and cannot but participate with it in a vivid and intense interaction . . . However, the discourse's internal dialogism is not exhausted here . . . The living and common discourse is directly determined by the future answer-discourse: it is the former that provokes this answer, foresees it and is based on it. The discourse, constituted in the atmosphere of the 'already said,' is orientated at the same time towards the answer-discourse that was not said yet but that was solicited and was already awaited."[11] In other words, the fat man's word sounds like an appropriation of the word of another (or of others)—populated with others' intentions—that become his own in varying degrees, since language, according to Bakhtin, "is populated or overpopulated with another's intentions. To dominate it and to subject it to one's own intentions and accents is a difficult and complex process" (Bakhtin 100).

From this standpoint, one can better understand the problem surrounding every act of literary creation that proposes to start from a text that is constructed through a dissonant dialogue of at least two narrative voices. This dialogue generates a discourse that often, when it lets the other's voice out, sounds strange coming from the sender's mouth. Such dialogism creates a point of flight toward other contexts that engender new narrations. Thus, the complexity of the narrative process (exemplified by the previously proposed axiom that indicates that a tale is always another and that a man is always another man) is highlighted through the assertion that the discourse is established in a boundary space. This boundary space is concretized in a context and a world vision that oscillate between what belongs to one and what belongs to others. These splits make possible an exchange of languages that expands into a permutation of identities. It is possible to speak for oneself in the other's language as well as to speak for the other using one's own language. This fact explains all the digressions that take place at the beginning of the text about distrust of the word as a reflection of reality, since not only is the word pregnant with subjectivity, but it is also produced in foreign territory.

One of the points of flight, through which another voice that creates a textual dissonance is clear, may be observed in the usage of a microstory inserted within the text. Such an operation is proposed here like a fissure lacking continuity. An example can be seen in the following fragment: "Leonardo hizo un león" ("Leonardo made a lion"; 256). This segment appears again immediately before the fat man starts to narrate his own death. This twofold reference to Leonardo da Vinci's mechanical lion incorporates the paratextual effects of a metaphor between the representation of reality and the search for knowledge. In this sense, the Italian artist integrated the Renaissance ideal of joining art and science. He tried to represent—through his paintings—an empirical observation of nature that, inscribed through ciphered symbols, could express the ineffable.

Some other characteristics of the alluded artist that are connected as a metaphorical intertext to the creation of a multidimensional and simultaneously contradictory narrative piece are related to da Vinci's superhuman attempt to obtain an inordinate professional diversity— painter, sculptor, musician, engineer, architect, physicist, biologist, fashion designer, inventor, geologist, cartographer, author of optical texts, garden designer, decorator, astronomer, town planner, mathematician, and philosopher—and to the impossibility of concluding his works. Freud attributed this incredible purpose to the tight link between art and science that Leonardo da Vinci pursued, which brought unexpected results for him: "An alien interest—in experimentation—at first reinforced the artistic one, only to damage the work later on" (Freud, *Leonardo Da Vinci*, 18). The idea that the work of art is an unfinished process is important for our reading of Roa Bastos's short stories because his works are characterized by the constant alteration and redistribution of textual elements. The notion of the unfinished work is a platform from which the rhizomatic text is constructed.

The allusion to the Italian Renaissance man, prototype of the "universal man," also aims, although in an inverted form, to insert a critical discourse about art and the social role of the artist. This issue does not refer to da Vinci's most famous paintings, but to the invention of a mechanical device whose symbolic interpretation, in contrast to that of his works of art, is not so difficult. This invention was conceived by Leonardo da Vinci in 1515, probably to celebrate the entrance of Francisco I to the city of Leon as well as the peace negotiations between the king of France and the Pope Leo X, which took place in Bologna.[12] On the one hand, within the historical context, the lion and the irises represent, respectively, the cities of Lyon in France and Florence in Italy. These symbols all share an onomastic identification with the Pope (Leo) and an association between the iris and the virgin. On the other hand, the allusion to Leonardo's mechanical lion announces the central character's imminent death in the story, a character who lets his audience see "una sonrisa muerta"("a dead smile"; 257). In this last case, irises link da Vinci's device to one of the motives of "To Tell a Tale": death as a spectacle.

The main narrative line of "To Tell a Tale" discusses literature itself because the story focuses more on digressions about writing than on events. This detour of the narration toward a secondary fact—such as details of the biography of the Renaissance painter—carries out a displacement that desanctifies immortal art. This demystifying function is a characteristic also present in Leonardo da Vinci's paintings and emphasizes the role of the artist as an entertainer, that is, one who offers his abilities to serve others. If we transfer this interpretation of the artist's role to that of the narrator in "To Tell a Tale," we once again confront a representation of the fat man as the teller of another's stories—as the one whose ultimate aim and fulfillment is to offer his voice to different identities—allowing them to speak through him. Thus, the writer understood as a compiler of oral stories loses his aura of demiurge to assume the function of a carrier of different voices. These voices participate in his narration, consciously creating a text that is presented as "a multidimensional space in which a variety of writings, none of them original, blend and clash. The text is a tissue of quotations drawn from the innumerable centers of culture" (Barthes, cited in The Norton Anthology, 1468).

Following this interpretation, we see that the allusion to Leonardo da Vinci's lion refers to a relation of formal inclusion between the names since *lion* (*león*) is contained in *Leonardo*, just as a text includes other texts.[13] This ability to multiply reappears in other points of flight of the story, for the narrative task is not only carried out through a diversification that allows the relation of inclusion (in which the different stories perform as an assembly), but also through an appropriation of crossed voices. The experience of simultaneously being one and being another, suggested by the exchange of voices, is implemented drastically in the tale "Settling Accounts." This story narrates a case of possession, not of the voice, but of the body of an individual to be utilized as the weapon for a crime. Thus, relations of complementation and of variation are established between the two stories. The relationship of variation is clear at both the theoretical and structural levels since both tales use variants of the oral story. However, the form of "Settling Accounts" has tighter relations with reality since it is about a crime, while "To Tell a Tale," as we have seen, explores the latent possibilities within the act of narrating.

This link vanishes when the boundaries between fiction and reality disappear. The evanescence of these boundaries is manifested textually in the phrase repeated in both stories regarding the way the fat man narrates: "Nunca se sabía cuando decía un chiste o recordaba una anécdota" ("You never knew when he was telling a joke or remembering an anecdote"; 257). The variant of this quotation reappears in "Settling Accounts." Another topic with respect to the variation between the two tales refers to the displacement of the fat man from protagonist of "To Tell a Tale" to a secondary character in "Settling Accounts." The fat man conserves his importance not only as a linking element between the two stories (due to the constant references to his figure in the second tale), but also as the guide to the operative key to the narrated crime. This transposition simultaneously corroborates some of his characteristics, such as his strangeness and his inventive ability to produce stories that demonstrate an indifference toward the facts of immediate reality. Such stories are only valuable when they are impregnated by imagination. Therefore, the fat man refuses to listen to the story of the crime. This same story, fertilized by the possibilities of fiction, becomes part of the repertory of "To Tell a Tale."

The complementary relationship between these two stories can be observed on both the theoretical and narrative planes. Both narratives experiment with Bakhtinian dialogic discourse, as already discussed in detail with regard to "To Tell a Tale." Moreover, a line of flight is opened up in the matrix tale ("To Tell a Tale"), which leads to the plot development of the complementary story "Settling Accounts." "Settling Accounts" fills in the narrative space opened up in "To Tell a Tale" by summarizing the previous tale succinctly: "Había empezado a relatar [un cuento] a propósito de unos emigrados que consiguen asesinar al embajador de su país con la ayuda de un ciego. El atentado y el crimen eran absurdos e increíbles" ("He had started to tell [a tale] about some emigrants that are able to murder the ambassador of their country with the help of a blind man. The attempt on his life and the crime were absurd and incredible"; 257).

Once the intratextual relationship is established between the two stories, a series of repetitions or variations of textual fragments creates a dialogue between the two texts that suggests that the protagonist of "Settling Accounts" is part of the audience gathered around the fat man to listen to his stories in "To Tell a Tale." The two stories manifest deeper conceptual connections with regard to man's inability to see reality because he is immersed in his daily routine, the relativity of truth, the impossibility of accurate expression through words, the unpredictability of human actions, and finally, the issue of the double already present in the figure of the protagonist of "To Tell a Tale," and developed to its extreme limits in "Settling Accounts."

Freud, in "The Uncanny," based on Rank's studies on the topic of the double, highlights that the presence of the double may appear in different forms. First, the double may present itself through an identical appearance; second, through a telepathic experience; third, through a total identification and confusion of someone with somebody else (an unfolding, splitting or permutation of the self); and fourth, through the permanent return or repetition of the same entity. These forms assure certain relationships between the self and the double, or alter ego, represented through referents like the mirror image in the shadow, the tutelary genies, animistic doctrines, and the fear of death. Freud discusses another important subject—that of the development of the psychological stage that starts as a protective provision against death, caused by a limited egotism or primitive narcissism, and ends with identification with the messenger of death: "But when this stage has been surmounted, the 'double' reverses its aspect. From having been an assurance of immortality, it becomes the uncanny harbinger of death" (Freud, *The UnCanny*, 940). This last point is illustrated by the splitting suffered by the protagonist of "To Tale a Tell" that not only permits him to foresee his own death, but also to present it as a macabre spectacle divided into narration and representation. In other words, the fat man tells his death as he dies. However, while the theme of the double appears metaphorically in "To Tell a Tale," this topic generates the central plot of the story in "Settling Accounts." Indeed, the theme of the double is so important in "Settling Accounts" that one might summarize it as the narration of an experience in which all the forms of the double mentioned by Freud are combined: the physical similarity, the telepathic experience, the permutation of the self, and the permanent return of the same entity performed in front of the mirrorlike image, thus producing the robbery of the identity of the blind man.

"Settling Accounts" starts with a reference to reality: the presence of the ambassador at a public event. The story superimposes science fiction (Sturgeon's novel), parapsychological phenomena (the power of clairvoyance), and the application of psychological theories (gestalt groups). This superimposition reveals that the narrated facts surpass the limits of reality and are mixed with fiction. It also suggests interpretative clues with regard to the narrated events: an inexplicable crime may be understood through perceptions that surpass reality.

Evidently, this approach is not linear since the text constantly plays with reality and superreality, putting the latter forward as an interpretative clue and at the same time invalidating it. The text compares what is being described with reality and then undermines this relationship by establishing doubt, not only with respect to the veracity of the narrated events, but also regarding our trust in the narrator. An example of this procedure can be found in a fragment strategically located in the text after the reference to a historical event—President John F. Kennedy's assassination—with which narrative events are compared. In this way, Kennedy's murder is linked to the crime in the text through the suggestion that it could also have taken place through identity theft. This is a critical approach because when we employ superrealistic elements to interpret Kennedy's murder, a crime whose authorship has been historically debated, the explanations offered by official history with regard to the president's murder are ironically questioned.

Another point that subverts the veracity of the narrated events and establishes the narrator's unreliability is the comparison of such events to the fictional readings of the narrator himself: "Le diría que aquel hecho ocurrió contaminado por la irrealidad de una mediocre ficción. Algo que únicamente se ve suceder en el ambiente enrarecido de los libros que me echaban en cara, burlándose de mí" ("I would tell you that that event was polluted by a mediocre fiction. Something that one only finds in the contaminated atmosphere of books. I was reproached and mocked for the reading of such books"; 425).

The key to the interpretation of the double—with regard to telepathy and the appropriation of another's identity—is manifested in a parallel fashion through a mirror image in the shadow, and as a textual mirage through which the imagined crime appears again in the textual reconstruction of its performance. In both cases, we confront a phenomenon of repetition through the unceasing return of the same element that constitutes the presence of the double. The mirror image consists of the ritual return of the blind man, carried out by the narrator every time he shaves in front of the mirror in the guesthouse where he lives. The description of this event mixes light and shadow, elements that lead to the identification of the image of the dead blind man with that of the narrator as the possible agent of the ambassador's assassination. In other words, there is a clear reference to the return of the dead blind man: "Permanezco en esta roñosa pensión [por] la calidad de la luz que tiene el baño . . . que da a las manchas del espejo un color muy especial, como el de las costras que agrietaban la cara del ciego sobre los pómulos" ("I stay in this dirty guesthouse (because of) the quality of the light in the bathroom . . . that colors very specially the stains on the mirror, like the scabs that cracked the blind man's face on his cheekbones"; 423). The textual mirage can be observed through the description of the imagined attempt on the ambassador's life by the narrator, which employs some elements of the possible execution of the "real" crime, and thus suggests that the narrator has led the blind man to carry out the murder through control by mental forces.

Thus, the first murder attempt takes place during the ambassador's public appearance, and this event is described as the possible fruit of the narrator's imagination: "Le volqué la cabeza contra el respaldo, hasta dejar la nuez al culo de pájaro en el buche peludo y sentir, bajo el pulgar, que palpitaba como la de cualquiera" ("I knocked his head over the back of the chair until I left his Adam's apple exposed in the hairy maw and I was able to feel under my thumb that his heart beat like everybody else's"; 424). This act of imagination, which was carried out through the liberation of the unconscious and interrupted by the abrupt return to reality, concludes in another act of imagination that culminates in the "real" murder of the ambassador. In other words, the crime attributed to the blind man is told not the way that it occurred, but the way it is imagined, thus making desire and its consummation coincide.

The repetition of the elements that constitute the two scenes (the actions of knocking the ambassador's head against the back of the chair and feeling for his Adam's apple in order to find the right place to stab the ambassador with the knife) allows a relation of continuity between such scenes. In the second scene, the imagination realizes its desire through the appropriation of another's identity. The superimposition of the two scenes suggests that the blind man, as the narrator's double, plays the role of the emissary of death, that is, of the one who completes an unfinished act of the imagination. In the same way, the text suggests that the execution of a particular crime can be activated by the imagination that desires it. In such a case, the double is a mere instrument of desire. These observations lead to the conclusion that a perennial pact exists between one and his double. It really is a peculiar pact since at the same time that the blind man becomes a double and dies—logical consequence of his criminal action—he comes back to life through the narrator's identity, which guarantees his survival when he recovers his shadows in the mirrorlike image.

The theme of the double connected to death is common in Roa Bastos's short stories. Nonetheless, "Settling Accounts" functions differently from the other stories that I comment upon here. This tale uses a ritual image that evokes complicity between the self and its double, whose aim is the execution of the perfect crime. In stories like "The Sawmill" and "He and the Other," there is a vision of destruction directed at the double itself (instead of a third party) as a way of recovering one's identity. "He and the Other" establishes an intratextual relationship with "To Tell a Tale," developing the axiom that affirms that one story is made out of others in the same way that the double infiltrates the original being. To demonstrate this fact, Roa Bastos experiments with the unfolding of a story in three tales that are thematically linked by the issue of the necessity of the absorption of the double. These stories share reflections of a philosophical nature that accompany the thought flow that imitates the cadence of the unceasing movement of a train ride. In this way, the story of the doubles that finally meet in a Buenos Aires subway station creates points of flight that lead us directly to "The Sawmill" and to the tale of the dwarf brothers who possibly share a passion for the circus's lion tamer. At the same time, the theme of the double generates connections with the theme of alienation. Here, the rhythm, as it evokes the movement of a train, inserts the stories within each other up to the moment when both—narration and trip— abruptly stop.

The agglomeration of the stories in a sole paragraph without any sign of punctuation achieves within the narrative structure the hallucinatory rhythm of rhizomes that move in an accelerated and ceaseless manner from one group to another. This movement may be registered in two directions: on the one hand, the lines of flight reterritorialize themselves to allow the continuity of the story, which is constantly interrupted. On the other hand, they cluster around the narrator's reflections about the fat man. The narrator's first consideration meditates on the ceaseless movement toward the origins that connects birth and death and displaces original time toward another world preceding birth. The result of this is an "ilusión de espacio y tiempo en que soñamos que nos movemos" ("illusion of space and time wherein we dream that we move"; 351). In this way, the narrated events annul time in two different ways. First, time is destroyed through the repetition of facts that return within diverse contexts, thus gathering all the stories into a single text that relates the execution of a crime as a form of eliminating the double. Second, time is destroyed through the narrator's contemplation of the origin's role of restoring the union between the self and its double, both still linked by a sort of umbilical cord. Thus, everything that happens becomes a linkage element that unites them. The text suggests (354) that only death is able to cut the "trozo de nervio placentario" (piece of placenta nerve) or, just the opposite, to join them inexorably since "cada cosa busca su perfección en la muerte" ("all things search for their perfection in death").

With respect to the annulment of space, we can perceive that there is an extension constructed by gradually chained elements, which suggest that what happened in the Buenos Aires's subway station can take place in any other place, whether in a distant and desert land, where two young men dispute a woman's love in a sawmill, or in a frail, domestic circus where a "tragedy of jealousy, incest, and death" is told. These elements also act in a rhizomatic way, blending the narrative spaces in which events take place by means of intermixing elements from one story to another. This circulatory movement is exemplified at the beginning of the tale through the iron gate, which evokes a cage, and also through the hands, which remind us of the circus's magician. In the same way, the reverie about the desert, a utopian dream of the man at the iron gate, and the mention of the sawdust on the ground at the circus allude to a nostalgia for the sawmill.

The suppression of time and the limitless openness of space that corroborates its annulations presuppose the abolition of the conscious subject that appears in one or two of the reflections of the fat man: "Todo este aspaviento al que ya no le queda más que el furor domesticado de la costumbre el vago rencor del hombre cosificado con el hunquito moral del yo aún sobre la coronilla" ("All these furious gesticulations that have only left the tamed furor of habit, the vague resentment of the objectified man with the moral poncho of the self still on the crown of his head"; 351). In this case, the topic of alienation emerges again, and, at the same time, the traces of a rhizomatic framework aimed at a mechanistic assemblage. According to Deleuze and Guattari, a mechanistic assemblage is oriented toward the strata that transform it into a type of organism, either a signifying totality or a determination attributable to a subject. This assemblage is like a body without organs "which is continually dismantling the organism, causing asignifying particles of pure intensities to pass or circulate, and attributing to itself subjects that it leaves with nothing more than a name as the trace of an intensity" (Deleuze and Guattari 4). It is precisely here where the rhizomatic characteristics of the Roabastian writing dwells. Roa Bastos's writing constantly sends one line of flight to another through an exchange of multiplicities and subjects that shift from one story to another.

It is possible that "He and the Other" is the best achieved experiment of this kind of writing, since the story neither attempts to produce an imitation of reality nor tries to create a psychological construction of characters. It is rather about moving multiplicities and intensities and exchanging mobile subjects that, when they go from one story to another, lose any remnant of individuality. In this sense, it is meaningful that the reference to the "objectification of man" is inserted between two characteristically rhizomatic animal formations: the ants' ceaseless movement and the cattle's arrangement.

Obviously, the loss of individuality in a social organization without any trace of similarity with communitarian life generates a contradiction whose most immediate result is alienation. For Roa Bastos, as for Marx, alienation is produced from a threefold separation that the human being experiences in modern society: the alienation from the product of his work, from nature, and from his fellow beings. The German philosopher explains the basis of alienation thus:

> When alienated labor tears from man the object of his production, it also tears from his species-life, the real objectivity of his species and turns the advantage he has over animals into a disadvantage in that his inorganic body, nature, is torn from him . . . It alienates from man his own body, nature exterior from him, and his intellectual being, his human essence. An immediate consequence of man's alienation of the product of his work, his vital activity and his species-being, is the alienation of man from

man. When man is opposed to himself it is another man that is opposed to him. (Marx 91)

This kind of alienation, which, according to Roa Bastos's text, results in "the objectified man," starts by recognizing that "somos peores que las hormigas . . . trabajamos para nada" ("we are worse than ants . . . we work to obtain nothing"; 264), and culminates in the declaration that monstrosity, that is, the crimes that happen in every story of "He and the Other," springs from a twofold ignorance: "Todo se confabulara para perderlos en la medida que simultánea-mente se ignoraran a sí" ("Everything conspires in order to make men feel lost as far as they simultaneously ignore each other"; 356). Such ignorance, which, in this quotation, refers to the story of two swindlers, extends to the other episodes, suggesting that nothing and nobody can escape from the fateful consequences produced by the sense of isolation that is created by modern social organizations.

Although social criticism is inherent in any interpretation of "He and the Other," the technique of its composition creates a distance that eliminates any kind of sentimentality or propagandist intention. Such a distance may be verified through the position of the narrator himself as an observer of events that he interprets with relative impartiality. One example of this is the total depersonalization of the characters of the main story to whom the narrator refers with pronouns or epithets. A second example may be observed in the text's obsession with the description of the approaching movement of the two characters, which integrates them completely into the crowd, accentuating even further the aforementioned depersonalization. The third instance resides in the idea of an excessive importance of chance as the motor of human actions. This results in a rupture in the order of things since human actions are prone to disorder, underscoring the representation of world as chaos wherein the subject's existence is devoid of importance.

The allusion to the characters as only traces of subjectivity is represented textually through an exchange of identity between them, carried out by means of a permutation between the pronouns that originally designated them. At the beginning of the text, *he* refers to the swindler who was at the station's iron gate, and *the other* signals the man in the long, camel fur coat who boarded the underground train later. In the middle of the story, *he* is abruptly identified with the second man. From this point onward, the text begins to name the characters by means of epithets: the one in the *Orion* and the one at the iron gate, respectively, showing that these characters' positions in the story—either with respect to the order of their appearance, or regarding their approaching movement—is more important than a personal identification. The characters may then be compared to the pieces of a chess game that act according to a determined position. The priority of the space occupied by them is implicit here, and is completely acknowledged at the end of the tale. Thus, the story is—like "Settling Accounts"—about the theft of identity evident in the mixture of the characters' countenances prior to the extirpation of the hands of "la verja" (the one at the iron gate), executed by the one "del abrigo y orión" (of the long coat and the *Orion*), and the consequent extermination of the former by the crowd.

Only after the crime (the consummation of the same ritual anthropophagic act carried out in "The Sawmill"), the man in the long coat reveals his identity as a swindler, executing what he intended to do at the beginning of the tale: "Ni ese caballero era lo que representaba ni esa mano correspondía al caballero que la enarbolaba" ("Neither that gentleman was what he represented nor that hand corresponded to the gentleman who raised it"; 352). This revelation shows the fallacy of the conscious and individual subject and hides the preeminence of chance, whose premise will be the natural denial of the order of things. This is patent in the ceaseless exchange of stories and identities. The twofold denial of the subject and of order not only proposes the refutation of the basis of rationalism, but also permits us to contemplate history's events and literature itself as results of mutations of an order made up by humanism: "Estos desajustes son lo que han llenado de cruces la historia y el arte" ("These disruptions are those that have filled history and art with crosses"; 357). Evidently, such disruptions cannot be carried out without the interference of chance, which disarticulates the order of similarities and repetitions, opening a breach through which difference escapes and the other is barely visible.

It is precisely this game between the self and the other that modulates the narration of "Nocturnal Games." The story agglutinates fragments in which the narrator recounts the fat man's readings about poverty in the United States—possibly *The Other America* by Michael Harrington—and awaits the arrival of a couple from a lower social class, who sustain sexual relations in the house's yard. Hence, the role of the voyeur and the role of the reader are associated, and this relationship between the two actions provokes the memory of events and dialogues of the central character with a group of friends. The expectations become frustrated in both cases since the reading does not fulfill the fat man's expectations and the couple does not perform as expected. For this reason, it could be asserted that "Nocturnal

Games" is about frustrated hopes that lead to an increasing alienation and indifference within the modern world. This idea is reinforced by the expansion of the central character's failures with regard to other characters and toward the reader himself. In other words, faced with an always disappointing reality, the story enumerates a chained series of disappointments, which join those of the central character: the frustration of Saint-Exupéry, who, instead of the myth, finds starvation during his visit to Asunción; that of the woman, who awaits a train that never arrives at the station; that of Campos Cervera, who sees the revolution indefinitely postponed; and finally, that of the reader himself, whose perceptions are constantly altered by the transformations of narrative planes that change his expectations on the sensorial and ideological levels.

Regarding the sensorial level, we confront a voyeuristic act that is canceled at the beginning of the text since we are dealing with a *sui generis* voyeur. In other words, even if the lovers did have sexual relations, we would not have been able to watch the scene, for the fat man was supposedly asleep. With respect to the ideological level, the two denials that frame the text are resolved either through a radical alteration of the initial proposition or by means of oblivion and indifference. That is, that, despite the text's suggestion of circularity between the inaugural negative phrase of the narrative and its repetition at the end of the story, there is an essential difference of degree between them since the text attempts to object to the former, whereas the latter contests any possible argumentation. Thus, "Nocturnal Games" is carried out as an intensive and extensive experience about alienation in the social and psychological senses.

In the Paraguayan writer's other stories, we observe a movement of lines of flight that lead the reader to other works of the same writer, whereas in "Nocturnal Games," such experience signals an intertextual relation with Harrington's *The Other America* and with Kafka's "Josephine the Singer, or the Mouse Folk." Roa Bastos's text establishes an explicit dialogue with Harrington's text, whose central axis refutes the thesis that poverty would spontaneously disappear in developed societies as a consequence of scientific and technological progress. Harrington shows that poverty survived in the United States in the conglomerates of marginalized poor people who were invisible to those who lived in affluence. In this dialogue, the fat man contests Harrington's thesis in three ways. The fat man's first attempt to contravene Harrington is by displacing material poverty to the spiritual world, which causes indifference, an attitude generated by "the force of habit" that distorts our vision of reality. This is a phenomenon linked to loneliness and alienation in the modern world. The platform of his refutations, in this case, is built on his personal experiences with Caroline and with the observation of the old woman at the station, whose existential aim consists of waiting for a train. The cases of the two characters refer to mental alienation as a result of emotional losses originated by the world wars.

The second form of refutation of Harrington's ideas presents starvation as a direct consequence of capitalist society's waste, which is not limited to wealthy people and extends to the less well-off neighborhoods. The framework for this objection is constructed by the insertion of the episode referring to the excursion made by the protagonist and his friends with the aim of inspecting the garbage in some of Buenos Aires's popular neighborhoods. The fragment's irony disarticulates any type of emotion that might suggest solidarity between different social classes, thus reducing the situation to a game motivated by a sort of morbid curiosity.

Finally, the fat man answers the proposition that myth and beauty conceal poverty through an inversion. The text introduces the episodes of Saint-Exupéry and Campos Cervera. In the first, the Frenchman seeks myth but finds poverty, revealed in the fact that Asunción's children eat dirt. The text counters the expectation that the commotion provoked by Saint Exupéry's observation of such a fact could cause some kind of demonstration against the social order in force and the unfair distribution of wealth. In short, the three forms of refuting Harrington's ideas refer to Kafka's text, whose theme relates to oblivion, which causes everything to evaporate in the shadow of indifference. In this way, the character's objections to Harrington's descriptions turn out to be a rationalization of poverty that, far from fighting against Harrington's ideas, seems to result in their affirmation.

Nonetheless, the fat man hides a letter that, apparently, could eliminate alienation, solitude, and the lack of solidarity among men. These ills are the result of an absolute indifference toward anything that goes against personal interests. I am referring to the young couple, poor but in love, that finds, in their love, the antidote for loneliness, poverty, and even the ever-frustrating reality. Thus, the character mistakenly generalizes from the idea of fraternal love among human beings that the couples' sensual love should be the ideological basis of civilization.

At this point, we can distinguish the development of another intertextual relationship that could be understood as another possible source for "Nocturnal Games": chapters five and six of *Civilization and its Discontents*. However, it is necessary to clarify that my suggestion about this relationship neither aims to examine possible influences nor attempts to prove that Roa Bastos read Freud's work. On the contrary, I am attempting to underscore one of the many meanings of communication between texts that modified the sociocultural heritage from which modernity emerged and developed. I defend this possibility of correlation between these texts in light of two arguments. My first argument is the similarity between the plot of the story and the development of the ideas of chapter six of Freud's text, and the second consists of the repetition of the Plutonian phrase *homo homini lupus* in both texts. In chapter six of *Civilization and its Discontents*, Freud's argument stems from Schiller's verses "hunger and love are what moves the world." Freud postulates a separation between the interior and the exterior worlds symbolized, respectively, by the terms *hunger*—representing the instinct of individual preservation—and *love*, which directs the ego toward the other, therefore carrying out a movement toward exteriority. Thus, the same Roabastian idea is psychologically explored here.

The idea of the opposition between love and hunger will eventually be undermined by Freud, who bases his argument on the theory that the concepts of narcissism and sexual sadism connect the ego to the libido. Even when he ventures outside the field of sexuality, the Austrian psychoanalyst proposes that a part of the death instinct turns off the ego and becomes the instinct of destructivity or aggression. This deviation once again inversely links the ego and Eros.[14] Hence, Freud concludes that the great force of destructiveness exceeds the necessity for common work. This impedes the task of civilization, understood as a process belonging to Eros, "whose purpose is to combine single human individuals, and after that, families, then races, peoples and nations, into one great unity, the unity of mankind" (Freud, *Civilization*, 69).

"Nocturnal Games" also uses, as a departure point, the same opposition between hunger, as a form of social segregation, and love, as an antidote for reality and as a force that can modify the world. This expectation gets frustrated since the couple does not consummate the awaited sexual act but instead acts out an episode of aggression performed by the man, an episode that suggests the couple's definite separation. Hence, Roa Bastos's story seems to echo Freud's words about the human capacity for aggression in chapter five of *Civilization and its Discontents*:

> Men are not gentle creatures who want to be loved, and who at the most can defend themselves if they are attacked; they are, on the contrary, creatures among whose instinctual endowments is to be reckoned a power

share of aggressiveness. As a result, their neighbor is for them not only a potential helper or sexual object, but also someone who tempts them to satisfy their aggressiveness on him, to exploit his capacity to work without compensation, to use him sexually without his consent, to seize his possessions, to humiliate him, to cause him pain, to torture and to kill him. *Homo homini lupus.* (Freud, *Civilization*, 58)

Another aspect of Roa Bastos's text that alludes, in a veiled way, to Freud is an ironic reference to the origins of mankind in the ocean, an abundant enough source of food to free human beings from starvation. Here, the reference to the Austrian physician is twofold, for it is directed both at the foundation of psychoanalysis and to the failures of civilization: "Porque . . . la invención de Ego o de la bomba . . . no nos han compensado bastante de lo que perdimos al desalojar de la placenta originaria" ("Because . . . the invention of the Ego or the invention of the bomb . . . have not compensated us enough for what we lost when we abandoned the original placenta"; 508). One notes an indirect mention of war, which plays a preponderant role in the story since it not only aligns the young woman attacked by her lover with other characters who are female victims, but also brings up the topic of mental alienation. In this respect, Caroline's episode illustrates and relates to the problems of the double and the transmutation of personalities between the fat man and Patrick, the English woman's husband, killed in war.

In addition to these connections, the quoted fragment allows a return to Freud's thought presented in chapter five of *Civilization and its Discontents*, with respect to the Communist revolution, cited briefly in Roa Bastos's text, too. This idea not only questions the ideal of integration among men, but also invalidates any Edenlike representation of the origin. That is, Freud considers that human civilization abolishes the hope for a better world, and is also an impediment to a more humanist civilization, which is suggested in the last quotation from "Nocturnal Games." This pessimistic vision of human nature extends to the premises of the Communist system, for, according to the psychoanalyst, these proposals would be illusory since the abolition of the system of private property would not alter "the differences in power and influences which are misused by aggressiveness, nor have we altered anything in its nature. Aggressiveness was not created by property. It reigned almost without limit in primitive times, when property was still very scanty" (Freud, *Civilization*, 60).

This thought is relevant here because the irony that the fat man uses to interrogate Campos Cervera about revolution, and the Paraguayan poet's disillusioned answer, coincide with the Freudian proposition: "¿Usted piensa que la Revolución les va a dar esta torta de hojaldre? ("Do you think that Revolution is going to give them that puff pastry?"; 509) The text proposes not only a relationship between psychical impulses and political options, but also creates the expectation that Eros's forces, either regarding sensual love or fraternal love, are the only way to survive within an unequal struggle between love and human instincts. For this reason, we can perceive the extent of the disenchantment of the protagonist's final denial and his return to indifference, which, although it has worked as the antidote for disillusions, has also been the seed that creates alienation.

Thus, "Nocturnal Games" appears as a supplementation of the critical, literary, and sociocultural discourse discussed in "To Tell a Tale." These stories maintain themselves within a rhizomatic system constructed by expansion between the plane of reality and the plane of fiction. These will meet and will merge into each other, invalidating any hierarchical separation. Evidently, this refusal of hierarchy is established as a sort of resistance against any oppressive model. Deleuze and Guattari describe this protest in the following terms: "Write, form a rhizome, increase your territory by deterritorialization, extend the line of flight to the point where it becomes an abstract machine covering the entire plane of consistency" (Deleuze and Guattari 11).

The forms adopted by this concept of resistance in the stories linked together by the character of the fat man are, nevertheless, ambiguous. Thus, the representation of this character as a support of a writing-in-gestation is susceptible to degradation, since his rhizomatic way of telling causes an increasing distrust reiterated by other characters' questioning of his narrative reliability and by his own reflections on writing. In this way, writing and telling become paradoxical forms of resistance since they use the material of words, the most unstable of all resources. Likewise, the representation of the fat man as writing's enclave deteriorates, thus accentuating the inefficiency of the literary task in two ways. First, when the fat man appropriates the other's discourse, the latter establishes a dialogue with what was "already said" and "already thought," which transforms literary creation into a tautology. Second, the displacement toward death as the final tale and the sole story that is really important emphasizes its sterility even more, annulling any idea of transcendence of the narrative act.

                    Fatima R. Nogueira

Notes

1. In the first place, this necessity of reorganization and redistribution regarding the brief story is proven by the republishing of the tales that integrate the first two volumes—seven among the seventeen of *El trueno entre las hojas* (*Thunder among the Leaves*; 1953) and nine among the eleven constituting *El baldío* (*The Vacant Lot*; 1966)—in five compilations that followed them. These compilations, organized by the author himself, are fashioned in the form of personal anthologies to which some new stories (ten during the twenty-seven years that separate the first and the last volume) and chapters or fragments of novels will be added. In this way, chapters one and five from *Hijo de Hombre* (*Son of Man*; 1960), whose titles are, respectively, "Macario" and "Hogar" ("Home") appear as short stories in *Los pies sobre el agua* (*Feet on the Water*; 1967) and in *Cuerpo presente y otros textos* (*Lying in State and Other Texts*; 1971), while the last of them appears again in *Antología personal* (*Personal Anthology*; 1980), along with a fragment of *Yo el Supremo* (*I the Supreme*; 1974), titled "Lección de escritura" (Writing Lesson). First, this characteristic permanent revision of Roa Bastos's work is exemplified by the story "Kurupí," published in *Madera Quemada* (*Burnt Wood*; 1967), which was originally conceived as the penultimate chapter of *Son of Man*, a piece that is added to the novel's 1982 new version. This same transferring of different literary genres may be observed in the adaptation of a fragment of *I the Supreme* in 1985 to a play with the same title as the novel. Second, we can see that, in the opposite direction, some of the stories are in fact initial projects for novels. This is the case of the five first tales of *Moriencia* (*Slaughter*; 1969), to which "Cuando un pájaro entierra sus plumas" (When a Bird Buries its Feathers; 1971) will be added later. According to the author, those five chapters were part of the novel *Contravida* (*Counterlife*; 1994), which was unfinished at that time. Third, some stories have different versions. Some examples of this re-elaboration are: "Ración de león" ("Lion's share"; 1969); "Función" ("Function"; 1972); "Moriencia" ("Slaughter"; 1969); "Chepé Bolívar" (1981); "Noche sin fin" ("Endless Night" 1957), and "La tijera" ("The Scissors"; 1966). On these versions, see Luna Sellés, *La narrativa breve de Augusto Roa Bastos*, 21. Also, Weldt-Basson's "Roa Bastos's 'Noche sin fin' and 'La tijera'" approaches minutely, from the perspective of genetic theory, the transformation of the story "Endless Night" (1957), originally published in the journal *Ficción*, to "The Scissors" published in *The Vacant Lot* (1966).

2. In the prologue to the second edition of *Son of Man* (1982), Roa Bastos sketches a definition of the "poetics of variations" as follows: "Corregir y variar un texto ya publicado me pareció una aventura estimulante. Un texto . . . no cristaliza de una vez para siempre ni vegeta como el sueño de las plantas. Un texto, si es vivo, vive y se modifica. Lo varía y reinventa el lector a cada lectura. Si hay creación, esta es su ética. También

el autor—como lector—puede variar el texto indefinidamente sin hacerle perder su naturaleza originaria sino, por el contrario, enriqueciéndola con sutiles modificaciones. Además . . . la letra se subordina al espíritu, la escritura a la oralidad. Esta poética de las variaciónes que subvierte y anima los 'textos establecidos,' forma los palimpsestos que . . . encantan a los lectores ingenuos . . . todo autor . . . debe proceder a la ética y la poética de las variaciones. Lo hace de todos los modos, aunque no se lo proponga, de un libro a otro, de tal modo que la última versión es exactamente, en la vuelta completa do círculo, la negación de la primera (The correction and variation of an already published text seemed to me a stimulating adventure. A text . . . does not crystallize at a time and forever or vegetate like the plant's dream. A text, if it is alive, lives and becomes modified. The reader varies it and re-invents it during each reading. If there is creation, this is its ethics. The author also, like the reader, may vary the text indefinitely, conserving its original nature and enriching it with subtle modifications. Moreover . . . the letter is subordinated to the spirit and writing to oral expression. This poetics of variations that subverts and animates 'established texts' forms palimpsests, which . . . delight naïve readers . . . every author . . . should proceed to apply the ethics and the poetics of variations. S/he does it anyway, although s/he does not intend it, from one book to another in such a way that the last version is exactly, like the turn of a circle, the negation of the first one; 2–3).

3. The prologues of *Cuentos completos* (*Complete Short Stories*) and *Slaughter* are about the referential nature of the story and the nature of the inconclusive work. The first presents a poem in the form of a preface whose verses remit to Paraguay's mythical world and erase the boundaries between reality and imagination. The poem concludes by asserting that the stories form a sole great text. The second prologue is about this great text's provisional nature expressed with the following words: "[Los demás cuentos] publicados parcialmente han sido retocados o reelaborados en su totalidad, por lo que provisoriamente al menos estas versiones pueden considerarse definitivas" ([The rest of the stories] already partially published, have been touched up or totally re-elaborated; for this reason these versions may be considered, at least provisionally, definitive; 7).

4. The absence of a clear boundary between the genres is noticeable through the constant intercommunication between the novels and the short stories. Such correspondences permit that some chapters or fragments of novels, in order to demonstrate certain autonomy, may be presented independently, or that certain situations that appeared before in the form of short stories are rewritten in a broader way in the novels. An example of this last case is the dismemberment of characteristics, such as the blindness and musical ability of Solano López, protagonist of "Thunder among the Leaves." This blindness and musical ability is later

divided between Macario Francia and Gaspar Mora in the first chapter of *Son of Man*. Another good example is the connection between the return of Aparicio Ojeda and Crisanto Villalba at the end of that same novel (Rovira 30). Moreover, the work's genre disruption was somehow encouraged by the author himself, since he published chapters of *Son of Man* in the form of stories, and also because he accepted that the tales of *Slaughter* were part of a larger project that would be completed with the novel Contravida (*Counterlife*; 7). Evidently, this conjunction between the novel and the short story was noticed by the criticism on this book that considered it as a project that "even having a certain unifying structure which relates its nine stories . . . is still a raceme of tales absolutely independent one from the others" (Herszenhorn 256). Trinidad Barrera also recognizes that "*Son of Man* is a book on horseback between a novel and short stories. There are nine tales of pain and anguish located in Paraguay, in an ample space of time, linked by Miguel Vera's fake memory" (107). With respect to *I the Supreme*, in 1976, Ángel Rama pointed out the book's unclassifiable hybridism with the following words: "esta desmesurada invención; este inclasificable libro (historia, novela, ensayo sociológico, filosofía moral, biografía novelada, panfleto revolucionario, documento justificativo, poema en prosa, confesión autobiográfica, debate sobre los límites de la literatura) que es en los hechos una infatigable requisitoria nacida de una conciencia en vilo, revuelta y convulsionada como su tiempo, a la que pone en llaga viva haber asumido todos los conflictos de un hombre latinoamericano." ("this excessive invention; this unclassifiable book [history, a novel, a sociological essay, moral philosophy, a fictionalized biography, a revolutionary pamphlet, a justifying document, a prose poem, an autobiographical confession, a discussion on the limits of literature] that is truly a tireless requisition born from a suspended consciousness, scrambled and convulsive as its time, which becomes an open wound due to the fact of having assumed every conflict of a Latin American man"; 21).

5. Deleuze and Guattari assert that the line of flight defines multiplicity, relating it to exteriority: "Multiplicities are defined by the outside: by the abstract line, the line of flight or deterritorialization according to which they change in nature and connect with other multiplicities. The plane of consistency (grid) is the outside of all multiplicities. The line of flight marks: the reality of a finite number of dimensions that the multiplicity effectively fills: the impossibility of a supplementary dimension, unless the multiplicity is transformed by the line of flight; the possibility and necessity of flattening all the multiplicities in a single plane of consistency or exteriority, regardless of their number of dimensions" (9).

6. For Deleuze and Guattari, "a rhizome has no beginning or end: it is always in the middle, between things, interbeing, *intermezzo*" (25).

7. The relationship between the lines of segmentarity and the lines of flight could be summarized as follows: every rhizome contains lines of

segmentarity—molar and molecular—and lines of flight. The molar segments (hard) are determined, predetermined, and codified by the state, whereas the molecular line of segmentation (malleable) is characterized by an ambiguity that permits it to oscillate between the hard lines and the lines of flight, with the aim of reconstructing at its own level all which it undoes. Therefore, the relationship established by these segments between themselves could be articulated as a fragmentation operated by the lines of flight—representative of an immanent social danger—in which the latter make explode the two segmentary series through movements of destratificatioin and deterritorialization. On this subject, see *A Thousand Plateaus*, 204–7.

8. All the quotations concerning Roa Bastos's stories come from *Cuentos completos*. All English translations are mine.

9. This perspective is also revealed by another teller-character, Macario, who, in *Son of Man*, affirms: "Man is born twice. First, when he is born, secondly, when he dies . . . He dies but he stays alive within the others" (33). A variant of this thought can be found in *Slaughter*, in the epigraph engraved by the master Cristaldo on Chepé Bolívar's coffin: "No hay más que el principio y lo que está antes del principio" (There is nothing but the beginning and what is before the beginning; 316). The theory of death as beginning is represented by Macario, buried in a child's coffin, and by Cristaldo, who had his face wrinkled like a newborn when he died.

10. About the unfolding of the axiom: a tale is fashioned by a series of other tales as a man is another man, see Aldana's *La cuentística de Augusto Roa Bastos*.

11. Bakhtin 88–89. The translations of Bakhtin's quotations are mine.

12. Carlo Pedretti points out that the mechanical device was probably made up for the reception of Francis I by the Florentine colony in the city of Lyons: "The occasion of the event can be clarified by a series of deductions. The triumphal entry of Francis I into Lyons took place on 12th July 1515. The chroniclers speak of great festivities organized by the Florentine colony. The line, at one time symbol of Florence (marzocco) and of Lyons, was commissioned by the *nazion fiorentina*, that is, by Lorenzo di Piero de' Medici, whom his uncle Leo X had elected governor of Florence on 24th May 1515. The symbolism of the mechanical lion is further explained by the presence of lilies in its chest: they are the fleur-de-lis of France. Thus the Florentine nation intended to show its devotion to the new king, whose aunt, Philiberta of Savoy, had just been married (January 1515) to the brother of the Pope, Giuliano de Medici. Finally, we must bear in mind that in December 1515 the Pope himself entered Florence on his way to meet Francis I in Bologna, and was received with great festivities in both cities" (341).

13. Gabriel Saad interprets the repetition of the four first letters of *Leonardo* within the word *lion* (*león*) as a reference to the mirror-like construction

of the writing practiced by Leonardo da Vinci. On this topic see Saad 145–52.

14. Here, Freud returns to the supposedly opposite impulses, analyzed in *Beyond the Pleasure Principle*, which are called, respectively, Eros and death instinct. The possibility that a part of this instinct might become aggression would connect the ego and Eros since the autodestruction instinct would become something's or somebody's ruin in the exterior world.

WORKS CITED

Aldana, Adelfo L. *La cuentística de Augusto Roa Bastos.* Montevideo: Ediciones Geminis, 1975. Print.

Bakhtin, Mikhail. *Questões de literatura e de estética: A teoria do romance.* 5th ed. Trans. Aurora Fornoni Bernardini, José Pereira Júnior etal. São Paulo: Hucitec/Annablume, 2002. Print.

Barrera, Trinidad. "Otra vuelta de tuerca a Roa." *Dos orillas y un encuentro: la literatura paraguaya actual.* Ed. Mar Langa Pizarro. Alicante: Centro de Estudios Iberoamericanos Mario Benedetti, 2005. 105–12. Print.

Barthes, Roland. "The Death of the Author." *The Norton Anthology of Literary Criticism.* Ed. Vincent B. Leitch. New York: Norton, 2001. 1466–70. Print.

Benjamin, Walter. *Illuminations.* Trans. Harry Zohn. New York: Harcourt, Brace & World, 1968. Print.

Deleuze, Gilles, and Felix Guattari. *A Thousand Plateaus: Capitalism and Schizophrenia.* Trans. Brian Massumi. Minneapolis: University of Minnesota Press, 2003. Print.

Freud, Sigmund. "The Uncanny." *The Norton Anthology of Literary Criticism.* Ed. Vincent B. Leitch. New York: Norton, 2001. 929–52. Print.

———. *Civilization and Its Discontents.* Trans. James Strachey. New York: Norton, 1962. Print.

———. *Leonardo Da Vinci and a Memory of His Childhood.* Trans. Alan Tyson. New York: Norton, 1964. Print.

Harrington, Michael. *The Other America: Poverty in the United States.* New York: Macmillan, 1962. Print.

Herszenhorn, Jaime. "Reflexiones sobre la temática de los cuentos de Augusto Roa Bastos". *Homenaje a Augusto Roa Bastos; variaciones interpretativas en torno a su obra.* Comp. Helmy F.Giacoman. Long Island City, NY: Las Américas, 1973. 251–66. Print.

Kafka. Franz. *The Complete Stories.* Ed. Nahun Norbet Glatzer. New York: Schocken Books, 1971. Print.

Luna Sellés, Carmen. *La narrativa breve de Augusto Roa Bastos.* Alicante: Instituto de Cultura Juan Gil-Albert, 1993. Print.

Marx, Karl. *Karl Marx: Selected Writings.* Ed. David Mc Lellan. Oxford; New York: Oxford University Press, 2000. Print.

Pedretti, Carlo. "The 'Pointing Lady.'" *The Burlington Magazine* 111.795, (1969): 339–46. Print.

Rama, Ángel. *Los dictadores latinoamericanos.* México: Fondo de Cultura Económica, 1976. Print.

Roa Bastos, Augusto. *Cuentos completos.* Asunción: El Lector, 2003. Print.

———. *Hijo de hombre.* New York: Penguin Books, 1996. Print.

———. *Moriencia.* Caracas: Monte Ávila, 1969. Print.

———. *Son of Man.* Trans. Rachel Caffyn. New York: Monthly Review Press, 1988.

Rovira, José Carlos. "Sobre los orígenes del universo narrativo de Augusto Roa Bastos." *Anthropos: Revista de Documentación Científica de la Cultura* 115 (1990): 28–35. Print.

Saad, Gabriel. "El árbol de la letra y el carnaval de la escritura". *Cuadernos Hispanoamericanos: Revista Mensual de Cultura Hispánica* 493–94 (1991): 145–52. Print.

Weldt-Basson, Helene. "Roa Bastos's 'Noche sin fin' and 'La tijera': Two Versions of the Same Story." *Revista de Filología y Lingüística de la Universidad de Costa Rica* 28.1 (2002): 93–105. Print.

C H A P T E R 6

GENDER AND THE STATE IN *HIJO DE HOMBRE*

TRANSGRESSION AND INTEGRATION

Katie MacLean

The first novel in Augusto Roa Bastos's trilogy on the "monotheism of power" narrates a particular vision of early twentieth-century Paraguayan history. *Hijo de hombre* (1960, revised in 1982) focuses on a twenty-five-year period between the sighting of a comet in 1910 and the Chaco War (1932–35). With such momentous events as bookends, it comes as no surprise that history figures as a major theme in the novel. The author develops a series of tensions that render historiography very problematic. These tensions appear between official history and that of the people, between the particular and the national, between oral and written discourse, between writing[1] and action, and between the moment and its precursors and consequences. At the same time, historical continuity in the world of the common people in the novel is not only underscored in the repetition of historical events such as peasant revolts, but is also assured, according to the elderly Macario Francia, in each new generation: "El hombre, mis hijos . . . es como un río. Tiene barranca y orilla. Nace y desemboca en otros ríos. Alguna utilidad debe prestar. Mal río es el que muere en un estero" (20) ["Man, my sons, is like a river, which has banks to keep it to its course, which is fed by other rivers and which in turn feeds them. Men, like rivers, must serve some purpose. It is a bad river which ends up in a bog" (18)].[2] Good rivers, then, merge and flow into the sea, completing the cycle. Even the title of the novel reinforces this notion of continuity and fatalism. This fatalism, however, should not be read as a sign of a Christian viewpoint that the title *Hijo de hombre* might initially indicate. Roa Bastos's narrative suggests that the "son of man" of the title is not synonymous with the son of God, but rather is evocative of the people who come together in solidarity at various points in the narrative. For instance, the role of a character like Cristóbal Jara in the history of his country—a constant and fruitless struggle to change the circumstances of rural laborers like himself—is preordained because he is the son of a very specific man (Casiano) who participated in the uprising of 1912. So the "utility" of this continuity can lead readers to explore the relationships between the role of an individual in history and his position with respect to the state.

Immediately, we are faced with an obstacle to the articulation of a unifying hypothesis that would describe the relationship between the characters of *Hijo de hombre* and the state. The female characters, the "daughters of women," at times follow very different trajectories in their relationship to history and to the state. Obviously, there are female characters in the novel, but it is not at all clear what they are doing there. Are all of them merely silent shadows whose lives evolve completely on the margins of the historical process? Are they simply a cast of archetypal and eternal "earth mothers"? Or, perhaps, do they just suffer in solitude a double tyranny of machismo and state repression? The purpose of this chapter is not to answer definitively "yes" or "no" to these questions. Rather, it is to examine the position of female characters with respect to the state, and, more specifically, to determine if there is any evolution on the part of these characters in terms of a gradual integration into, or a separation from, the events of a national history and the apparatuses of state power. If it is possible to tease out such trajectories, then further exploration into their meaning is necessary, especially if they do not coincide with the experiences of the male characters.

At first glance, the women in the novel appear as a sequence of images (they speak even less than the laconic male inhabitants of Sapukai) that have been read as a series of variations on the archetype of the mother (earth mothers, virgin mothers) that nourish the bodies and satisfy the sexual desires of men (Busquets 208–210), or as a reduction and spiritualization of women's physical presence in the narrative (Ostrov 128). Admittedly, the glaring repetition of Christian imagery in women's lives, such as the sculpture of the crucified Christ by Gaspar Mora and the subsequent placement of the murdered Melitón

Isasi on the cross, may tempt the reader to extend the allegory so that every female character is reduced to a succession of Marys (the virgin, the Magdalene, and so forth). The fact that many of the female characters are named *María* contributes to this reading. Nonetheless, further analysis is needed in order to see whether a purely archetypal interpretation of the female characters is the only one possible. How do we explain Juana Rosa's escape or the activities of Sor Micaela? In effect, they cannot be accounted for if we view the female characters as merely figures that populate the narrative's background.

These characters are not just figures or images—they work. In addition, their labor is not confined to the traditional "women's work." For example, when the Jaras are recruited to work in the *mate* (mate tea) plantations in the upper Paraná, Natí also finds work in the local store in an attempt to eliminate their growing debt. There, she works like a man and thus becomes an active participant in the local economy of the *yerbal (mate tea plantations)*. The labors of characters like Natí, Juana Rosa, and the gravedigger María Regalada are barely alluded to, but they undertake tasks that put them in direct contact with historical events. Does this labor constitute a form of assimilation or resistance to the machinery that upholds the political regime? The case of María Regalada is illuminating because, at first glance, her existence seems to be confined to a very marginalized space (that of the cemetery). This space, however, is closely linked to the people's history. If we extend Benedict Anderson's interpretation of the tombs of unknown soldiers, both the cemetery and the mass grave in Sapukai distill "imaginings" of a shared history and identity (Anderson 9–10). Thus, María Regalada becomes a kind of custodian for the history of Itapé, and from that position, is able to undermine the efforts of the army by hiding Cristóbal Jara. Consequently, from her apparently unthreatening position as a woman, and through her work that is both marginalized from, and constitutive of, her community, she mounts a kind of resistance to the repressive operations of a state that seeks to suffocate all traces of rebellion.

The marginalized position of women with respect to the state at times leads them to fade almost completely from the historical process narrated in the novel. While male characters gain increasing signifying power as they fall victim to illness or insanity (as in the cases of Macario or Gaspar Mora), women who lose their mind disappear almost completely. Of the two characters who have knowledge of Gaspar's story, only Macario's voice, old and inebriated, is heard: "Si [María Rosa] hablaba, nadie le hacía caso porque era lunática" (24) ["if she (María Rosa) had spoken, no one would have paid any attention, because she was a lunatic" (22)]. Not only are these women voiceless, they are invisible: "Los hombres aparentaban no verla" (37) ["The men did not seem to see her" (34)]. They do not appear to display any agency in history. After going mad following the death of Gaspar, María Rosa abandons her two professions as *chipera* and prostitute; she loses her productive function in the communal economy. She is deprived of both her economic potential and her authority as a witness to history. The mad women are transformed into images or objects whose presence is hardly noticed in the background of the actions of men. Years later, María Rosa continues to be the demented grandmother who guards the Christ figure. Madness and illness completely isolate these women, offering them a partial defense against the violence while depriving them of an active role in events.

The beginning of the Chaco War with Bolivia alters the relationship between the characters and the state on many levels. An interesting result of the outbreak of an international armed conflict is the voluntary and enthusiastic participation of a sector of the population that previously engaged in a continuous struggle against the same soldiers. They are now all considered comrades-in-arms. It becomes apparent in the chapter titled "Misión" that, while the strong bonds among townspeople persist, the imperatives of military order and discipline have assimilated these rebels into the great war-machine of the state.

Should we consider this sudden nationalist sentiment a profound contradiction in the Salpukai rebels' revolutionary ideology? After all, why not merely observe, with delicious equanimity, the defeat of these troops who were so abhorrent in the past? In the novel, we find a nationalist spirit that seems to override internal class conflicts. This radical change in the relationship between the characters and the state deserves greater attention, specifically in the context of the Chaco as simultaneously a national territory and the mass grave of a marginalized people. From this perspective, a study of the role of female characters in the conflict will point to new clues in our analysis of the relationship between women and the state. It remains to be seen whether the Chaco War provokes a change in the women similar to the movement toward integration undertaken by the male characters. Two characters in particular, Sor Micaela and María Encarnación (Salu'í), perform roles that are very different from their previous ones. So this analysis will center on them in an attempt to shed light on the tensions between their role as marginalized women excluded from the historical process and their active participation in the institutions and actions of the state.

The character Sor Micaela is presented to the reader as the narrator of a statement that forms the chapter "Madera quemada," part of a larger story narrated by another character, Miguel Vera. In the novel, her narrative serves to fill in the gaps in Vera's story about events surrounding Itapé's political leader, Melitón Isasi, during the war. She is one of two female characters who are indirectly able to have their own voice preserved by the written word.[3] Somehow, Sor Micaela has managed to have the right, the power, and the voice to contribute to the writing of history—the history of politics, of the state, of men. How did she come about this power and this privileged position? After all, Vera himself reduces her to an old gossip: "Las mujeres empezaron a parlotear todas juntas en el corro formado en torno a la vieja [sor Micaela] de la cofradía, que al fin consiguió imponer su habilidad de oracionera" ["the women began to chat all together in the chorus formed around the old woman (Micaela) from the sisterhood, who finally managed to impose her praying ability" (322; my translation)]. This view of women's talk as superficial prattle notwithstanding, Sor Micaela goes on to demonstrate superior knowledge about the deeds of the former leader.

Sor Micaela herself characterizes her role in Isasi's story as secondary. Her participation is limited to that of consoling Isasi's wife, Brígida, who can only "sufrir y aguantar en silencio junto a ese hombre que golpeaba al pueblo como a una peste" ["suffer and hold up in silence next to that man who struck the village like a plague" (306; my translation)]. Isasi brings his wife to this town where she knows no one and leaves her to keep house while he pursues other women. Brígida, confined to this lonely space, spies on her husband's sexual conquests and affairs through a crack in the door. This "gozo triste" ["sad enjoyment"] (306; my translation) in turn provokes spasms and trembling that Sor Micaela alleviates by massaging Brígida's naked body until she is "tranquila, los ojos cerrados, suspirando muy hondo" ["tranquil, her eyes closed, breathing very deeply"] (309; my translation). These scenes of sensuality and eroticism between the two women are repeated each time Melitón Isasi has sexual relations with a young woman from town, and they allow Sor Micaela a glimpse into the political leader's evolving drama.

The nun's position here is not merely that of a bystander who observes the action from an objective distance. Even she realizes that her relationship with Brígida de Isasi has placed her in a situation that is not typically that of a woman: "Le hablo [a Vera] hasta de lo que yo pensaba ahí con Ña Brígida dormida en mis brazos, hamacándola y diciéndole cosas al oído a través de su sueño. Ah mundo, ah vida . . . *Todo tan al revés*. Ña Brígida en mis brazos y Melitón a caballo por esos andurriales buscando hasta dónde llegaba la punta de su deseo

["I spoke to him (Vera) even about what I was thinking there with Ña Brígida asleep in my arms, rocking her and telling her things in her ear through her dreams. Ay world, ay life . . . Everything backward. Ña Brígida in my arms and Melitón on horseback around those boondocks looking for where the tip of his desire extended"] (309; my translation). Indeed, Sor Micaela has brought about a substitution. While Melitón goes about his business of laying down the law and bedding young women in the area, the nun is occupying his place in his own home. A little further along in the story, when one of his lovers becomes pregnant, there is a moment when Isasi himself defers to Sor Micaela and relinquishes his power to shape his own future: "Usted sabrá qué hacer, [Isasi] me dijo desgallado, la omnipotencia para abajo" ["You will know what to do, (Isasi) told me undecided, his omnipotence buried underneath"] (310; my translation). As a result, Sor Micaela achieves a privileged perspective not simply by being the confidante of Isasi's wife, but by also replacing this rather important male character in his role as husband and man in charge.

Sor Micaela's rise to this new position in relation to male power destabilizes a series of gender binarisms that other aspects of the novel appear to uphold. First, this woman is a nun and therefore has effectively removed herself from a sexual economy where women are traded among men for their sexual and reproductive functions. Then, by occupying the place of the husband in his relationship with his wife, she changes her "practices" with respect to feminine gender norms.[4] According to Valerie Traub, the supposedly natural differences between men and women are the result of the recasting of concepts that should remain very distinct: "In a move that obscures the constructedness of subjectivity, gender and sexuality, the female subject is defined in terms of a desire that is implicitly passive, heterosexually positioned in relation to man" (Traub 85–86). The "practices" of Sor Micaela reveal this heterosexual norm to instead be a construct reinforced by a society that seeks to obscure the very processes of its construction. She acts on her desire (and perhaps Brígida's) by replacing the male and blurring the boundaries by which we tend to delineate gender and sexuality.

Apart from surpassing the limits imposed by traditional notions of the feminine, this nun's transgression can also be considered a fundamental threat to the patriarchal nation-state. Women's designated roles can be divided into two categories. Floya Anthias and Nira Yuval-Davis point to a series of functions that women fulfill within the family: the reproductive one to sustain the population (with its divisions intact); and other functions that serve to preserve and transmit the social values of the community" (Anthias and Yuval-Davis 7). On the other hand, women may participate in the economic, political, and even military activities of the state, but usually in an auxiliary capacity: "They are seen to be in a supportive and nurturing relation to men" (Anthias and Yuval-Davis 10). Sor Micaela does not fulfill her traditional female obligations to the state. Instead, she steps forward to offer her own narrative voice in order to represent her version of events in Itapé within the discursive framework of the official (written) history that Vera attempts to construct.

Sor Micaela's case is one of defiance and transgression concerning the roles that society has deemed appropriate for women. She stands in for the husband in the Isasi marriage and for Vera's voice in the writing of history. The problem of the relationship between women and the state is further complicated, however, with other instances of instability in gender identity. At another point in *Hijo de hombre*, this interesting issue again comes to the foreground. In the midst of the Chaco, Salu'í, another female character, undergoes a transformation that leads her to participate in a very untraditional way in the defense of the nation.

The moment when the conflict between Sapukai peasants and state power is replaced by a war between Paraguayans and "the *bolís*" is when nationalism is mobilized to pacify and homogenize antagonist groups within the nation. The new meanings of "we" and "them" are dramatized in the military jail in Peña Hermosa where Miguel Vera writes in his journal: "Así que las divergencias se han superado de golpe. Ya no hay discusiones políticas. Colorados, liberales y apolíticos están en paz . . . Todos de acuerdo, eufóricos, como si realmente hubiéramos recuperado la libertad" (222) ["All our differences have suddenly disappeared. There are no more political arguments . . . All in sympathy, in a state of euphoria, as though we were free again" (173)]. So all the former "traitors" are off to the front. This phenomenon, explored by Benedict Anderson, underscores the power that the idea of the nation exerts on its citizens: "Regardless of the actual inequality and exploitation that may prevail in each, the nation is always conceived as a deep, horizontal comradeship. Ultimately it is this fraternity that makes it possible, over the past two centuries, for so many millions of people, not so much to kill, as willingly to die for such limited imaginings" (Anderson 7). The idea of the nation, then, brings together a community of fellow countrymen as well as the corresponding geographical territory. In the novel, both are threatened by an external enemy.

Two women arrive in the middle of this fervor. The narrator attempts to explain their presence in a war zone as a story of women in search of their beloveds: Juana Rosa has left Itapé to escape her "dishonor" and search for her husband, Crisanto Villalba, while María Encarnación, also known by her nickname "Salu'í", has come to the area to work as a prostitute. When she falls in love with Cristóbal Jara in the military camp, she decides to give up prostitution and finds work in the infirmary. Thus, the two women assume the auxiliary role of supportive female outlined above. Salu'í also identifies with the idea of women as men's property, and so wishes to erase the traces of other men in order to be worthy of Cristóbal's love: "En lo más hondo de su degradación habría sentido resucitar su virginidad como una glándula, renacer, purificarse, bajo ese sentimiento nuevo y arrollador, que no nació, sin embargo, para ella en un deslumbramiento" (260) ["Her regeneration, which had seemed inconceivable, began. Something in her ardent, abused femininity, something that had never got quite corrupted, began to grow" (201)]. In this context, then, although the two women find themselves in the middle of a war, they remain strictly within the state's parameters for female agency.

When Salu'í discovers that Cristóbal is being sent on a dangerous, and probably suicidal, mission, she offers to accompany him as a stretcher-bearer in order to be by his side. The mission consists of reaching a group of soldiers trapped behind enemy lines with a convoy of trucks carrying water. Not surprisingly, Jara forbids her to go: "Cada uno en su puesto"(285) ["Everyone should stick to his own job" (198)]. Evidently the military's structure precisely defines and controls access to the field of combat and to power, even more so for its female personnel. Salu'í does manage to join the convoy despite the prohibition, but only after reinventing herself in secret during an aerial attack.

During the time her activities went unnoticed due to the darkness, panic, and general confusion of the attack, Salu'í steals a uniform from a dead soldier. By cutting her hair and dressing as a soldier, she joins the other participants on the mission. The immediate effect of this cross-dressing is that she passes for a man: either a deserter or a Bolivian soldier, according to the first impression of her comrades. Once her real identity is confirmed later on by fellow soldiers, her appearance continues to have a disquieting effect. Silvestre declares that now she really is "reborn" (277), and Cristóbal, the object of her affections, is dumbstruck: "Pareció fijarse en ella, como si la hubiera visto por primera vez" ["he seemed to notice her as if he had seen her for the first time"] (216). Although the men realize who she is, they still do not recognize her as the woman they thought they knew. The identity of the Salu'í whom everyone knew as a prostitute or a nurse was articulated by means of a "performativity," in the sense that Butler accords it, that reiterated and reinforced a specific feminine position: "This suggests that 'sexed positions' are not localities but, rather, citational practices instituted within a juridical domain—a domain of constitutive constraints. The embodying of sex would be a kind of 'citing' of the law, but neither sex nor the law can be said to preexist their various embodyings and citings" (Butler 108). Her cross-dressing marks the end of a reiterated "citing" whereby Salu'í's identity can be read in the previous way as "capricious," "prostitute," and "*Pequeña Salud.*" By not continuing to "cite" this version of Salu'í, she provokes immediate confusion in those who attempt to locate her within the usual norms that differentiate masculine and feminine.

This character now manifests an unstable subjectivity. Suddenly she is "citing" a masculine position. However, her transformation is not limited to her physical appearance. When she finds herself in the middle of the action, her behavior resembles more that of a seasoned medic than that of a prostitute-turned-nurse:

> Sacó un botiquín de primeros auxilios, cargó en un brazo medicamentos, paquetes de venda, todo lo que pudo, y regresó a escape hacia el bosque, en momentos en que el avión hacía una nueva pasada ametrallando el abra. La rápida estela de nubecitas de polvo cruzó mordiendo en camino muy cerca de ella. Apuró el paso y se alejó culebreando entre los destrozos en llamas del aguador y el cadáver del camillero. (275)
>
> She picked up a first aid box and filled her arms with medicines, packets of bandages, everything she could carry. She climbed out again and was running toward the wood when the plane came over and swept the clearing once more with guns. Puffs of dust rose all round her. Quickening her pace, she picked her way between the burning ruins of the water-truck, and the stretcher-bearer's corpse (213).

In effect, the "performativity" of this new subject position resides not only in the way she dresses her body; it consists of a series of strategies and behaviors as well. Salu'í does not stop at dressing as a male soldier; she makes a convincing display of *hombría* (manliness). In the episode described in the quote above, not only does she rescue critical supplies from a truck in danger of exploding, she must also zigzag through a veritable obstacle course of burning vehicles and machine gunfire. Later on, she ensures the survival of the mission by tying Jara's hands to the steering wheel of the truck while she herself is bleeding from a fatal bullet wound. Both bravery and indifference to pain are traditional masculine traits. In this process, she is subverting an array of binary oppositions imposed on the sexes. She passes from a feminine to a masculine position, she travels from the periphery (an auxiliary function in the camp) toward the center of combat, and moves from passivity to action. By transgressing the limits that distinguish gender identities, Salu'í participates fully in the Chaco conflict.

Her incursion into the combat zone by means of cross-dressing brings with it a transformation in her relationship to the state. Previously relegated to the confines of the military encampment because of her sex and her profession, she joins a mission with strategic objectives. She becomes an active participant in the war machine of the state. This apparatus is fundamental to state power and, perhaps for that very reason, is the male space *par excellence*. Once there, she displays the same commitment and valor as her comrades. She joins the collective in this nationalist struggle.

By incorporating herself in the state in this manner, Salu'í does not become a foremother to a mass participation of women in the Paraguayan armed forces in this novel. She has no rank and will never be decorated for her courage. In fact, no one will ever know of her, no one will miss her because she abandoned her post amid the chaos of an enemy attack. Even the suicide mission releases her from many military conventions. When she is discovered by her comrades, dressed as a male soldier, she worries about the consequences:

> "Ahora puede hacerme fusilar . . ."
> "'Sólo se fusila a los desertores,' dijo Aquino riéndose."
> "'Soy una desertora . . .' dijo ella, seria."
> "No se deserta cuando se va a un bautismo de fuego." (269)
> "Now he can have me shot . . ."
> "We only shoot deserters," said Aquino laughing.
> "I am a deserter . . ." she said seriously.
> "Going to meet the enemy for the first time is hardly deserting." (208)

And sure enough, she dies with everyone else on the mission. She dies in the mud of the Chaco after tying Cristóbal to the steering wheel of the truck so that he may attempt to complete the mission alone. Her foray into the male space of the national army ends abruptly in an anonymous silence.

Dying this way in the Chaco, Salu'í's character is joined in the fate of thousands of Paraguayans. The novel insists, over and over again, on the omnipresence of suffering and death in that war. Thirst tortures everyone: "La sed, la *muerte blanca* trajina del bracete con la otra, la *roja*, encapuchadas de polvo" (233) [Thirst, the White Death, walks among us arm in arm with the other, the Red Death, both of them cloaked with dust" (179)]. Thirst and bullets destroy the combatants until it is impossible to bury or forget them. As Cristóbal looks upon two fallen comrades, he makes an observation that could very well stand for the totality of victims:

> recogió un puñado de tierra seca del desierto. La dejó caer sobre ellos, en un vago gesto de despedida, acaso de instintiva rebelión. Infancia y destino, el tiempo de la vida, lo que quedaba detrás y lo que ya no tenía futuro, se desmenuzaban en ese chorro árido que caía de su mano, en la fatal pesantez que todo lo devuelve a la tierra, pensando quizá que toda la tierra muerta del Chaco no iba a alcanzar a cubrirlos, a tapar esos agujeros del tamaño de un hombre. (280)
>
> He stooped and picked up a handful of the dry desert earth. He let it fall on them, in a vague gesture of farewell, and perhaps of rebellion. Childhood and fate, the whole course of his life, what had been and what could never be, sifted through his fingers with the dry stream of dust, returning to dust as everything is bound to do. He was thinking, no doubt, that all the sterile earth of the Chaco could never cover them, never conceal those holes in the shape of men. (216)

Through the sacrifice of so many, the earth of the Chaco and remains of the dead are fused into one. The corpses that litter the ground are now an integral part of this contested region. Now, if the Chaco has been made to represent the national territory for the purposes of waging this war, then this mass grave becomes coextensive with the nation-state.

The anonymous death on a mass scale that often characterizes modern warfare is frequently presented as the price that citizens must pay in order to preserve the sovereignty of the state. The fallen acquire a symbolic meaning that goes beyond the historical event in question. The Chaco has been transformed into a tomb by this defense of the nation, and consequently acquires the same symbolic weight that Anderson attributes to tombs of the Unknown Soldier: "Public ceremonial reverence [is] accorded these monuments precisely *because* they are either deliberately empty or no one knows who lies inside them . . . one has only to imagine the general reaction to the busybody who 'discovered' the Unknown Soldier's name" (Anderson 9). The Chaco has become this monument. On one level, anonymity guarantees this kind of national identification. Salu'í remains buried in this enormous tomb like one more unknown soldier. Her body is part of a national monument.

This female character begins her adventure with cross-dressing in order to join a combat mission. She infiltrates the male sphere of the state and participates alongside the men. Her death in combat immortalizes this integration into the Chaco as both a tomb and monument; a testimony to the geographical territory and temporal continuity of the state: "a secular transformation of fatality into continuity, contingency into meaning" (Anderson 11). Her body will forever remain integrated into this symbolic dimension of the Paraguayan nation. In this sense, Salu'í's assimilation into the state is irrevocable and complete.

The two female characters, Sor Micaela and Salu'í, who have allowed us to explore the relationship between women and the state in *Hijo de hombre*, have been able to transform that very relationship. If, at first, they exist and act within typically female roles and spaces in society, they then undertake a movement toward, and even integration into, the structures of male power: Sor Micaela with the writing of history and Salu'í with the War of the Chaco. It must be pointed out, however, that the two women do not follow parallel trajectories. Although there are certain elements in common, there are important differences in the nature of their positions within the structures of power.

Both Sor Micaela and Salu'í change their relationship to the state through instances of transgression. Each, in her own way, crosses the gender boundaries imposed by society. In both cases, we can observe two decisive moments when the characters take steps toward the realms of state power. For Sor Micaela, these moments occur when, first, she replaces the husband in the sexual realm of the Isasi marriage, and then, she is one of the voices that narrate the history of the community. For Salu'í, her cross-dressing and her death in combat make her an active participant in a national drama. The fact that these transformations in these women's relationship to the state result from transgressions of this type is no fortuitous coincidence. In the world of these two characters, women's spaces and roles are strictly defined and removed from political power. For a woman to approach any position of power, she must abandon the elements of a "performativity" normally associated with the feminine: sexual passivity, silence, women's garb, and fear.

Although both women enter into the discursive and institutional spaces of state power through transgression, their subsequent situations are not identical. Through her challenge to the limits of her gender role (her sensual and sexual relationship with Brígida), Sor Micaela gains what one might call a representational power. Her voice speaks for the marginalized who normally do not figure in the discourse of history (women and oral culture).[5] In the novel, this is a temporary position. While her voice in the historical narrative is a permanent testimony to her incursion into lettered culture, she herself goes back to her previous role as guardian of the Christ figure and marginalized woman. Salu'í's case is very different. She never goes back to dressing as a woman, nor does she return from the war. While Sor Micaela's words are preserved for posterity, Salu'í's physical body remains in the Chaco as a monument to the nation-state. There is no return to a former feminine subject position; she is forever incorporated into the state.

Even though both sexes have some kind of relationship to the state in this novel, there are stark differences between those who have political power and those who do not. At the same time, other divisions are apparent, such as the one between those who have direct access to the spaces and institutions where power is concentrated and those who are permanently on the periphery. In *Hijo de hombre*, class, ethnicity, and also gender determine the individual's relation to the state. Women only gain direct participation in that sphere when they successfully blur the borders that distinguish masculine from feminine. The state defines itself in masculine terms, thus keeping power in the hands of men. However, this appears to be a precarious position that requires the constant reinforcement of gender norms in order to marginalize women. Two female characters in the novel challenge these norms by taking advantage of the instability of these categories in times of tension and crisis.

Near the end of the novel, Miguel Vera laments his people's apparent inability to transcend the cycle of injustice and violence: "Alguna salida debe haber en este monstruoso contrasentido del hombre crucificado por el hombre. Porque de lo contrario sería el caso de pensar que la raza humana está maldita para siempre" (342) ["Men cannot go on crucifying one another forever. There must be an end to it. Otherwise one must come to the conclusion that the human race is forever accursed, that hell is here and now and that there is no hope of salvation" (262)]. The cyclical nature of violence related to class and ethnic hierarchies suggests that these—like gender identities—must be constantly rearticulated and "reiterated," at times with the use of force. The fatalism that pervades *Hijo de hombre*, with respect to class struggle in Paraguay, is by no means offset by the representations of the two female characters examined in this chapter. However, if we look at gender as being an integral part of a web of identities that have often marginalized individuals and communities, then we can no longer ignore the constructed – and therefore vulnerable—nature of these hierarchies.

Notes

1 Weldt-Basson explores the focus on writing throughout the trilogy as one of several postmodern practices.

2. Note that all English translations of *Hijo de hombre*, unless otherwise noted, are taken from: Augusto Roa Bastos, *Son of Man* (New York: Monthly Review Press, 1988).

3. At the end of the novel, there appears a fragment of Rosa Monzón's letter accompanying Vera's manuscript. She explains the abrupt end to Vera's political career and how she came to possess the manuscript. At the same time, she lets the reader know that she has also censured the manuscript in order to erase any reference to herself. In a potentially powerful move, she has gained control of written history, but only in order to eliminate any sign of her own agency in it.

4. In order to emphasize the volatility of the concepts of masculine and feminine, several theorists, notably Judith Butler in *Bodies that Matter*, propose that gender is not a natural attribute; instead, it must be constantly reiterated: "To the extent that the 'I' is secured by its sexed position, this 'I' and its 'position' can be secured only by being *repeatedly* assumed, whereby 'assumption' is not a singular act or event, but, rather, an iterable practice" (108).

5. For a detailed study of oral history in *Hijo de hombre*, see the essays by Loreto Busquets, María Caballero Wanguemert, and Ana María Sánchez.

Works Cited

Anderson, Benedict. *Imagined Communities: Reflections on the Origin and Spread of Nationalism*. Rev. ed. London: Verso, 1991. Print.

Anthias, Floya, and Nira Yuval-Davis. "Introduction." *Women-Nation-State*. Eds. Yuval-Davis and Anthias. New York: St. Martin's Press, 1989. 1–15. Print.

Busquets, Loreto. "El realismo impresionista de *Hijo de hombre*." *Cuadernos Hispanoamericanos* 493–94 (1991): 199–215. Print.

Butler, Judith. *Bodies that Matter: On the Discursive Limits of "Sex."* New York: Routledge, 1993. Print.

Caballero Wanguemert, María. "*Hijo de hombre*, de la tradición oral al mito." *Augusto Roa Bastos: Antología narrativa y poética: Documentación y estudios*. Ed. Paco Tovar. Barcelona: Antropos, 1991. 183–88. Print.

Ostrov, Andrea. "En el nombre del Padre (Lectura de *Hijo de hombre* de Augusto Roa Bastos)." *Hispamérica* 28.83 (1999): 125–31. Print.

Quiroga Clérigo, Manuel. "Un pueblo en busca de su libertad: Relectura de *Hijo de hombre*." *Cuadernos Hispanoamericanos* 493–94 (1991): 225–38. Print.

Roa Bastos, Augusto. *Hijo de hombre*. Barcelona: Plaza & Janés, 1994. Print.

———. *Son of Man*. Trans. Rachel Caffyn. New York: Monthly Review Press, 1988.

Sánchez, Ana María. "Oralidad e Historia en *Hijo de hombre* de Augusto Roa Bastos." *Cuadernos de Literatura* 7.13–14 (2001): 160–68. Print.

Tovar, Paco, ed. *Augusto Roa Bastos: Antología narrativa y poética: Documentación y estudios*. Barcelona: Antropos, 1991. Print.

Traub, Valerie. "Desire and the Difference it Makes." *The Matter of Difference: Materialist Feminist Criticism of Shakespeare*. Ed. Valerie Wayne. New York: Harvester Wheatsheaf, 1991. Print.

Weldt-Basson, Helene C. "Augusto Roa Bastos's Trilogy as Postmodern Practice." *Studies in Twentieth-Century Literature* 22.2 (1998): 335–55. Print.

VERBA VOLANT, SCRIPTA MANENT

ORALITY AND LITERACY IN *I THE SUPREME*

Gustavo Verdesio

In 1992, I published an article on Augusto Roa Bastos's *Yo, el Supremo* that discussed one of the issues that I was interested in at that time: the centrality of the dichotomy orality versus writing for the history of Latin American discursive production. Today, my interest in that problem has not waned completely; however, but it would be fair to say that it has mutated into something related, but different, to it. Said mutation has its origin in my growing interest in indigenous societies both in Latin and North America.[1] For this reason, what you will read in the following pages can be best described as a rewriting of that paper, or, if you prefer, as an updating of it that makes it reflect my changing ideas about the field of Latin American literature and cultural studies.

In *Yo el Supremo*, the main character, José Gaspar Rodríguez de Francia (a legendary dictator of Paraguay in the first half of the nineteenth century), voices a series of concerns. One is the way in which official history represents him. His discourse is full of insults to his critics, and sarcasm is the predominant tone of his invectives. In several occasions, the compiler of the volume includes some of the original testimonies against the Supreme Dictator, giving the reader the chance to compare both versions: the predominant version, registered by the dominant historiographic tradition, and Rodríguez de

Francia's, which challenges it. Another evident concern relates to language. His reflections on language's nature and essence, as well as on its uses, are frequent and abundant in the book. These reflections take, on occasion, the form of a theorization and are mostly focused on a very specific issue: the relationship between oral and written language.

The dictator often appears worried about, when not plainly indignant with, the lack of fidelity with which Policarpo Patiño (sometimes called "fide-indigno"—wordplay with the expression "fidedigno," and "infiel de fechos, another pun based in a distortion of the archaic expression "fiel de fechos," by Rodríguez de Francia)[2] transcribes his speech when he dictates it to him. The Supremo reproaches his scribe: "Lo que sucede es que tu maldita memoria recuerda las palabras y olvida lo que está detrás de ellas" (90) ["What happens is that your wretched memory remembers the words and forgets what is behind them" (83)]. Behind the condemnation of the poor scribe lies a more profound reflection that deals with the problem of transcription in general:

> Le cuesta a Patiño subir la cuesta del contar y escribir a la vez; oír el son-ido de lo que escribe; trazar el signo de lo que escucha. Acordar la palabra con el sonido del pensamiento que nunca es un murmullo solitario por más íntimo que sea; menos aún si es la palabra, el pensamiento del dictare. (26)
>
> [It costs Patiño an effort not to allow himself merely to coast downhill, to follow instead the uphill path of the telling and write at the same time; to hear the dispari-son of what he writes; to trace the sign of what his ear is taking in. To attune words to the sound of thought, which is never a solitary murmur, however intimate it may be; less still if it is the speech, the thought involved in dictating. (18)]
>
> Cuando te dicto, las palabras tienen un sentido; otro, cuando las escribes. De modo que hablamos dos lenguas diferentes . . . Escribes lo que te dicto como si tú mismo hablaras por mí en secreto al papel. Quiero que en las palabras que escribes haya algo que me pertenezca. (63)
>
> [When I dictate you, the words have a meaning; when you write them, another. So that we speak two different languages . . . You write what I dictate to you as though you yourself were speaking in my place in secret on the paper. I want there to be something of myself in the words that you write. (57)]

The Supremo's anxiety has its cause in the discrepancy between his oral speech and the written transcription produced by Patiño. The latter's incapacity to be faithful (fiel) to his master's speech makes him not only anxious, but also angry. His utmost desire is to achieve an exact transcription of what he dictates to the poor scribe—that is, a faithful rendering of his oral speech. He would like, in other words, a writing in which he could recognize his own speech. He wants Patiño to capture the sound-gone (*el son-ido*)—the words that the wind has taken with it—which is an actualization of the old Latin proverb *verba volant, scripta manent*. In some other passages of the book, the dictator seems to aspire to get his speech transcribed in a way that captures all the overtones and nuances of oral expression:

En lugar de trasladar al estado de naturaleza lo que te dicto, llenas el papel de barrumbadas incomprensibles . . . Te alimentas con la carroña de los libros. No has arruinado todavía la tradición oral sólo porque es el único lenguaje que no se puede saquear, robar, repetir, plagiar, copiar. Lo hablado vive sostenido por el tono, los gestos, los movimientos del rostro, las miradas, el acento, el aliento del que habla. (62)

[Instead of transcribing what I dictate to you in its natural state, you fill the paper with incomprehensible barbarisms . . . You feed on the carrion of books. You have not yet destroyed oral tradition only because it is in the language that cannot be sacked, robbed, repeated, plagiarized, copied. What is spoken remains alive, sustained by the tone, the gestures, the facial expressions, the gaze, the accent, the breath of the speaker. (56)]

In his view, speech cannot be ruined or corrupted, and it is the only language that resists copying: no matter how much Patiño distorts it, the dictator seems to suggest, speech will survive outside his transcription. This is an important point, as we will see later, because in the battle between orality and literacy, between speech and writing, the Supremo seems to believe that the former will have the last word. However, in light of the dialogues he has with Patiño throughout the novel, this is somewhat paradoxical, because the dictator's obsession with writing (that is, with leaving a written record of his thoughts) seems to contradict his apparent faith in the incorruptible nature of oral expression. His desire is to leave a record of his opinions, of his version of history, and of his worldview, to posterity, but in order to accomplish that, he does not seem to trust the incorruptible nature of speech and has recourse, instead, to the written word.

As it seems clear from the previous quote, the results he expects from his scribe are very difficult to achieve through the written record. The limitations of writing are pointed out and fiercely criticized by the Supremo: "Yo sólo puedo escribir; es decir, negar lo vivo" (100) ["All I can do is write; that is to say, deny what is alive" (92)]. Writing, then, is a negation of what is alive—of what speech is able to convey almost naturally.

In this context, the only way to accomplish what the dictator desires is to have recourse to a fictional instrument: a magic pen the character himself has created. This pen simultaneously writes words and projects their corresponding images on the paper:

> Escribir al mismo tiempo que visualizar las formas de otro lenguaje compuesto exclusivamente con imágenes, por decirlo así, de metáforas ópticas . . . Pienso que en otro tiempo la pluma debió también estar dotada de una tercera función: reproducir el espacio fónico de la escritura, el texto sonoro de las imágenes visuales; lo que podrá haber sido el tiempo hablado de esas palabras sin formas, de esas formas sin palabras. (207)

> writing while at the same time visualizing the forms of another language composed exclusively of images, of optical metaphors, so to speak . . . I believe that at one time the pen must also have possessed a third function: reproducing the phonic space of writing, the sound-text of the visual images; which could have been the spoken time of those words without forms, of those forms without words. (197)

In the Supremo's opinion, this artifact (which Roa Bastos has taken from Raymond Roussel's "La vue," as Weldt-Basson has pointed out) is the only means through which to achieve a full and faithful rendering of oral speech, a kind of perfect translation of what has been said.[3] This aspiration shows the Supremo in an attitude that is not new in the framework of our Western philosophical tradition: the privilege of oral discourse over the written word.

As is well known, the privilege of the phonic over the written is part of a worldview that Jacques Derrida called, a long time ago, phonocentrism. This term describes one of the aspects of logocentrism, which is the term Derrida uses to name one of the consequences of the search for an order of meaning understood as foundation—as something that exists in and by itself. Logocentrism is a consequence of what has been called the metaphysics of presence. In this conceptual framework, oral language appears as something present and actual. This is due to the fact that oral language has traditionally been understood as an adequate representation of the workings of our sequel because it appears as simultaneous to our thinking. The fact that speech is not something perceived as material makes it, in the context of this conception, an adequate vehicle, without any hindrances, for the concepts that come from our mind. Writing, on the contrary, is considered as a graphic representation of that "natural" language and, therefore, as an unwanted and disturbing mediation.[4]

Having said that, I think it is important to point out that this position vis-à-vis oral language is mostly confined to the philosophical and religious realms. It is also important to remember that when Derrida came up with his analysis of phonocentrism, he was not thinking of how this love for oral discourse took shape in concrete historical situations. He was not thinking, for instance, of Latin America during colonial times. In that era, writing was, as some scholars (among them Walter Mignolo—*The Darker Side of the Renaissance*—and Martin Lienhard) have pointed out, the foundation upon which European domination of the lands and peoples of the new territories was based. It was the model for the occupation of the territory and a tool for domination. Oral discourse was not, then, dominant or much appreciated for, at least, the first two centuries of the colonial regime. On the contrary, manifestations of the oral traditions of indigenous peoples were particularly repressed by colonial authorities. This is why every time an indigenous subject raised his or her voice, the phonocentric attitude analyzed by Derrida was nowhere to be seen. So in the realm of the social, indigenous orality was not privileged the way speech was in the works of, say, Plato.

Having clarified this issue, let us now go back to those who did embrace phonocentrism in the framework of Western culture. It can be safely said that the standpoint of those who privilege orality over writing is best illustrated by the following statement: thinking relates in a very special way to sound (Ong, *Orality and Literacy*, 7). This statement is related, in my opinion, to the beliefs and aspirations of the Supreme. As can be seen in the passages quoted above, the belief that oral language is a "pure" vehicle for thinking inspires the dictator's reflections on the subject. It also inspires or supports the idea that written language is a mere transcription of another system—a secondary modeling system is the expression used by Ong (Ong, *Orality and Literacy*, 8). What the dictator is afraid of, then, is that dangerous distorting effect that characterizes the written word. Its pathological nature, its tendency to induce lying and distortion, make writing a medium completely unsuitable to meet his goals or to fulfill his needs. The most important of those goals is one that has to do with the image of him as an object of historiographic discourse. This kind of discourse, because it is a written one, does not offer him any guarantee that the written words will be faithful to his idea of truth. Rodríguez de Francia, throughout the narrative, contradicts historiographic texts that refer to him, while he offers, in turn, his own version of things. Yet, his efforts at contradicting those texts are not enough to counter them because what those books say about him remains written and, therefore, said. The authors of those texts may be dead, but as Ong points out, one of the defining traits of written words is that they can be resuscitated, so to speak, as many times as readers decide to read them (Ong, *Orality and Literacy*, 81). In contrast, oral discourse is more suitable for a more humane kind of communication, for example, for the initiation of a dialogue, for the clarification of doubts, or for the rectification of opinions (Ong, *Orality and Literacy*, 32). The intention to express his own thinking with fidelity, his ideas about the fate of his country and Latin America as a whole, will be better served by that kind of oral language whose traits have been enumerated above by the Supremo himself (richness of tone, of accent, of gesture, the possibility of feeling and perceiving the breathing of the speaker, etcetera). All this reflects a search for clarity, a perspicuity that could vehicle his message in a way that the expressed may be as close as possible to the original—that is, what was created by the mind of the speaker.

Another one of the Supremo's goals is foundational in nature, and it can also be achieved more easily through the use of oral language. The Supreme Dictator proposes himself as the founder of Paraguayan nationhood.[5] This foundational desire or drive is an aspect characteristic of the metaphysics of presence and, therefore, of logocentrism. His desire is to postulate himself as origin, as something given (in the sense of not being created), as foundational, insofar as it is a logocentric desire of a phonocentric support. Oral language is, then, the best possible, as well as the most "natural," means to incarnate, propagate, and actually fulfill the Supremo's desire. However, the dictator appears as possessed by an imperious need to write, and his main battle seems to have to take place in the realm of written discourse.

This conflict between orality and writing is juxtaposed to another one of similar nature, but one that manifests itself on a different plane. The above-mentioned tension between the two poles (writing and oral discourse) takes place in the very discourse of the Supremo himself. It is a tension perceived from his own point of view or, if you prefer, from his own situation of enunciation as a character in a novel. Yet, his discourse appears encapsulated by another one whose limits are not the field defined and circumscribed by the discourse of the dictator himself: it takes place in the context provided by the novel as a whole. It is what another critic has called the "outer text," which is the terrain in which said conflict between orality and writing manifests itself: "What is of central interest is the production of a text, the production of an 'inner' text by Francia, either by his own pen or through the medium of dictation to his secretary, and the production of an 'outer' text, the novelistic framework that presents Francia in the process of satisfying his verbomania" (Foster 102). Such a text cannot be other than a written one. I am saying this because, as Ong has suggested, the word "text" should only be applied to written messages: "When literates today use the term 'text' to refer to oral performance, they are thinking of it by analogy with writing" (Ong, *Literacy and Orality*, 13)

Although *Yo el Supremo* exhibits all the characteristics of writing, several critics have seen an attempt in the novel to recover its opposite: orality. I must clarify, first of all, that some of them do not use the expression "orality," and those who use it do not always give it the semantic range that it has in this article, which is the following: an oral organization of society and culture.[6] Therefore, it seems convenient to make explicit the exact range I give to this term here. For this reason, we should begin by establishing what kind of society the novel is trying to portray. As is well known, Paraguayan society is a bilingual one.[7] In it, diverse kinds of language coexist, but above all, there are two that are of interest to us here: the educated one (Paraguayan Spanish or Castilian[8]) and the popular one: Guarani. The historical society described in the novel must have belonged, already, to what Marshall McLuhan called the Gutenberg Galaxy (the world dominated by printing). This same historical society is also marked by Guarani culture and language, which gives it a number of traits more typical of communities where orality predominates as an organizational principle. In this kind of society, then, alphabetic writing does not completely replace the oral world. On the contrary, what it does is to invoke it: "The function of the original model was not to replace a prior knowledge of spoken speech but to trigger a recall of that knowledge" (Havelock, *Origins of Western Literacy*, 55) It is for this reason that I believe it is possible to understand the opinions and desires of the Paraguayan people—that inform and traverse the discourse of the Supremo—as oral in nature. It is necessary, then, to insist on the importance of Guarani oral culture, which is, in the text, emblematic of the Paraguayan people as a whole. For this reason, every time I write the expressions "collective identity," "choral expression," "collective voice," and "collective memory," the reader should remember that those notions and expressions are used with the intention of alluding to an oral culture: the one that developed in Paraguay in the times when the Supremo was dictator.

A society where oral forms of organization predominate does not work in the same way as a literate culture does. For those of us who grew up in the framework of an alphabetic, literate culture, it is very difficult to imagine a culture founded on patterns so different from ours: "We—readers of books such as this—are so literate that it is very difficult for us to conceive of an oral universe of communication or thought except as a variant of a literate universe" (Ong, *Orality and Literacy*, 2).

This is what Havelock tried to demonstrate when he tentatively described the Greek prealphabetic thought.[9] This author traces a complete panorama of what he calls the psychodynamics of orality—that is, the way in which this culture functions socially. The characteristics of that kind of culture that Ong identifies are the following: language is a mode of action; it is performative; it verbalizes knowledge with respect to human life, not to abstractions; there is an empathic participation in social life; there is a tendency to create heroes and memorable men, due to the fact that knowledge in an oral culture, in the absence of a fixed record, is based on mnemotechnics; and there is a tendency to rely on ritual and mythical thinking (Ong, *Orality and Literacy*, 31–68). Some of these characteristics will manifest themselves in the novel, but some will not. The way in which they appear takes different forms that will take the shape of what Ong calls residues of orality (Ong, *The Presence of the Word*, 79–87), or better yet, traces, in a Derridean sense.[10] These traces can be detected in the discourse of the dictator as well as in the text that encompasses it: the totality of the novel. In this way, the submission of the popular voices (that belong to an oral culture) to the powerful discourse of the Supremo appears as only apparent. The very same discourse of Rodríguez de Francia is a tapestry comprised of traces of that oral discourse that is supposedly absent. Yet, in a system or sequence, nothing is merely present or absent: a text is a composite of traces and differences.

I have chosen to comment on only some of the multiple traces or residues of orality that appear in the novel. One of them is a procedure that tends toward the recovery of orality (which is not representable but that can be suggested): carnivalization. The character of this operation is undoubtedly popular, and it conveys a sense or feeling of orality. Juan Manuel Marcos detects different cases in which the carnivalization procedure takes place in the novel. He puts emphasis on its parodic and desacralizing character ("contrapersonificador," in his own terms): "La parada militar que, con Fulgencio Yegros a la cabeza, luciendo como medallas los agujeros de su fusilamiento, carnavaliza la fanfarria castrense que hubiera conmovido al general Moreira César" ["The military parade that, with Fulgencio Yegros at the forefront, who exhibited the holes produced by the shots he received at his own execution, carnivalizes the military fanfare that would have moved General Moreira César."][11] Another case of carnivalization is the following: "El Supremo menosprecia al mismo Roa como 'un mediocre escriba' y a *Hijo de hombre* como 'una de esas novelas que publican en el extranjero los escribas migrantes'" ["The Supremo looks down at Roa himself as a 'mediocre scribe' and at *Hijo de hombre* as 'one of those novels that some migrant scribes publish abroad.'"][12]

Related to this procedure of strong popular roots, there are references made to a certain kind of picaresque tradition in Spanish literature that consists of making an animal speak. More concretely, the animal who speaks is a dog in a celebrated text written by Cervantes: "Coloquio de los perros."[13] Yet another significant trace of oral culture that can be found in the novel is the transcription of fragments of what Marcos calls Castellano Paraguayo, and that I prefer to simply call Paraguayan Spanish language. Because I am not a native speaker of Paraguayan Spanish and have not had a close relationship to that linguistic universe, I have no choice but to have recourse to the work done by specialists on the subject. "En *Yo el Supremo*, Roa Bastos jerarquiza el castellano paraguayo y, además, estudia algunos principios de filosofía del lenguaje, sin abandonar el plano de la ficción" ["In *I the Supreme*, Roa Bastos privileges Paraguayan Castilian and, also, studies some philosophy of language's principles, without abandoning the plane of fiction" (Marcos 51).] He insists on reaffirming the presence of Paraguayan Spanish in the text, a presence he characterizes as one of the most remarkable technical aspects of the book: "una jerarquización del castellano paraguayo, a través de una inspirada recreación del habla popular, al lado de neologismos, innovaciones morfosintácticas, sutiles arcaísmos y cierto amaneramiento verbal dieciochesco y neobarroco propio del protagonista, y no pocas meditaciones acerca de graves problemas de la lingüística actual" ["a hierarchization of Paraguayan Castilian through an inspired recreation of popular speech side by side with neologisms, morphosyntactic innovations, subtle archaisms, and certain eighteenth-century-like, neobaroque verbal mannerisms that characterize the protagonist's speech, as well as some meditations about some of the most serious linguistic problems of today" (Marcos 58).]

In order to shed light on this matter, I will cite some remarks made by Ferrer Agüero on the influence of Guarani language on the Spanish spoken in Paraguay. He offers the following example of this influence: "Yo malicio que uno de estos mis animalitos podría aliviar los males de Su Excelencia" (33) ["I suspect one of these (sic) my animals will be able to alleviate your Excellency's ills"]. His explanation is as follows: "Estamos ante un doble caso de influencia del guarani: a) malicia, voz del castellano arcaico se ha incorporado al guarani verbalizándose (aquí aparece en un contexto castellano pero verbalizada); b) volvemos a encontrar un posesivo superfluo ('. . . Estos mis animalitos')" ["We are before a case of double influence of Guarani over Spanish: a) "maliciar," a voice taken from archaic Castilian, has been incorporated into Guarani (it appears here in a Castilian context in a verbalized way); b) we find again a superfluous possessive" (Ferrer Agüero 429)]. He explains the meaning of "superfluous possessive" like this: "El guarani tiene tendencia a abusar del posesivo cuando se refiere a objetos de pertenencia personal" ["Guarani has a tendency to abuse of the possessive when it refers to objects of personal possession" (Ferrer Agüero 428)]. According to this, the following passage "Tu mamá de usté te malcrió demasiado mal luego, niño Josué" ["your mother of yours (sic) spoiled you too bad, niño Josué" (157)] is a clear case of intrusion of Guarani structures in Paraguayan Spanish.

For the sake of brevity, I will offer only one more case that shows, eloquently, the presence or traces of Guarani language in what these authors call Paraguayan Castilian:

"Silencio demasiado" (*Yo el Supremo*, 21; Ejemplo de Bareiro Saguier).

> El paraguayo que habla en castellano suele confundir (como le sucedía al hebreo antiguo) la idea del superlativo con la idea de exceso, que ya resulta defecto, usando del adverbio "demasiado" en vez de "muy"; señal de que en guarani el sufijo ETEREI puede significar los dos adverbios "muy" y "demasiado" . . . En el habla popular es frecuentísimo el empleo de ETEREI como "masiado" o "masiao."
>
> La expresión correcta en español sería entonces "Mucho silencio" y el "Silencio demasiado" sería traducible por "Silencio ETEREI." Estamos pues ante una estructura guarani.

["Silence too much" (*Yo el Supremo*, 21; an example by Bareiro Saguier].

> The Paraguayan subject who speaks Castilian usually confuses (as it also happened to the speakers of ancient Hebrew) the idea of the superlative with the idea of excess, which is a mistake, using the adverb "too much" instead of "very;" this is a sign that in Guarani the suffix ETEREI can mean both adverbs ("very" and "too much.") . . . In the popular version of this spoken language, the use of ETEREI is very

frequently used as "masiado" or "masiao" (n.b.: these are popular versions of "demasiado").

The correct expression in Spanish should be, then, "mucho silencio" and "silencio demasiado" could be translated as "silencio ETEREI." We are, then, before a Guarani structure—"silence too much" (Ferrer Agüero 428).

Yet, the presence of Guarani language is not limited to the way in which it mixes itself with expressions in Paraguayan Spanish. It also manifests itself in its original form, or at least in a transcription of its original (oral) form, through the use of the Roman alphabet—which represents the "spirit" of that language in a way that I suspect is incorrect. This is another form in which the author's intention of not leaving the Guarani (one of the languages that are part of the bilingual or diglossic culture of Paraguay) substratum outside the discourse of the novel is made clear. A good example of this is the passage in which we find out that the popular classes called the Supremo "Karaí-Guasú." It is through this name that the echo of a collective voice reflects, once again, the worldview of an oral community.

Another fragment of said worldview can be found in the verses of a popular song composed in Guarani and Paraguayan Spanish: "pasaba el tiempo/pasaba y pasaba/pasabá avá avá/avá avatisoká" (152) ["time passed/passed and passed/happened avá avá/avá avatisoká" (my translation)]. The presence of the words "avá" (Indian) and "avatisoká" (mortar stick), two Guarani elements, make this composition an undeniably bilingual one. It should be noticed that the presence of Guarani voices in this novel is not limited to those expressions quoted by the protagonist: they appear, at least once, in the discourse of the Supremo himself. When he gets angry at one of the Robertson brothers and he decides to deport them, he gives the order in Spanish, but at the end of his speech, he adds an invective in Guarani: "Ko' à pytaguá tekaká oñemosé vaerá jaguaicha!" (333), which means, according to the translation provided by the compiler, "¡Estos gringos de mierda deben ser echados como perros!" [these fucking gringos must be expelled like dogs (my translation)]. In this bilingual society, even the supreme dictator uses Guarani language when he feels like expressing his most personal feelings.

Closer to the end of the book, Guarani language appears on its own, without the framework provided by bilingual expressions, where it appears side by side with Paraguayan Spanish. This happens on occasion of one of the Supremo's birthdays, during which a big popular feast takes place, in which the anonymous choir of voices sings the following song: "Oe . . . oé . . . yekó raka' é / ñande Karaí- Guasú o nacé vaekué . . ." (398), which means "oé . . . oé . . . hace mucho tiempo / nuestro Gran Señor dicen que nació" [oé, oé, they say our Great Lord was born a long time ago (my translation)].

Guarani presence, however, does not limit itself to appearing as linguistic intrusions throughout the novel. On the contrary, traces of that oral culture interweave with the written world through the most representative vehicle of preliterate consciousness: myth. Let's examine two myths that Ferrer Agüero detects in the novel. The first one is a Mbyé myth, narrated by a Nivaklé Indian (184)[Ferrer Agüero 436-37]. The myth is narrated in a way that intends to resemble the oral modes of storytelling. Another myth appears on page 411: it is the myth of the double, which, as Ferrer Agüero remarks, "es común a la literatura oral guarani . . . y a la literatura fantástica occidental y oriental" ["it is common to both Guarani oral literature and Western fantastic literature" (Ferrer Agüero 437)]. This is a very functional myth in the novel, for it is clear that it alludes to the ways in which the personality and voices of Rodríguez de Francia are split throughout the novel.

It seems evident to me that the uses or quotes of myths of Guarani origin contribute to making the absence, or marginal position, of that oral culture more conspicuous. However, the way in which the Paraguayan people are best represented in the novel is through the discourse of the Supremo. This character, who appears to be pure presence, is, in actuality, a complex text (in its etymological sense: textile) made of traces and differences. Moreover, it can be said that the myth of the dictator, the *El* (He) the novel speaks of, the alter ego or the other side of *YO* (I), is a product of the popular imagination. As Marcos suggests, "Ya sabemos que esta novela está basada, no tanto en el personaje histórico del doctor Francia, como en el mito que le ha sobrevivido. Y es que los mitos no se transmiten y perduran a través de los libros de historia, los documentos ni clase alguna de escritura, sino a través del lenguaje oral, de voz en voz, de generación en generación" ["We know that this novel is based not on the historical figure, Dr. Rodríguez de Francia, but in the myth that has survived him. Myths are not transmitted and preserved by history books, documents, or any kind of writing, but through oral language, from generation to generation" (Marcos 55; my translation)].

The transformation of the dictator into myth is not a strange occurrence. We have already seen that in one of the historical interpretations of this figure, Francia was, for the people, a hero and a founder of Paraguayan nationality. I would even go a little farther and say that Rodríguez de Francia was also the founder and mentor of the national project that continued with the governments of two other dictators: the Lópezes. The Paraguayan people adhered massively to this national project. Their reaction to the various attempts by foreign powers to deviate it from its course attests to this adherence (like the failed Belgrano expedition and the Triple Alliance War). Marcos defines that project in these terms:

> Elecciones nacionales sin manipulación de los criollos, abolición de la esclavitud, ejército nacional de jefes campesinos, persecución sistemática de los patricios y los clérigos españolistas o porteñistas; educación popular masiva, envío de jóvenes de familias humildes para cursar estudios técnicos y humanísticos en Londres y París a sueldo del Estado; desarrollo del periodismo, las letras, las artes, y las instituciones superiores de enseñanza; confiscación de los bienes eclesiásticos, estancias de la patria, catecismo patrio reformado, solidaridad federalista y antineocolonial en la política exterior del país, instalación del primer ferrocarril de Sudamérica, los primeros altos hornos, el primer gran hospital público, concurso de profesionales europeos contratados por el Estado, etc.

> National elections without manipulation by the Creole elite, abolition of slavery, a national army that included peasant officers, systematic persecution of the patricians and of the pro-Spanish or pro-Buenos Aires clerics; popular education for the masses, scholarships to London and Paris provided by the State for children from families of humble origin; the development of journalism, the belles lettres, the arts, and tertiary education institutions; confiscation of the Church's possessions, estancias de la patria, national-reformed catechism, federalist solidarity, and a foreign policy against neocolonialism, installation of the first train of South America, of the first great public hospital, European professionals hired by the State, etcetera (Marcos 90).

José Gaspar Rodríguez de Francia, as a founder of that social system, the factotum of that national project, and a proponent of independence and Paraguayan nationality, was a great candidate to become a popular myth. The image we get of this character in *I the Supreme* is the image that takes shape, in a subtle manner, through the interweaving of traces. The Supremo is not, then, an absolute presence. He is not original as he pretends. He is a product of a system of differences, of a combination of traces of an oral community that struggles to survive in the context of the lettered city.[14]

There is yet another form in which collective voices make themselves present in the novel. In this case, I am not referring to traces of Guarani voices but to an intangible and impersonal, yet omnipresent, form of public opinion: rumor. Already in the first few pages of the novel, we learn about a rumor that spreads some false news successfully: the death of the Supremo—a rumor so effective that a funeral is celebrated in Villa Franca (19–20). Although the dictator maintains, from the beginning of the novel (13), that the only valid and lasting form of memory is the popular one, in this case, confronted with the rumor that announces his death, he seems to be a little less enthusiastic about it. The collective and popular voice, then, in order to be legitimate, must be in favor of the Supremo—or at least not contradict him.

His reaction is in clear contrast to what he states in another part of the book, where he affirms that the only sacred writer is the collective one (71). His ideal book should resemble those of a very prestigious series that includes the Bible and the epic poems of Homer (71). This is interesting, among other reasons, because it reminds us that the West not always wrote and not always postulated an order like the one proposed by the lettered city: there was a time when the West trusted other forms of knowledge transmission. However, that is ancient history, and it happened before the collective books the Supremo talks about crystallized as written messages and, as such, stopped being part of the knowledge reservoir of those societies that organized themselves in an oral way.

This is a good time to ask what kind of relationship exists between the idea of collective voice and people's voice and the role Guarani Indians play in this scheme. It is also a good time to ask what place the Supremo gives to indigenous peoples in his conception of the populace. It would be important to figure out how the main character views them. Let us see, then, a few passages in which the dictator talks about Amerindians, so that we can focus on how he represents them.

Throughout the novel, like most Latin American leaders, Rodríguez de Francia invokes the people numerous times. As I suggested above, his idea of the people seems to be based on the elements that can be found in societies where orality predominates. This does not mean that the oral can be assimilated to the indigenous, but it can be said that many of the forms of social and cultural organization that he identifies as typically popular are very likely to be found in the way in which indigenous societies of Paraguay organized themselves in the times of the Supremo. As Martin Lienhard states, these societies expressed the fundamental things of their cultures verbally, in the framework of a predominantly oral system (Lienhard 15). If this is the case, it will be useful to analyze the ways in which the character refers to, or conceptualizes, indigenous peoples.

After a perusal of the ways in which Amerindians of Paraguay appear in the framework of the discourse of the dictator, it is evident that he shows at least three attitudes toward them: praise or positive allusion, criticism (sometimes with racist overtones), and paternalism. An example of the first attitude is the following fragment: "Hoy por hoy los indios son los mejores servidores del Estado; de entre ellos he cortado a los jueces más probos, a los funcionarios más capaces y leales, a mis soldados más valientes" (47) ["Nowadays the Indians are the best servants of the State; it is from such cloth that I have cut the most upright judges, the most capable and loyal functionaries, my most valiant soldiers" (40)]. Other examples can be found in the fragments where Rodríguez de Francia puts Guarani knowledge and conceptions on the same plane with those of classical antiquity. An instance of this attitude can be seen when the dictator states that the dualism Plato talked about is not very different from the one postulated by the belief systems of Guarani Indians (139). An occasion when the respect the Supremo feels (or at least declares) for the beliefs and narratives of indigenous origin manifests itself is the fragment in which he orders the Nivaklé cacique to tell him all he knows about some of the complex beliefs of his tribe in relation to human nature, to its duality, to the nature of its soul, as well as questions about other equally metaphysical topics (178–80). Another illustrative case is that moment when he approves the Guarani ritual used to scare a mythical character: the Vieja-Demonio or Old lady-Demon (146). This case takes us directly to an issue that is very important for the elucidation of the relationship of the Supremo with indigenous worldviews: his position vis-à-vis indigenous ritual and magic.

It is my opinion that in Roa Bastos's novel, Rodríguez de Francia appears as a character that really, truly believes in Guarani knowledge—even when that knowledge takes the place of those practices that, in Western culture, are called magic. Moreover, I believe that it can even be said that the authorial voice, and the narrative in general, seems to believe in, and endorse (as does another Latin American creation: the film *Cabeza de Vaca*[15]), said practices, affirming their legitimacy and effectiveness. This becomes clear when the magic of the Payaguás really works: a sick person (a character named Echevarría, whose hands were "crispadas" or badly contracted) recovers after having been treated by an Indian *curandero* (230). The indigenous knowledge that from this side of the cultural divide is considered magic is also presented as real and effective in the episode in which a fantastic cacique/tiger materializes before the presence of many witnesses. This is the story of the visit of a cacique-sorcerer-prophet of the Kaiguaa-Gualachi—an indigenous group that had not yet been defeated either by Conquistadors or by missionary priests—to the festivities organized in 1804 to celebrate the inauguration of Manuel Godoy as perpetual regidor (256). In this episode, the cacique-sorcerer-prophet turns into a blue tiger who, to the public's surprise, plays all kinds of stunts and undertakes extraordinary acts of magic in front of an audience comprised of many members of the elite, who are amazed by his feats (256–58). This story, which had not been recorded by official history (the one that emanates from the lettered city), is told by this novel—which seems to indicate an interest in filling the blanks and silences left by the written history penned by dominant culture. This scene, which is part of oral tradition, does contain—if we are going to agree with the Supremo's logic—a more profound truth than the one offered by official history.

There is yet another case in which Guarani magic is presented as something that works—that is, as a tool that obtains the results that magic acts pursue. I am referring to an episode where a *curandero* from Lambaré is called by the dictator to get his opinion about the birth of some deformed twins. The Payé Payaguá prophesizes that those twins are going to become soothsayers or fortunetellers and that they, therefore, will be of great service to the Supremo's regime (421). What is important here is not whether the *curandero* is right or not, but the belief in indigenous science that the dictator shows.[16]

However, throughout the novel, the opinions of the Supremo about indigenous peoples are not always so uniformly positive. On the contrary, there are several moments in which his position can be qualified as, at best, paternalistic, for example, when he says, from a very pronounced existentialist attitude, "Quiero que tengan bien vestidos y alimentados a esos indiecitos" (131) ["I wish those little Indians to be well dressed and fed" (123)], or when he says, "La población de indios, especialmente las mujeres de los naturales, merecen especial protección" (383) ["The Indian population, the wives of the Natives in particular, deserve special protection" (361)]. This idea that indigenous peoples need to be protected as if they were handicapped deprives them of agency, and it turns them into subjects under tutelage of the state or the dictator.

Sometimes the dictator's words about indigenous peoples go beyond paternalism and take the shape of an evolutionary glance that puts them in a time and a place that are considered as less advanced than, or plainly inferior to, those in which Western culture develops. This is patent in the opinion he has on hunter-gatherers and agriculturalists. He puts them in a continuum or narrative that is informed by an evolutionary gaze: agriculturalists are less barbaric than hunter-gatherers (79). This gaze presupposes a narrative in which humankind progresses from simple forms of organization to others that gradually develop increasing complexity, until they reach the peak of civilization that coincides with the stage at which the culture that enunciates the narrative has arrived. In the novel, the peak is Western modernity, as understood in the nineteenth century. In other occasions, the position of the Supremo, vis-à-vis the indigenous peoples of his country, is simply and candidly negative: he calls them barbaric or savage ("gentiles bárbaros" ["gentle barbarians"], 348). This is consistent with those moments when he sees, with preoccupation, the indigenous insurrections that take place in his country—he seems to think those insurrections are not legitimate (88).[17]

These fragments complicate the picture the dictator himself offers about his relationship with the indigenous peoples from Paraguay:

> Acabé con la injusta dominación de los criollos sobre los naturales, cosa la más natural del mundo puesto que ellos como tales tenían derecho de primo-genitura sobre los orgullosos y mezclativos mancebos de la tierra. Celebré tratados con los pueblos indígenas. Les proveí de armas para que defendieran sus tierras contra las depredaciones de tribus hostiles. Mas también los contuve en sus límites naturales impidiéndoles cometer los excesos que los propios blancos les habían enseñado. (46)
>
> I put an end to the unjust domination and exploitation to which the Creole subjected the natural-born citizens of the country, the most natural thing in the world since the latter as such had the right of primo-geniture over the proud mingle-blooded lordlings of the land. I concluded treaties with the indigenous peoples. I provided them with arms so that they might defend their lands against the depredations of hostile tribes. But I also contained them within their natural limits, thereby preventing them from committing the excesses that the whites themselves had taught them. (39)

In the character's own words, the Indians needed to be helped, but they also needed to be contained and disciplined so that they did not go beyond the limits established by the Supremo. Insofar as they respected the order imposed by Rodríguez de Francia, they were going to be helped. Otherwise, they would be repressed like any other group or individual that did not behave as the leader of the nation expected and demanded. The formula through which to deal with indigenous peoples seems to look like this: they are offered security and protection in exchange for respect for the state system promoted by the dictator. This is a very far cry from a progressive attitude of subalternist inspiration. It is, rather, a protectionist and paternalistic attitude in the framework of a dominant system that is foreign to the indigenous societies that dwell in its territory. At least this is what the novel seems to be saying in a rather direct fashion. Thus, his apparent, declared love for oral traditions (an element characteristic of indigenous societies) must be taken with a grain of salt in the light of fragments as the ones quoted above. The words penned by the scribe (who could very well be the Supremo himself, or his conscience—something that is treated in an ambiguous fashion that continues to the final pages of the novel), who sneaks in the text that Rodríguez de Francia is writing, are very critical: the dictator has forgotten his people; perhaps he never believed in them and kept them well fed, protected, educated in fear, but always at a distance; in the end, he is accused of having read incorrectly the will of the masses (445).

This way of presenting the relationship of the Supremo with the indigenous peoples of Paraguay contrasts with the attitude they have vis-à-vis the dictator when they are told that he died (a death that, as we saw above, was only a lie spread by a rumor): more than twenty thousand Indians attend the funeral in Villa Franca (20). So the novel is ambiguous in its presentation of the dictator's relationship with indigenous peoples. There is a tension between the Supremo and the Amerindians, but the latter seem to love him or, at the very minimum, to respect him enough to mourn for him.

The novel presents itself, then, as a text where the complexity of the relationship between the dictator and the indigenous peoples under his power is rather ambiguous and not easy to elucidate. The novel presents, every time it has the chance, traces or residues of orality. Part of the project behind this novel seems to be to allow the oppressed indigenous societies to express themselves in their own terms. However, the form chosen to achieve that goal is none other than writing.

At this point, it seems opportune to make some reference to the different statuses of the diverse forms of cultural production in Latin America. There exists, on the one hand, the cultural production of the Spanish-speaking elite, executed in the different variations of the language inherited from the Spanish conquistadors, and on the other, a marginal production in indigenous languages. The latter is comprised of ethnic literatures in vernacular languages and of popular literatures (regardless of linguistic affiliation) that, according to Antonio Cornejo Polar, are orally formalized (Cornejo Polar, "Las literaturas marginales," 93). One of the terrains in which the division between these two kinds of textual production develops is in the basic structures of the aforementioned two modes of discursive production: orality and writing (Cornejo Polar, "Las literaturas marginales," 97).

Roa Bastos's novel is very aware of the contradictions prevalent in Latin American cultural production. These contradictions are those that produce what Cornejo Polar called heteorgenous literatures: "Aunque las literaturas heterogéneas son excepcionalmente complejas, el concepto que las define es, más bien, simple: se trata de literaturas en las que uno o más de sus elementos constitutivos corresponden a un sistema socio-cultural que no es el que preside la composición de los otros elementos puestos en acción en un proceso concreto de producción literaria" (although heterogeneous literatures are exceptionally complex, the concept that defines them is rather simple: they are literatures in which one or more of their constitutive elements correspond to a sociocultural system that is not the one that presides the composition of the other elements put in action in a concrete process of literary production (Cornejo Polar, *La novela indigenista*, 60). I believe we can safely place this novel within the boundaries of the latter category because although it is presided by the principles that regulate highbrow literary production—in this case, written in Paraguay's hegemonic language, Spanish—it also presents an abundant oral substratum that remits to another kind of cultural production. The heterogeneity of this novel is not based only on the frequency with which oral Paraguayan and Guarani expressions appear in it, but also on the presence of diverse traces of oral culture that include, among other manifestations, a mythology and a worldview that are not those that predominate in Western culture.

The aesthetic option that consists of adopting a scriptural model by an author is determined and inspired by one of the other important objectives of the novel: the deconstruction of historiographic discourse. Just like Rodríguez de Francia, the author is very interested in deconstructing the official history so that he can offer his own version of history. As Walter Mignolo explained many years ago, "La ficcionalización del discurso historiográfico sería una de las maneras de poder explicar la 'apropiación del sistema de signos codificados . . . en la cristalización ideológica de una cultura': el discurso de la historia ficcionalizado y apropiado por el discurso de la ficción literaria" (209) ["The fictionalization of historiographic discourse would be one of the ways to explain the 'appropriation of the system of codified signs' in the ideological crystallization of a culture: the discourse of history fictionalized and appropriated by the discourse of literary fiction" (Mignolo, "Ficcionalización," 209; my translation)].

I said earlier that besides this objective (the desacralization and deconstruction of historiographic discourse), the novel has another one: the recovery of elements of an oppressed popular culture. As we saw, fictional writing offers itself as a useful tool for the appropriation of historiographic discourse. Now we will see that that very same device is also useful for the achievement of another goal: the vindication of a marginal popular culture. Although I provided an explanation of how this strategy works, I will make it a little more explicit here.

The author of this novel positions himself within the system of writing—more specifically, the realm of fiction writing—in order to deconstruct it with its own weapons, so that the most profound manifestations of an oral culture can be retrieved from oblivion through the recovery of traces or residues of oral culture. That is, he positions himself at the heart, at the entrails of, the Western, capitalist system—a system that can only be defined as a product of historical forces that operate, according to Derrida, within logocentrism: "To name them 'historical forces' is to name them in the grammar and in the syntax of logocentrism. There are things that happen before they can be named, before we can choose names for them, because all names are marked by logocentrism" (Mignolo, "Ficcionalización," 209). From the terrain dominated by logocentrism, the capitalist mode of production imposes certain rules on Latin American authors: to write in Spanish, to publish a book, to enter the market and the world of cultural industries. That is, the system sentences him to produce heterogeneous literatures. This price is precisely the one Roa Bastos is willing to pay in order to be able to undertake his complex task. He enunciates his message from the world of writing (from the historiographic discourse and from fictional writing) to be able to use it, to appropriate it in an operation that resembles that executed by the deconstructionist. The deconstructionist also positions himself or herself in the very center of the system to be deconstructed, in order to undermine—through the laying bare of the system's structure and rhetoric—the foundations upon which it rests. In Latin America, that center is, in Ángel Rama's words, the lettered city. The traces of what the city negates (that is, oral culture) are precisely the tools with which Roa Bastos deconstructs it. In other words, it is the interweaving of presence and absence (that is, lettered culture and the traces of repressed orality) that produce this text that deconstructs a system of domination from within. In sum, what it produces is yet another version of both Paraguayan history and the referent "Gaspar Rodríguez de Francia."

NOTES

1. The critics are Gladys Vila Barnes, Monique du Lope, Saúl Sosnowski, Carlos Pacheco, Juan Manuel Marcos, Graciela Maturo, Josaphat Kubayanda, Enriqueta Morillas, Bartomeu Meliá S. J., Ana Maria Gazzolo (in reality, this article deals with the topic but from a perspective that differs a lot from mine), Salvador Bacarisse, and Linda Hutcheon.

2. These two expressions refer to the Roman legal tradition, where some documents, in order to have publicity and validity, had to be faithfully transcribed by a scribe, who was conceived and understood as a faith-giver.

3. This artifact has the ability to record images and sounds at the same time. It also has the ability to show everything that exists in the world, which makes it something like a portable aleph.

4. For more complete description of logocentrism, see part I of *Of Grammatology* by Jacques Derrida.

5. This has been pointed out by Roa Bastos himself in "Algunos núcleos generadores," 71, and by Ezquerro, "Fonction narratrice et idéologie," 109, and Bacarisse, "Mitificación de la historia y desmitificación de la escritura," 156, 159.

6. The critics are those mentioned in Note 1, and the terms they use are: "pueblo" (people) "pueblo paraguayo" (Paraguayan people), "cultura popular" (popular culture), and "oralidad" (orality), among others. Kubayanda, for example, borrows Ángel Rama's expression "nuestras masas" (our masses), to which he gives the following meaning: "all those outside the centers of authority, especially the Blacks and Indians and the several women and their children who populate *Yo el Supremo*" (Kubayanda 132). Among the different meanings of the word "orality" (understood, on the one hand, as oral expression, and on the other, as oral culture), see Mignolo "Tradiciones orales." In the article by Gazzolo, "Escritura y oralidad en *Yo el Supremo*," both meanings seem to be conflated. For this author (like for the Jesuits Melia and Ong), oral expression qua medium seems to be considered as better than writing. On page 314, Gazzolo seems to subscribe the belief that oral communication is more faithful to the thoughts of the speaker than writing is, due to its immediacy and to a certain communicational insufficiency that characterizes the written word. However, it is my contention that in order to criticize literate culture, it is not necessary to resort to the metaphysics of presence, which is an important tool for domination in the hands of dominant culture. In other words, it is not necessary to praise the oral *medium* from a philosophical perspective in order to vindicate (from an anthropological and ethical perspective) indigenous, oral *cultures*.

7. Meliá makes reference to this situation throughout his article.

8. There is no reason to privilege Castile, just one little region of the Spanish-speaking world, at the time of naming one of the languages spoken in Paraguay.

9. See Havelock, *Preface to Plato*.

10. To attempt to explain the complex notion of trace as it appears in Derrida would take a considerable amount of space, so I will try to be as succinct as possible. It is valid to say that both the elements of oral discourse and those of the written one are incapable of functioning as signs without having to relate to other elements that are absent from the text itself. This relationship means that each element is constituted with reference to the traces of other elements of the linguistic sequence or system. That relationship is the text itself, which can only be produced through the transformation of another text. It is because of this that it can be said that none of the elements of the system is simply present or absent. The text or system is always made of traces.

11. Marcos, *Roa Bastos*. This translation, and all others, unless otherwise noted, are mine.

12. Ibid., 72. On the same page, Marcos offers other cases: "En otros pasajes la carnavalización es más directa. A menudo, se basa en el uso coloquial del estilo, para ironizar la solemnidad pedante de los historiadores. "Belgrano y Echevarría – narra el Supremo –Echevarría tuvieron que sufrir en el purgatorio de Corrientes un largo plantón.' A veces la sátira se despliega como juego de palabras: 'Cuando Buenos Aires se convirtió en flamantes ruinas, Asunción la refundó. Buenos Aires se avanza ahora a querer refundirnos.' La risa se cierne a veces sobre individuos concretos. Como en el carnaval, desfilan en el texto una y otra máscara" (In other passages, carnivalization is more direct. Often, it is based on the colloquial use of style to make ironic the pedantic solemnity of historians. 'Belgrano and Echevarría —the Supremo narrates—had to suffer in the Corrientes purgatory a long wait.' Sometimes satire is deployed as wordplay: 'When Buenos Aires became brand-new ruins, Asunción refounded it. Buenos Aires advances now to refund us.' Laughter looms sometimes over concrete individuals. Like in Carnival itself, one mask after another; my translation).

13. The tradition of speaking animals goes back very far in time, to the fables of Aesop, the Latin version of it (Fedro), and the Golden Ass by Apuleius. In Roa Bastos's novel, this popular tradition conformed by proverbs and "decires" takes shape in the speaking parts of the dogs Héroe and Sultán.

14. Ciudad letrada (lettered city) = Spanish, Western, literate culture (which irradiates its power from urban centers). See Rama's *La ciudad letrada*, especially pages 1–68. Kubayanda's work seems to promise an analysis of this topic, but he ends up mentioning it only in passing.

15. See Verdesio, "Verba quoque manent," for an analysis of that film.

16. Indigenous practices are not the only alternative knowledge forms that the dictator believes in: he also manifests great interest, and seems to have faith, in the study of the occult—which, despite being of European origin, it is also a corpus of knowledge marginal to the knowledge

the West considers as scientific and, therefore, as valid. This can be seen throughout the novel, but it is made very clear on page 54.

17. He also sometimes has negative views about other ethnic minorities: the mulatto. They are accused of duplicity (206) and of having an innate tendency to behave as traitors (216).

Works Cited

Bacarisse, Salvador. "Mitificación de la historia y desmitificación de la escritura: *Yo el Supremo* de Augusto Roa Bastos." *Bulletin of Hispanic Studies* LXV (1988): 153–61. Print.

Cornejo Polar, Antonio. "Las literaturas marginales y la crítica: una propuesta." *Augusto Roa Bastos y la producción cultural americana*. Ed. Saúl Sosnowski. Buenos Aires: Ediciones de la Flor, 1986. Print.

———. *La novela indigenista*. Lima: Lasontay, 1980. Print.

"Deconstruction in America: an Interview with Jaques Derrida." *Critical Exchange* 17 (Winter, 1985): 1–33. Print.

Derrida, Jaques. *Of Grammatology*. Trans. G. Chakravorty Spivak. Baltimore: Johns Hopkins University Press, 1976. 6–73. Print.

du Lope, Monique. "Le statut ideologique de la lecture." *L'Ideologique dans le texte*. Toulouse: Université de Toulouse-le Mirail, 1984. 133–38. Print.

Ezquerro, Milagros. "Fonction narratrice et idéologie." *L'ideologique dans le texte*. Toulouse: Université de Toulouse-le Mirail, 1984. Print.

Ferrer Agüero, Luis María. *El universo narrativo de Augusto Roa Bastos*. Diss. Universidad Complutense de Madrid, 1981. Print.

Foster, David William. *Augusto Roa Bastos*. Boston: Twayne Publishers, 1978. Print.

Gazzolo, Ana Maria. "Escritura y oralidad en *Yo el Supremo*." *Cuadernos Hispanoamericanos* 493–94 (1991): 313–27. Print.

Havelock, Eric. *Origins of Western Literacy*. Ontario: The Ontario Institute for Studies in Education, 1976. Print.

———. *Preface to Plato*. Cambridge: Harvard University Press, 1963. Print.

Hutcheon, Linda. *The Politics of Postmodernism*. New York: Routledge, 1989. Print.

Kubayanda, Josaphat. "Order and Conflict: *Yo el Supremo* in Light of Rama's Ciudad letrada Theory." *The Historical Novel in Latin America*. Ed. Daniel Balderston. Gaithersburg: *Hispamérica*, 1986. 129–37. Print.

Lienhard, Martin. *La voz y su huella*. La Habana: Casa de las Américas, 1990. Print.

Marcos, Juan Manuel. *Roa Bastos, precursor del post-boom*. México: Katún, 1983. Print.

Maturo, Graciela. "*Yo el Supremo*: la recuperación del sentido." *Megafón*, Buenos Aires II, 3 (July 1976): 151–56. Print.

Meliá, Bartomeu, S. J. "Una metáfora de la lengua en el Paraguay." *Cuadernos Hispanoamericanos* 493–94 (1991): 65–73. Print.

Mignolo, Walter. "Ficcionalización del discurso historiográfico." *Augusto Roa Bastos y la producción cultural americana*. Ed. Saúl Sosnowski. Buenos Aires: Ediciones de la Flor, 1986. Print.

———. "Tradiciones orales, alfabetización y literatura (o de las diferencias entre el corpus y el canon)." *IX Congresso Internacional da Associaĉåo de Lingüistica e Filologia da America Latina*. Campinas: Brazil, 1990. Unpublished.

———. *The Darker Side of the Renassaince. Literacy, Territoriality and Colonization*. Ann Arbor: University of Michigan Press, 1995. Print.

Morillas, Enriqueta. "Roa Bastos, Hispanoamérica y la novela." *Cuadernos Hispanoamericanos* (1991): 43–51. Print.

Ong, Walter. *Orality and Literacy*. New York: Methuen, 1987. Print.

———. *The Presence of the Word*. New Haven: Yale University Press, 1967. Print.

Pacheco, Carlos. "Yo/El: primeras claves para una lectura de la polifonía en *Yo el Supremo*." *Augusto Roa Bastos y la producción cultural americana*. Ed. Saúl Sosnowski. Buenos Aires: Ediciones de la flor, 1986. 151–78. Print.

Rama, Ángel. *La ciudad letrada*. Hanover, NH: Ediciones del Norte, 1984. Print.

———. *Transculturación narrativa en América Latina*. México: Siglo XXI editores, 1982. Print.

Roa Bastos, Augusto. *Yo el Supremo*. Asunción: Servilibro, 2007. Print.

———. *I the Supreme*. New York: Vintage, 1987. Print.

———. "Algunos núcleos generadores de un texto narrativo." *L'ideologique dans le texte*. Toulouse: Université de Toulouse-le Mirail, 1984. Print.

Sosnowski, Saúl. "A propósito de Roa Bastos y la producción americana ante la historia." *Augusto Roa Bastos y la producción cultural americana*. Ed. Saúl Sosnowski. Buenos Aires: Ediciones de la Flor, 1986. 9–17. Print.

Verdesio, Gustavo. "Verba quoque manent: *Yo el Supremo* como deconstrucción de la ciudad letrada." *Hispamérica* 22.66 (1993): 31–44. Print.

———. "*Cabeza de Vaca*: una visión paródica de la épica colonial." *Nuevo Texto Crítico* 19–20 (1997): 195–204. Print.

Vila Barnes, Gladys. *Significado y coherencia del universo narrativo de Augusto Roa Bastos*. Madrid: Orígenes, 1984. Print.

Weldt-Basson, Helene Carol. *Augusto Roa Bastos's I the Supreme. A Dialogic Perspective*. Columbia: University of Missouri Press, 1993. Print.

CHAPTER 8

TYRANNY AND FOUNDATION

APPROPRIATIONS OF THE HERO AND REREADINGS OF THE NATION IN AUGUSTO ROA BASTOS AND JEAN-CLAUDE FIGNOLÉ[1]

Javier Uriarte

Podría fundar, sin embargo, en la negrura, algo. Ver de ver algo, ahora: algo que, sin ser el comienzo, sirva, sin embargo, para comenzar, o como ejemplo de lo que, comenzando, seguiría.
(I could found, however, something in the darkness. To see from seeing something, now: something that, without being the beginning, might serve, however, to begin, or as an example of what, by beginning, would follow.)

—Juan José Saer, "La mayor"

LITERATURE AND "COUNTERHISTORY": DICTATORSHIP, HERO, FOUNDATION

In his insightful essay "Algunos núcleos generadores de un texto narrativo" ("Some Generating Nuclei of a Narrative Text"; 1977), Augusto Roa Bastos (1917–2005) discusses some of the problems dealing with the genesis of his novel *I the Supreme* (*Yo el Supremo*, 1974). He then mentions his original "project" when he started the writing process, which consisted of "escribir una contrahistoria, una réplica subversiva y transgresiva de la historiografía oficial" (177) ["writing a counterhistory, a subversive and transgressive retort of the official history"]. It is not my intention to argue here what seems evident: that this "counterhistorical" impulse effectively takes place in the novel. Rather, I attempt to explore the forms that this project adopts, that is to say, to analyze the ways in which we can speak of "counterhistory" and how we can understand this concept within Roa's novel. When Roa affirms he wants to write "against historians' history" ("contra la historia de los historiadores") [Roa Bastos, "Algunos núcleos," 177], I see in his words a gesture that deals with property or appropriations. In other words, a central idea that in many ways inhabits this chapter is that the ways in which history is narrated, and in which the national hero is described and constructed, are directly linked to ideological or political projects that deal with the present and with the future of the nation. These problems are not only related to the always uncertain and problematic boundaries between literature, fiction, and history, which are constant throughout the novel, but also mainly to symbolic battles over the discourse.[2] Roa's project is then basically an "appropriative" one, in the sense that it tries to make a given object its own against other discourses that operate with different and opposing logics of appropriation. He is struggling to construct a historical figure according to specific projects and to introduce the former within the latter. In order to achieve this, he needs to perform a reinterpretation, a rereading of the nation, its origins, and its heroes.

In relation to Roa's work, I am interested in exploring the ways in which the text approaches the historical character José Gaspar Rodríguez de Francia (who is not directly mentioned as such even once in the whole novel), and both reads and appropriates him as part of his revisionist project. I suggest that from this perspective, it is possible to clearly understand the concept of "counterhistory," which Roa does not thoroughly explain in the aforementioned essay. What the reader does know is that he is writing "against" "la irrealidad historiográfica fraguada en los moldes del pensamiento reaccionario y liberal" (the historiographic unreality forged within the molds of reactionary and liberal thinking)[Roa Bastos, "Algunos núcleos," 79]. This confrontational and polemic element sets the tone of the novel. It would be necessary, then, to identify those discourses against which the novel is written and, above all, to ask ourselves how is it possible to appropriate Francia's figure.[3] The reading of the historical figure of Francia that is present in *I the Supreme* is related to—and this is explicit in the essay by Roa—his role as a founder of the Paraguayan nation. This look at the dictator as founder (or at the founder as dictator, depending on the case) and, in this sense, as national hero, is—as I see it—the most original and controversial element in this text.

Throughout these pages, I discuss the ways in which the tyrant and the foundational hero within the character of El Supremo dialogue with each other both in the novel by the Paraguayan author, and in the much more contemporary work, *Moi, Toussaint Louverture . . . avec la plume complice de l'auteur* (2004) [*I, Toussaint Louverture, with the complicit author's nib*] by Haitian writer Jean-Claude Fignolé (1941). Fignolé's novel poses some questions that relate in an interesting way to the South American text.[4] When is the nation founded? Who founds it and how does he or she do it? Who is legitimized to do it? Which are the legitimizing discourses of the nation? "Official" versions of history have tried to give definite and unambiguous answers to these questions—answers that would match the occidental and liberal version of democracy. The texts I analyze here propose new answers that disturb that impression of clarity and reflect on the figure of the dictator as founder and, in that sense, as national hero.

I would like to examine, then, how it is possible to critically vindicate these characters as national heroes. I am particularly interested in showing exactly how both novels make use of a critical narration of the national history. I will discuss the ways in which these texts claim the right to a complex historical discourse for the Latin American nation that assumes the problematic and ambivalent as an essential part of itself. In this sense, I will argue that these novels represent history in ways that are far from the hagiographic impulses to which "official" versions of history have been prone.

Through which mechanisms are the main characters of the novels by Roa and Fignolé constructed as heroic and totalitarian at the same time? To a certain extent, both texts escape from the logic of traditional liberalism, which believes in nothing else than the paths opened by democracy (conceived mainly as electoral rights) and free market as "regulators," establishing a sharp and unequivocal opposition between freedom and dictatorship. Thus, these novels critically demand the possibility that tyranny and liberation—conceived by traditional liberalism as mutually exclusive—can share a similar logic and can coincide in some specific points.

These texts perform parallel operations. Both of them aim to problematize major historical figures, thus questioning key concepts such as foundation, hero, nation, memory, dictatorship, liberation, and history. Nevertheless, each project—through similar operations—takes opposite directions, since the appropriations that take place in each of them have opposite departure points. In other words, each of the texts is written against previous discourses whose projects do not coincide: while Roa conceives his text as a vindication (even if a critical and problematic one) of the dictator[5] José Gaspar Rodríguez de Francia against the "black legend" (as Roa [1977] and Fernández Retamar call it) that had imposed the common thought of him being a despot, Fignolé seeks to problematize the figure of Toussaint Louverture, traditionally seen as the perfect liberator, in the service of the Haitian people (i.e., the black slave population). Throughout these pages, I focus on the textual operations that the novels perform in order to represent these historical figures as characters, and to grant them a new place, always problematic and ambivalent, within the symbolic space of the nation.

The strategies by which the novels achieve their respective construction-appropriation of the hero are projected mainly in two directions: genesis and genealogy.[6] On the one hand, I consider what I call the discourses (or politics) of origin, both of the hero and the nation, whose apparent definitive and unmovable condition is undermined by both novels. On the other hand, I discuss the genealogies and specular processes by which the main character of each text is constructed.

The issues related to the origin deal with the ways in which the discourse seeks to erase and/or establish (sometimes simultaneously, sometimes successively) a point of origin both for the nation and the hero. To a certain extent, these processes tend to identify both elements: the origin of the nation *is* the hero, but the hero cannot be a real "hero" without the nation he creates. At the same time, the idea of the "hero" as creator is complemented by the idea of the "non-generated" or "autogenerated" hero: he is his own origin as well as that of the nation (hence the identification between both). The idea of autogeneration is possible thanks to the use of mythical discourse, which makes possible the erasure, the clouding of an exact "point" of origin. In opposition to the traditional historical discourse, mythical discourse ignores measurable and precise time. As a result, the characteristics of the hero change as well. He is enlarged by this conception of time, and thus becomes eternal.

The character is constructed in the midst of a web of heroes and discourses, in relation to which he constantly positions himself. It is a process of continuous dialogue and modeling, through which the character finds his place while the narrative discourse appropriates some discourses and rejects others (it is important to remember, in this respect, the "counter" nature of this discourse). In some way, the narration is constructed from many different discourses in the same way as the character is modeled by contemplating himself in the "mirror" of other heroes who precede and succeed him. The discourse seeks to legitimate itself and the character through the search for a genealogy: the hero establishes who will be his "parents" and "sons," and thus he situates himself in a particular genealogical line, offering a reading, an interpretation of himself.

GENERATION AND AUTOGENERATION: THE DISCOURSES OF THE ORIGIN

The epigraph that opens this chapter comes from a short story by Juan José Saer (1937–2005), who constantly reflects upon time throughout his work. His text does not deal, like the texts I study here, with problems related to interpretative battles around different versions of history or historical characters. The plot of his narration is very reduced and purely centered on the "I." It deals with the concerted efforts made by a conscience to find memories within itself. The need to remember seems to take over the protagonist and cause him to suffer different anxieties, one of which deals with the possibility of finding a beginning, a point in which to "found" oneself in order to continue to remember. In this view, the beginning is always an invention, something that "without being the beginning" is nevertheless a way to point it out. In other words, the idea that there is an objective, unique "origin" *per se*, which preexists the discourse that founds it, is—according to the epigraph and to my reading of history throughout these pages—a construction. As the epigraph shows, that constructed origin is of great importance because, to some extent, it determines what comes afterward, by imposing a reading of successive times and events. Not only does it make possible the act of remembrance, but it also indicates what will be remembered and how.

These considerations regarding foundation and the interpretation of the past are also essential with respect to the Latin American nation. Roa's and Fignole's texts are clear examples of this, since a crucial part of the articulation and structure of the novels deals with a debate over foundation. If Latin American literature has been—in an obvious way during the nineteenth century, and perhaps in a more sophisticated way later on—largely obsessed with giving origins and limits to the nation, these texts are not different in this respect, although they do appear as polemic interventions in the battle for interpretative power and present new approaches to an old topic.

The act of establishing a starting point for the independent life of the state (and the nation) is still a debated issue in some Latin American countries, and the fixation and celebration of the event is crucial in order to define these divergences. "Official" histories have sought to present the point of origin as an unproblematic and easily identifiable moment. Thus, the celebration of independence (or the hero's birthday) that exists in every country works as an element that, through its annual repetition, produces and fixes meanings while establishing certain dates as unmovable in the national imaginary and, at the same time, generating, paradoxically, a feeling of absence of temporality. Celebrations and dates, which are generally linked to a temporal dimension, work thus to erase any idea of the course of time. It is as if those dates had always been there, with a heavy symbolic meaning that is seen as natural to them, respected by everyone since the beginning of time, which almost amounts to mythologizing the past.[7] For the national discourse, it seems to be of great importance to know how and when each state is inaugurated in order to make impossible any rereading of the origin by dissident or problematizing voices.[8]

The voices that speak in these novels by Roa and Fignolé seek precisely to destabilize this discourse of origins that seems static and unmovable. To begin with, the Supreme's voice[9] seems obsessed with the idea of giving itself an origin and a genealogy, since it repeatedly comes back to these notions. If a given genesis produces a genealogy (perhaps the Bible is the most striking example in this sense), maybe both ideas should be considered in dialogue with each other. Here, I particularly think of the idea of "counterhistory" in relation to the problem of origins. Roa's vindication is not aimed only at Paraguayan history, but also at the modes of construction and representation typical of every hagiographic discourse that considers itself "official," which constitutes a point in common with the Haitian novel. One of the operations that Roa's novel performs consists of blurring the boundaries between history and literature by creating a character who is, and is not, fictional; who is, and is not, Francia—a character who, in other words, cannot be defined or explained. Besides the nonexplicit identification with José Gaspar Rodríguez de Francia, the central voice is not a uniform one, which prevents the reader from identifying it with any particular speaker, either historical or fictional.

This is possible because the character's own genesis is clouded by the text. The main character seeks to erase any trace of his parents: there are various names for his mother and father (Roa Bastos, *I the Supreme*, 332–33), and he even argues that he has not been born from a woman: "Yo he podido ser concebido sin mujer por la sola fuerza de mi pensamiento" (165) ["I was able to be conceived without woman with the power of thought alone" (132)].[10] Moreover, two possible dates of birth are given—January 6, 1756, and the same one in 1766:

"¿No me atribuyen dos madres, un padre falso, cuatro falsos herma-
nos, dos fechas de nacimiento?" (165) ["Do people not credit me
with two mothers, a false father, four false brothers, two birthdates?"
(133)]. The character thus becomes impossible to apprehend and
seems to situate himself in a distant and mythical dimension, far from
the accidents of life and death. In this way, he positions himself as
eternal and multiple (the echoes of the Catholic dogma of the Holy
Trinity are almost obvious to me here), which is an essential characteristic of the dictator whose presence dominates everything and whose
government cannot be perceived as having a beginning or end.

At the same time, in a parallel operation, the text identifies the
Supreme with the nation, since it problematizes both the dictator's
and the nation's origins. The nation also lacks a clear date of birth.
This strategy makes it possible for the character to impose a new beginning for the state that is thus identified with him. In this respect, the
text seeks to destabilize a certain meaning and to propose a different
one in its place. However, this new date is not always clear since, on
many occasions, the Supreme refers, using similar expressions, to the
"la mala época de los comienzos" (365) ["bad days of the beginning"
(302)], meaning the years before he was given extraordinary power.
There is an almost mythical way of perceiving those times, which the
historical discourse cannot narrate. Milagros Ezquerro has discussed
these problems insightfully, showing the ways in which "hard" historical discourse becomes myth (for Ezquerro, the story narrated by the
character is actually a mythical relation of the country's origins), since
the account of the foundation works at the same time as the beginning of a tradition. The Supreme's discourse works as a relation of the
nation's origins because it seeks to transmit a narration that will be
adopted and perpetuated as a reading of the past (Ezquerro 54–55).

These two parallel and complementary processes seem to coincide
with the different registers the narrative voice presents throughout
the text. The "Circular Perpetua" uses a discourse that seems to do
battle in the field of history, of which it proposes its own polemic version. Carlos Pacheco has defined it as "una rehechura de la historia
pasada, presente y futura" ("remaking of past, present, and future history") [Pacheco xxvi]. Dates and concrete events are problematized
here, while in the "Cuaderno de Apuntes," we can find a different type
of reflection, that refers to the writing process and to the narrator's "I,"
to his obsessions and ghosts, his internal conflicts and duplicities. Here
it is possible to find statements that seek to erase the notion of origin,
such as the ones referred to above. The Supreme's discourse, then, contradicts itself: the zeal with which it intends to point out a single date

(thus identifying himself with it) is undermined by the subsequent impossibility of establishing it.

This element is part of the character's ambivalence, which has been clearly studied by Milagros Ezquerro in her introduction to the novel. Within this ambivalence, contradiction is possible and even desirable. It is possible to find, within the same discourse, the intention of presenting oneself as "official" and proposing a new beginning while erasing other memories and imposing one's own. This practice, together with the use of an ahistorical, and almost mythical, logic, makes impossible the idea of a "politics of origin" (univocal and fixed) that the protagonist's voice seeks to establish. As I have suggested above, both discourses relate to the structural division within the Supreme's voice between HE and I, which has been neatly explained by Carlos Pacheco in his very Bahktinian introduction to the novel. While "I" is "un ser humano concreto y cambiante" ("concrete and changing human being"), "HE" is "una imagen abstracta, eterna, invariable, infalible y omnipotent" ("an abstract image, eternal, invariable, infallible, omnipotent") [Pacheco xxi]. In this sense, Pacheco points out the mythical nature of this second voice. However, when thinking of proposing a new national starting point a new contradiction appears, since the assertive, imposing, and decided discourse of the "Circular Perpetua," anchored in history, is simultaneously a mythical, that is, ahistorical, time. How can the mythical also be historical at the same time? Pacheco's clear division is undermined by the fact that, in *I the Supreme*, both the mythical and historical dimensions coexist in the "I" and the "HE."

The construction of oneself as lacking an origin and based on contradictory facts works in the same way as Jorge Luis Borges indicates that Walt Whitman proceeds. He constructs himself through contradiction ("I contradict myself? Very well, then, I contradict myself"), as a figure of mythical dimensions. In his essay "Nota sobre Walt Whitman," Borges meditates on the embracing and totalizing ambition that characterizes Whitman's "I." It is a voice that constantly and tirelessly multiplies itself: "Así se desdobló en el Whitman eterno, en ese amigo que es un viejo poeta americano de mil ochocientos y tantos y también su leyenda y también cada uno de nosotros y también la felicidad" ("Thus he managed to unfold himself in the eternal Whitman, in that friend who is an old American poet of the eighteen something and also his legend and also each of us and also happiness") [Borges 253]. Putting aside differences of projects and poetics, the operations both multiple voices perform are not far away from each other. The Supreme's voice works, in general terms, in the same way within Roa's text: we have a man—actually a voice—without an origin that was part of an ahistorical time, but who, at the same time (and maybe for that same reason), is capable of establishing a new beginning, of founding historical time. Here, contradiction appears as a generating, multiplying, and productive principle.

Roa has said that the Guarani expression "Karaí-Guasú," applied here to The Supreme, has a mythical meaning, and that the figure of the Founding Father (whose role Francia adopted) has traditionally been an essential element of the Paraguayan national imaginary and Guarani cosmology. Then, given that Francia's central presence has never been overlooked in the country's culture, the novel seeks to make explicit its importance in Paraguayan life. It is also impossible— within the Guaranis' imaginary—to leave aside the figure of the Karaí-Guasú, even if the references to him might seem not direct enough. The novel puts both unavoidable presences next to each other, and they are thus identified, conjugated, and contained by the Supreme's voice. However, at the same time, as Sibylle Fischer (1991) explains, it performs this identification through the appropriation and deformation of Guarani myths of origin (there are, then, two simultaneous appropriations: throughout the novel, Roa Bastos appropriates the figure of Dr. Francia through his character, while The Supreme appropriates the indigenous discourse in order to legitimize himself). The character carries on partial readings of this cycle of narratives in order to position himself as the absolute origin, something he never entirely achieves.[11]

Without using exactly the same strategies, the central voice in *I, Toussaint* seems to construct itself in a surprisingly similar way. Here, there is the same tendency to erase one's own past and to position oneself as an absolute new beginning. First of all, the ambivalence dealing with the date of birth is evident in Fignolé's text: "Je suis né en 1743. D'autres disent en 1745" (17) ["I was born in 1743. Others say in 1745"].[12] Toussaint strongly believes in the idea of autoconstruction; it is almost a mise-en-scène of the I. This first person portrays him as being obsessed by the future. In this sense, he proposes a mythical narration of his own origin: "Écrivez-moi quelque chose de grandiose en accord avec le destinée que le Seigneur me réservait"(17) ["Write me something grandiose according to the future that the Lord reserved for me"]. Not only is the date erased, but also the parents. The character lacks real or lasting affective relationships, and his discourse (like The Supreme's) is a catalogue of loneliness. This relates to the absence of his mother (20). However, when he talks about his father, the feeling of hate expressed is close to that of

Roa's novel: "Quant à mon père! Était-il ce nègre misérable que se soûlait chaque soir, après le travail aux ateliers, pour mieux assortir sa nostalgie de l'Afrique . . . ?" (20–21) ["Regarding my father! Was he that miserable negro who got drunk every evening, after working at the studios, in order to better match his nostalgia for Africa . . . ?"]. This rejection is coherent with his attitude of ignoring his African inheritance, which is despicable and counterproductive according to the modern, liberal, and capitalist logic that guides him. The fact of having been born of an unknown father and mother (66) makes it possible for him to affirm, "Je suis né du néant" (66) ["I've been born from nothing"]. This conclusion opens[13] in two directions: on the one hand, it leads him to invent a genealogy, to choose his own "parents" and "sons." I shall discuss this aspect later. On the other hand, Toussaint goes beyond the logic of history and becomes mythical (67). This mythical nature is what gives him supernatural powers (106) and makes possible for him "être ici et ailleurs en même temps" (106) ["to be here and somewhere else at the same time"].

That is why he manages to have a broad vision of his country's history and to identify himself with the revolutionary mythical origin, thus substituting Mackandal. Mackandal was a slave who escaped and was later caught and publicly executed in a bonfire, although he was mythically believed to have escaped from the execution through a metamorphosis.[14] While Toussaint's voice becomes mythical, other voices (Mackandal's, for example) are stripped of that characteristic. Instead of considering Mackandal as a revolutionary, he sees him as a sanguinary man who sought only vengeance and whose aim was to "tuer tous les blancs" (114) ["kill all whites"]. In some way, here we again see a contradictory operation: the mythical discourse is used in order to erase the mythical nature of the African imaginary and replace it with a "modern" logic. The protagonist is horrified before the possibility of being compared with Mackandal, from whom he intends to differentiate himself: "On a voulu associer mon action à la sienne. Erreur! Nous n'avons rien de commun" ["They have wanted to associate my actions to his. Wrong! We don't have anything in common"]. While Mackandal is a rebel, Toussaint is a visionary (115).

Interestingly, while the protagonist denies Mackandal the possibility of having supernatural powers, he attributes them to himself. For example, when somebody tries to kill Toussaint, he survives because he manages to multiply himself before the killers: "Ils virent dans mon entourage trois fois plus de Toussaint qu'ils n'avaient d'hommes disponibles. Je me serais multiplié par cent et ils ne savaient pas lequel de ces cent Toussaint était le bon. Était le vrai" (161) ["Around me they saw three times as many men than what they had available. I would have multiplied myself by one hundred and they would not know which one of those hundred Toussaints was the good one. The true one"]. Of course, the character's capacity to multiply himself (274) is mainly symbolic, since it refers to the multiple faces that he adopts in order to seize power, an idea that is reinforced by the strong alliteration in "ces cent Toussaint." As the quotation suggests, there is nothing more difficult than to find the true Toussaint. This uncertainty is not only his enemies', but is also very strong among his subjects, friends, and, of course, among the readers. It is a consequence of the plurality of voices, faces, and ideas that integrate and filter into this apparently solid voice.

A second, more obvious, moment, in which Toussaint uses his powers in order to escape from certain death, can be read as the exact opposite of Mackandal's metamorphosis. Mackandal, according to Carpentier (51), would have jumped over the bonfire, almost flying, disappearing afterward among the multitude. In Fignolé's novel, the protagonist glides through the air on horseback to avoid oncoming bullets. Undoubtedly, the protagonist knows very well the consequences of exploiting this narration for his own benefit. While he dismisses the possibility that Mackandal could have escaped magically from death, he does not problematize his own ability to fly (161). This is actually the substitution of one foundational hero for other: the articulated and scheming discourse prevails, a discourse that attributes to itself mythical features because it can obtain practical benefits from doing so, against the other discourse that has its origins in magic, orality, and tradition.[15] There is also a struggle on two levels: Toussaint's discourse silences Mackandal's voice while at the same time trying to eliminate the silence that was imposed upon his own discourse.

Heroes or Antiheroes? The Breaking of the Pantheon

In the same way the novels destabilize the certainty of the date of origin, they undermine the stability of the pantheon of national heroes. Again, these fluid discourses transmit their fluidity to ideas conceived as unmovable and permanent. This is possible because both texts propose certain genealogies that explain the new origin: an origin that, at the same time, makes possible those genealogies. An important element, to which I have referred above, deals with the dialogue and interaction of voices and historical accounts that coexist in tension throughout Fignolé and Roa's pages. The centrality of voice and dialogue[16] is, thus, a point we should underline from this perspective.

There is one particular element that unites both characters: the fact that each of them is a "spokesman" ("vocero"). I am interested in this word in many senses—in the first place, because both characters are, above all, voices.[17] Also, if the "spokesman" is, according to the *Diccionario de la Real Academia Española*, the "persona que habla en nombre de otra, o de un grupo, institución, entidad, etc, llevando su voz y representación" ["person who speaks on behalf of another, or of a group, institution, entity, etc, carrying his/her/its voice and representation"],[18] this definition brings up many questions. On behalf of whom are these protagonists speaking? Whose is the will that their words communicate? Which are the voices transmitted by these "spokesmen" and where have they originated? Even if the relationship between the Spanish words "voz" (voice) and "vocero" (spokesman) seems obvious, my aim here is to problematize it. The "spokesman," within these texts, seems woven by different, contradictory, and plural voices. If the spokesman, in general, tries to faithfully and clearly communicate a unique and monologic discourse (the case of politics would be the clearest in this sense), these spokesmen undermine that intention, since they make possible (and even create) various filtrations and instabilities. They speak for themselves and for others who, at times, are not easily identifiable. Maybe it would be possible to rethink the "spokesman" as one who carries voices and weaves them while being, at the same time, constructed by them. This importance of the voice implies, obviously, the centrality of dialogue.

In neither of these texts does the central discourse work in a disconnected or independent way, but rather it is always surrounded by other discourses that complete it and make it more complex. Both *I the Supreme* and *I, Toussaint* unfold within a network of texts, and it is this dimension that I intend to discuss here.

In *I the Supreme*, the dialogue is already present from the very intertextual structure of the novel, which tirelessly suggests meanings in different directions, rewriting and resignifying historical texts, political figures, travelogues, and novels. The Supreme's discourse—full of holes, penetrated by various discourses that establish conflicts and tensions with it, that "invade" it and even appropriate its word—nevertheless manages to destabilize and create confusion within different systems of discourses.

I return here to one aspect I have briefly mentioned in the first pages of this chapter and that I believe is essential to the dialogical nature of these texts. The idea that these discourses are generated as a resistant and alternative reaction against previous ones is key within the "counterhistorical" project that is at the roots of these novels. Each of the novels, as it has been said above, takes a different path in order to fulfill a common purpose: while Roa's text seeks to transform the figure of an unquestionable dictator into a foundational hero, Fignolé's works around a historical figure traditionally considered as a hero in order to reveal his ambitions, his intrigues and betrayals, through which the liberation of his country does not seem a sincere priority.

Moreover, each of the novels originates as a polemical answer to different preceding discourses. *I the Supreme* faces, on the one hand, the liberal historiography, which originates during the nineteenth century with the work of Bartolomé Mitre (1821–1906),[19] called, ironically, "Tacit-Brigadier" by the Supreme. This tradition, which counted on the support of the aristocratic and liberal Paraguayan elites, was largely built relying on the accounts by the "civilized" European travelers and by those who had, in the neighboring countries, interests opposed to those of Dr. Francia.[20] The classical book by John Lynch, *The Spanish American Revolutions, 1808–1826* (1973), is a contemporary version of this same project.[21]

There is another front on which Roa's "counterhistory" fights, always seeking to appropriate the hero. Although Dr. Francia is, from a liberal perspective, an execrable character, for the official historical account during the years in which the novel was written, he was also a hero. Paraguay was then under Alfredo Stroessner's dictatorship (1954–1989), the longest in the country's history. This regime viewed Dr. Francia as the founder of the nation and positioned him within a pantheon that was also occupied by the two presidents that succeeded him, Carlos Antonio López (1844–1862) and Francisco Solano López (1862–1870). The latter has been considered a martyr by many, since he died in battle during the War of the Triple Alliance. In relation to this particular appropriation, Francisco Tovar affirms that "el Supremo ha sido utilizado como justificación y ejemplo de un gobierno dictatorial, sin reparar en escrúpulos de conciencia ni considerar la falsedad del símbolo que ofrece al pueblo como si su significación fuera la original" (136) ["the Supreme has been used as a justification and example of a dictatorial government, without having any scruple of conscience or considering the falsehood involved in the act of offering the symbol to the people as if its meaning were the original"].[22] It is difficult to accept that Stroessner's regime, which expelled Roa from his native country, could recognize as its own the voice that dominates *I the Supreme*.[23] This struggle for the appropriation of the hero goes along with another one, which takes place in a different dimension: the struggle for the place of the hero within the pantheon.

Fulgencio Yegros (1780–1821), considered by some (mostly by Francia's opponents) as the Paraguayan national hero, is called a series of names by the Supreme, including "gaucho ignorante" (199) ["ignorant gaucho" (161)], "animal" (200) ["stupid animal" (161)], "traidor-conspirador" (412) ["conspirator-traitor" (343)], and, last but not least, "infame traidor a la patria" (49) ["infamous traitor to the Fatherland" (34)]. Again, we are before a symbolic battle for the central place of the founding hero. The fact that the fictional characters were also historical enemies places the departure point for this struggle at the very beginning of Paraguayan independent life. Consequently, the battles for the interpretation and appropriation of history remain constant all throughout the history of independent Paraguay.[24] Thus, the choice between one or the other hero will imply a different interpretation of history. At the same time, national history will be constructed through this debate.

According to the Supreme's logic, the erasure of Yegros would constitute the necessary step before proposing himself to that post, which is now vacant: if every nation needs to have (according to the discourse of the origin) a founding father, and if Yegros can no longer be considered as such, it is necessary then to put someone else in that post. The rereading of history that takes place in the text, together with the identification with the "Karaí-Guasú," constitutes the best argument in order for the Supreme to occupy that position.

If the ideas of dictator and founder are really that close to each other in the Paraguayan novel, it is important to point out that this is possible because there was also a clear, original, and successful social and political project. During José Gaspar Rodríguez de Francia's dictatorship (1814–1840), the foundations for a project based on social policies (focusing on education with the well-being of the population as a central goal) were established. Regarding international affairs, the main obsession of Francia was to preserve the country's sovereignty against Argentina's and Brazil's imperialist ambitions, and also against European diplomacy. Some of the features that characterized Francia's government were continued by the two presidents that succeeded him, who also ruled for long periods, until 1870. The project sought to carry on a significant industrial development, accompanied by a strong policy of isolation with respect to the region, and included the creation of an autarkic market and the elimination of illiteracy. This project, however, ended dramatically with the War of the Triple Alliance. The country could never again resume the interrupted process, and its history followed a different path. Nevertheless, there continued to be dictatorships whose projects changed drastically, of which Alfredo Stroessner's government is a striking example.

Francia was the one who inaugurated the process, and that is why he conjugates for Roa the figures of the dictator and the founder. The Supreme's philosophy also encompassed European readings and concrete examples of different types of thinkers. Robespierre appears as an example to be followed (I shall return later to the character's Jacobin ideas), but Rousseau, Pascal, Machiavelli, Montesquieu, Voltaire, Franklin, and Napoleon appear as well. It is from this point of view that the novel is not only about the character's genesis, but also about his genealogy. References to thinkers, men of action, and politicians abound in the text. Two different genealogical lines lead to the Supreme and, in some way, found him. On the one hand, there are ideological, political, and philosophical readings, which correspond to a protosocialist (or maybe Jacobin) European tradition. On the other hand, there are Latin American politicians among whom the character is included.

The expulsion of Yegros from the position of national hero occurs in the text next to the inclusion of certain characters that work as "examples" of true heroism. Thus, the Supreme positions himself within a new and different line. San Martín and, above all, Manuel Belgrano are the Latin American heroes recovered by the text. Simón Bolívar, on the contrary, is regarded with a certain reticence by the Supreme. This is partly because the Pan-American project cherished by Bolívar was not shared by the Supreme, who never joined initiatives that would involve associations with other territories, even though the desire for a true federation is mentioned in the Supreme's discourse.[25] The Supreme dislikes Bolívar because the "Libertador" expressed his intention of invading Paraguay in order to "free" it, motivated by reports that Aimé Bompland was allegedly being held a prisoner there (Roa Bastos *I The Supreme* 296, 299). The Supreme's preference for San Martín over Bolívar is made clear when he mentions their famous meeting in Guayaquil: "No contento [Bolívar] con haberlo fastidiado a San Martín en Guayaquil" (363) ["(Bolívar was) not content with having tripped up San Martín in Guayaquil" (300)].

In this respect, it is particularly interesting to think of the place that José Artigas (1764–1850) occupies within Roa's text. This historical figure, considered Uruguay's national hero, shares some interesting characteristics with Francia. He was opposed to Buenos Aires' centralist ambitions; he planned, as explained above, a federation that could eventually prosper only fugaciously; and he was also the victim of what was called a "black legend" in Uruguay (significantly, the same expression used by Fernández Retamar), created by the Argentine official historiography during the nineteenth century. This "black legend" portrays Artigas as a "gaucho," a "barbarian" that led the mob according to his will (this last characteristic, that of cunningly molding the masses, is part of those attributed to Francia by Lynch). Finally, Artigas has also been appropriated by the Left as having revolutionary ideas or at least as someone who sought to promote social equality.[26] However, he could not carry out the changes he had planned or stay in power for a long period. Unlike Francia, his political life and government were short, and he never thought of himself as a dictator in the same terms as Francia did.

There is one more point of similarity between Francia and Artigas: it deals with historical and biographical events. After being defeated by his enemies, Artigas decides to escape and enter Paraguay as a refugee, were he lived in exile from 1820 to 1850, without ever returning to his country. In *I the Supreme*, there are various references to that event and to the obscure relationships between both characters. To some extent, it is not easy to determine whether Artigas was free or kept as a prisoner. While Lynch interprets Artigas's Paraguayan exile (and that of Bonpland) as an imprisonment,[27] in *I the Supreme*, the narrator's voice says that Paraguay was actually a kind of wall that protected Artigas from his enemies, who repeatedly asked the dictator to put the Uruguayan into their hands (76–78, 308). Throughout the Supreme's discourse, it is possible to notice a certain respect toward Artigas, who is nevertheless sometimes treated as a barbarian, and even as medicine man (!) (21).

In the case of *I, Toussaint Louverture*, the text is itself a dialogue, that is, its external structure consists of something that could be called an interview between the "author" and the central voice of the narration, which would be that of a possible Toussaint Louverture. Moreover, the text makes this dialogue visible, since the protagonist's discourse includes frequent references to a "you" that could be the "accomplice" author but also the reader, considered an accomplice as well, since he is identified with the former (to a certain extent, we find the same dialogic structure that we find between the Supreme and Patiño, who writes his dictation). The fictitious voice of Toussaint introduces—sometimes to ratify his opinions, other times to criticize them—others' points of view and historical narrations, as he adopts a twenty-first-century perspective. This makes it possible for him to draw parallelisms and comparisons with contemporary political situations and characters, from Mao to the U.S. invasion of Iraq in 2003.[28]

I, Toussaint opens three battlefronts in this struggle for the discourse. Like Roa's text, which is aimed at the same time "against" the "anti" and "pro" Francia discourses, that of Fignolé opposes the silencing and the "excessive" ones. The latter, mainly represented by versions of the revolution preceding the second half of the last century, is exemplified by Pauléus Sannon, the author of *Histoire de Toussaint Louverture* (1933), who is referred to as "*votre plus zélé hagiographe,*"(193; italics in the original) ["your most zealous hagiographer"]. In this sense, the novel seems to reject the hagiographic discourse. This is why it constructs a character that is selfish, cynical, and calculating; in other words, human. For this reason, the character is presented as complex and full of contradictions and insecurities; he blames himself and repents for his (and general Rigaud's) actions and their consequences (231–32).

From a contemporary perspective, the character in the novel frequently shows that he has precisely what he lacked in the past: this ability to clearly see and evaluate different historical events. He almost obsessively tries to insert himself into a broader historical discourse. He shows himself as being strongly aware of posterity and of how he can be written and rewritten by history. The voice, which speaks from a present of enunciation situated on April 7, 2003 (14), is able to evaluate his own administration from this perspective and to give his version of it in dialogue with the opinions of historians, politicians, and thinkers. However, the fact that this voice remains the same through time goes along with its protean character: "J'ai survolé deux siècles d'histoire, qui m'ont donné la certitude de mes propres mutations" (149) ["I have flown over two centuries of history, which have given me the certainty of my own mutations"]. These alterations can be seen in the character of the novel, whose faces change constantly.

The character's voice dialogues with many historical characters. This discourse seems more worried about establishing a genealogical line than that of the Supreme, even if here the lines are multiple and contradictory and do not follow a uniform and clear path.[29] In the first place, the text is full of a certain tension regarding the relationships between the main character and Napoleon, who is an enemy, a "father," and a "son,"[30] all at the same time. The identification is explicit: "Je suis le Bonaparte de Saint-Domingue. La colonie ne peut exister sans moi" (239) [I am Saint-Domingue's Bonaparte. The colony cannot exist without me"]. His authority is acknowledged even during the moments of greatest conflict (272). This bond, based on military hierarchies, is respected and maintained. In this sense, the character is a disciple or follower of the French hero. However, the inverse operation is strong as well, and shows the character's "appropriative" logic: Bonaparte is, actually, thanks to his aim to possess the island, his pupil and disciple (226). The idea of the precursor is strong throughout the text and, at a certain point, turns into an absolute. Toussaint would thus be something like a great precursor, the one who initiates everything that succeeds him. Everything that comes after himself is, in this way, explained by him. He understands in absolute terms the idea of causality associated with succession: *post hoc, ergo propter hoc.* He is eventually the origin and cause of everything: "Pourquoi m'appelle-t-on un précurseur sinon pour avoir précédé tous les autres en tous les domaines, pour avoir ouvert toutes les voies"? (150) ["Why do they call me a precursor if not for having preceded everyone else in every domain, for having opened all paths?"].

The fact of being, simultaneously, Napoleon's successor and precursor is clearly part of the character's aim to be included within the discourse of "civilization" that fascinates him. Within this context, France is not the enemy, but an example to follow. Thus, Fignolé's text seems to agree with what Laurent Dubois affirms: "Louverture had not in fact declared independence, and he seems to have still believed that the colony would, and should, remain tied to France" (Dubois 253). The fictional character seems to seek a more discreet revolution as well, a less "revolutionary" one. His "moderate" attitude in comparison to that of Mackandal, and the preference for the European discourse over the African one, from which he distances himself, are some previously discussed examples of this.

This point is of importance because it denies a third reading of the revolution (the silencing and hagiographic discourses being the other two): the reading that, in the sixties, connected the Haitian revolution to the African processes of independence and related these events to the idea of Panafricanism and *négritude.* Fignolé's character tries to distance himself not only from the African process, but also, and more precisely, from the *theoretical* approaches to it, which see in the Haitian Revolution the origin of the twentieth-century events.[31] The character defines himself as being born in Saint-Domingue and claims the island as his origin: "Je n'ai rien à voir avec cette Afrique qui ne peut pas être celle de mes ancêtres" (23) ["I don't have anything to do with this Africa that cannot be that of my ancestors"]. Immediately, this distance is expressed ideologically: "Notre quête de filiation demeure pour eux une coquetterie d'intellectuels et d'artistes à la recherche d'identité, faute de savoir, de pouvoir, de vouloir s'enraciner là où ils sont. Une fantasie de petits-bourgeois" (23) ["Our search for a lineage remains for them a coquetry of intellectuals and artists in search of identity, who do not know how to, do not want to, and cannot root themselves where they are. A petit-bourgeois fantasy"]. The text adopts thus a perspective that, on the one hand, is much more "Haitian," since it is centered on the country's process without assigning an extrinsic meaning to it, without evaluating it for being the cause of *something else.*

On the other hand, there is a broader, and mainly European, historical perspective, the aim to insert the island's history within dialogues and processes to which it had never been related. Thus, the text includes references to the European Union, Charles de Gaulle, Bismarck, Hitler, Vietnam, Cuba, the Paris Commune, Mao, the Industrial Revolution, the cold war, the U.S. hegemony, and many more. The center of attention is not here, however, but in the relations of power and the different plots between Toussaint and the other revolutionary leaders, those who preceded and succeeded him (Sonthonax, Christophe, Dessalines, Laveaux, Pétion, Bouckman, Moyse, and Rigaud). The character is constructed through his relationships with all of them. His voice narrates the history of his own construction as a historical character, all the plots that were necessary in order to seize power, and, finally, his downfall. However, the decolonizing process in Africa is mentioned only in order to separate it from the Haitian Revolution. The character seeks to speak from a different place.

One example is interesting in this sense. It deals with the religious policies imposed by the character, who seeks to abandon the African pagan rites in order to embrace the Roman Catholic faith: "J'imposais pratiquement le catholicisme comme religion d'État" (256) [I practically imposed Catholicism as the State religion]. This goes along with the prohibition to perform family ceremonies in homage to ancestral spirits and the erasure of the African memories in general (257). Thus, the character's intention deals not only with the country's insertion within a Western and European line (Judeo-Christian, we may call it), but also imposes a clear politics of origin. In the same way as the character portrays himself as an absolute founder, Haiti seems not to seek for roots outside of itself and the revolution is self-explanatory. Later on, however, Fignolé's character admits the failure of these policies when he notices that the population subjected the Catholic symbols and rites to those of their own religion; that is to say, that they would continue to interpret and practice religion according to their previous beliefs, disguising the Catholic rite with elements of voodoo (257). The project for a sociocultural homogenization of the island (254) was doomed to failure. The discourse that seeks to erase the African religion and origin (256) is, paradoxically, appropriated by the targets of that operation, who subvert it while eliminating—through the inverse operation of appropriation—the desired artificial homogeneity and creating syncretic practices charged with new and richer symbolic power.

While it would be difficult to define the character of Toussaint Louverture as a dictator, I believe that many of the characteristics I have mentioned here show a considerable distance from the image of the "liberator" that history has frequently associated him with. They show a character in which liberation coexists with authoritarian features and with the desire for absolute power. The celebration of the act of lying (38) and that of Machiavelli's ideas (140) show a ruler who knows, despises, and manipulates the popular mind. For the character's logic, the ends always justify the means—and the end is, precisely, to increase his own importance and power: "Quel homme d'état n'est pas à un moment ou à un autre pris de folie par besoin de se hausser?" (172) ["What statesman does not at some point or another go mad under the desire to elevate himself?"]. Thus, the text carefully narrates the different plans to get rid of his enemies, to erase them from the political map, and to eliminate the opposition in order to reach his goals.

In this sense, it is clear that the will of the population is regarded as secondary or looked at with indifference and disdain. There is always a considerable distance from the people, whose struggle and liberation seem extraneous to Toussaint's voice: "une cause, l'anti-racisme, à laquelle je me crois étranger" (67) ["a cause, anti-racism, to which I feel an alien"]. The "I" even agrees with slavery and justifies his taking part in the slave trade (108). In this sense, the regime he imposes, once in power, does not seem to be too far from the one he has just abolished. Dubois refers to this situation when he explains the polemical nature of this decision taken by the historical character: "Louverture decided that he must preserve the plantation economy and encourage the return of white planters who had fled. Locked in conflict with ex-slaves who had a very different vision of what freedom should mean, he maintained and perfected a coercive system that sought to keep them working on plantations" (Dubois 4). The capitalist and business logic that guides Fignolé's character leads him to justify these decisions and to feel misunderstood by the ex-slaves, who cannot comprehend that these political decisions—alien to them— have been actually taken for their benefit. While he obsessively pursues accumulation of capital, he even dares to suggest "enterrer les libertés accordées et conquises" (265) ["burying the liberties already agreed upon and conquered"]. Toward the end of the novel, a final judgment of his administration shows the conservative character of the revolution: "Qu'est-ce qui avait changé? La direction du pouvoir seulement. Les rapports entre les groupes sociaux demeuraient les mêmes. La société, sans être juridiquement esclavagiste demeurait de type servile" (270) ["What had changed? Only the direction of power. The relationships between social groups remained the same. Society, without being legally proslavery still remained a servile system"].

It is impossible not to think here of the Supreme's model when the character seeks to obtain power (or the presidency at a different moment in the novel) for life (241). The need for peace and stability justifies everything. That is why the slaves, believing to have been freed, cannot understand the disciplining policies imposed upon them by the new government; they cannot fully grasp the paradox inherent to a newly obtained freedom that implies the loss of some rights for which they fought: "Je lui enseignais qu'au nom des droits de l'homme promulgués par la grande Révolution en France en 1789, pour son bien je le privais de quelques-uns de ses droits fondamentaux" (237) ["I taught him (the tiller) that in the name of the rights of man promulgated by the great Revolution in France in 1789, for his benefit I deprived him of some of his fundamental rights"]. The presumption—indeed very typical of "civilized" thought—that the "barbarian" hates to work and cannot be efficient without being coerced is what guides this policy. Moreover, the character refers to "l'horreur du vagabondage" (205) ["the horror of vagrancy"], which has to be repressed. "La malice originelle des nègres, leur sens inné de la comédie" (255) ["The original mischief of negroes, their innate sense of comedy"] would be, in this context, another obstacle for Toussaint's project. Here, the character speaks from a "civilized," white, and, to some extent, racist perspective. This is probably the reason why he holds Henri Christophe as his most legitimate successor, or the least evil of them. While all his successors have been traitors, the character believes that Christophe shared "mon projet de transformer une bande d'esclaves en un peuple de civilisés" (283) ["my project of transforming a band of slaves into a civilized people"].[32]

CLOSING REMARKS:
JACOBINISM AND APPROPRIATIONS

Roberto Fernández Retamar, in his essay "Cuba defendida" (1997), draws a timeline that starts with the experience of the Haitian Revolution, continues with nineteenth-century Paraguay, and ends with the Cuban Revolution. The critic reads the three processes as parallel mainly because of their revolutionary connotations and the fact that these three had a "black legend" built around them by different foreign powers: France, England, and the United States, respectively. Thus, the relationship he draws is objectified in the name "Haipacu," which he uses to baptize an imaginary country whose name consists of the first syllable of each of the three countries, in chronological order (Fernández Retamar 203).

While Fernández Retamar considers the Haitian Revolution as a founding moment within a Latin American context, C. L. R James sees it as a starting point in relation to the African processes of independence and to Pan-Africanism (however, he also sees the Cuban Revolution as the last link in this chain). As I see it, the inclusion of Paraguay, or of the African countries in the second link, signals an important difference of perspective—and of political project—that is worth pointing out. As I have shown above, Fignolé's text also works in this double perspective: even though the character tries to escape from his African past, his successive attempts are always followed by this ghost, in what could be read as a kind of return of the repressed from which he cannot escape (the workers prefer to die than be forced to work). To them, death means a return to Africa, the only land they identify with freedom: "Soucieux de leur proposer l'avenir, je leur en avais fermé la porte. Ils s'étaient remis à rêver au passé, à fantasmer sur une époque lointaine qui les ramenait à l'Afrique mythique de leur mémoire. Elle aura été finalement ma pire ennemie" (237) ["Concerned with proposing them the future, I had closed the door to it. They had started again to dream of their past; to fantasize about a remote age that brought them back to the mythical Africa of their memory. Eventually, this would be my worst enemy"]. The same happens, as we have seen, with the religious aspect.

Fernández Retamar's essay can be read as a particular interpretation, as a construction. The Cuban critic proposes new filiations and genealogies in a manner similar to "official histories," but in an effort to contradict them. This is what *I the Supreme* and *Moi, Toussaint Louverture* do as well. They also destabilize and question, while suggesting new canons, new genealogies, and accounts for the nation. As Carlos Pacheco puts it, Roa's novel implies "un rechazo de lo oficial, de la verdad indiscutida, de lo estático, de lo establecido" ["a rejection of the official, of the never questioned truth, of the static, of the established"] (Pacheco ix). In the appropriation that Fernández Retamar carries out, the Haitian and Paraguayan processes are useful because they legitimize the Cuban Revolution. The Cuban Revolution is conceived in this discourse as a natural consequence, almost inevitable, of the preceding ones, even if at the same time it resignifies and completes them, working thus as their definitive objectification. Actually, this is what the reading of history is about: it happens always in a given present, and in relation to it. Retamar's reading is, just like any other, an interpretation and an attribution of a specific meaning performed from a given discursive place, from which the discourse cannot separate itself. I have tried to point out some of the symbolic battles in which these texts take part, or that occur within them. The discourses of both central characters remain polemical, contradictory, elusive, and perform appropriations while being appropriated by interested readings.[33]

The connection between the Haitian and the Paraguayan processes can be partly attributed to the figure of the "Jacobin." The link between the French and the Haitian revolutions is clear (as well as problematic, tense, changing, as Laurent Dubois and Sibylle Fischer [2004] have showed in different ways). The title of C. L. R James's well-known text refers as well to this connection. If the Haitian Revolution was carried out by "Black Jacobins," I find important to remember that this reading implies a selection within the process of the French Revolution. Since the French Revolution went through profoundly different stages, it is worth pointing out that that the line James draws refers only to the Jacobin period, significantly called the "Terror" by some. Fignolé's novel underscores the importance of Robespierre's principles to the Haitian Revolution, and immediately after doing so, it makes a comparison between Sonthonax, a revolutionary chief admired by the central character, and the French leader: "En cet homme qui savait être intolérant, inflexible, pour atteindre ses buts se cachait un Robespierre" (175) ["Within this man who knew how to be intolerant and inflexible in order to reach his goals there was a hidden Robespierre"]. That which the character admires about Sonthonax is exactly what he himself boasts of having: also for Sonthonax (constructed here as the character's own image and likeness), the end justifies the means. The identification with Jacobinism is later on even clearer: "Je décidai d'unifier l'Éle sous une administration centrale française en conformité avec l'idéal jacobin. Elle serait placée sous un commandement militaire unique. Le mien," (224) ["I decided to unify the island under a central French administration in accordance with the Jacobin ideal. It would be placed under a single military command. Mine"]. As can be seen here, Jacobinism is, for the character, something that goes beyond its ideological aspect and reaches centralism, militarization, and absolute power. This particular reading of Jacobinism performed by the character is interesting, since there are plenty of contradictions within it. The character is a "rebel," even if, at the same time, he seeks to preserve the *status quo*. He is a liberator and an absolutist, an antislavery advocate and the creator of a system based on forced labor. Very much like in the case of the Supreme, we are here before a complex and *sui generis* "Jacobinism."

Many of the interpretations of Gaspar Rodríguez de Francia go in this direction. Ares Pons, Carlos Pacheco, and Fernández Retamar, among others, have pointed out the importance Robespierre had for Francia. These references are also clear in the novel, when the main character speaks to his scrivener: "Fíjate en el busto de escayola de Robespierre a la espera de una palabra" (78) ["Concentrate on the plaster bust of Robespierre and wait for it to speak" (58)]. Ares Pons has read nineteenth-century Paraguayan history from a Socialist perspective; for him, Robespierre's influence (and that of the Jacobin period as a whole) on Gaspar de Francia, has to be understood in this context.[34] C. L. R James, in the 1963 edition of his *Black Jacobins*, adds an appendix titled "From Toussaint L'Ouverture to Fidel Castro," where he affirms that "the Cuban Revolution marks the ultimate stage of a Caribbean quest for national identity" (James 391). In a parallel operation to that of Fernández Retamar, and inversely to him, James reads the Haitian and Cuban processes together, even if he does it within a Caribbean context. I would like to point out, however, that the Cuban Revolution is seen, once again, as the culminating stage within a sequence of revolutionary events, even though it is not itself finished. The central voice in Fignolé's novel seems to be aware of this parallel: "Je réussis ce que tentera plus tard le Che, malheureusement mollement épaulé par Castro" (48) ["I succeeded in doing what the Che tried to realize afterward, unfortunately shyly assisted by Castro"]. Significantly, this quotation performs a subtle inversion of influences. The Cuban Revolution is not the event that closes the process; rather, the process has already been fully completed in Haiti. Through this operation, the precursor is, at the same time, the one that culminates the process, its beginning and end. Everything is read and resignified from the place of the precursor. Later on in the novel, Castro's figure is implicitly cited: "Si l'Histoire doit faire la part équitable entre nous deux, sans aucun doute, elle m'absoudra" (271) ["If History has to make the equitable part among the both of us, undoubtedly, it will absolve me"]. Within the character's obsession with building a historical judgment for himself, with situating himself in a certain way before the historical discourse, and with projecting himself within that discourse and being legitimized by it, it seems that

Fidel Castro's discourse (about which the oscillations I discuss here are permanent) offers, in its aim to be reread by historical discourse, a plausible rhetorical choice.

The Haitian and Paraguayan revolutions[35] have been especially silenced. In the Haitian case, Michel-Rolph Trouillot has showed different operations that have made the revolution "unthinkable" for many years for different political discourses, as well as a "nonevent" for the majority of historical discourses (Trouillant 82, 98), since history books and political processes—like many other discourses that have been analyzed by Sibylle Fischer (2004)[36]—have preferred not to look at it, downplaying its significance and condemning it to the margins or to a passing, dispensable, almost insignificant reference.[37]

Something similar happens with Paraguay. The easy identification of Gaspar Rodríguez de Francia with a "tyrant" or a "despot" quickly eliminates all interesting elements from a character who has a problematic place in the pantheon of heroes and in the foundational moment of the nation. Or, given that his presence is inevitable, it is dissimulated, hidden, played down. Miguel Ángel Pangrazio, in his *Historia política del Paraguay*, explains the achievement of independence as a process carried out by shared responsibilities, although he affirms that "cometen un gravísimo error de concederle todo el mérito de nuestra soberanía a José Gaspar Rodríguez de Francia. Un solo hombre no decide el curso histórico de un pueblo," ["they (he wouldn't say who) commit a terrible mistake when giving all the merit for the achievement of our sovereignty to José Gaspar Rodríguez de Francia. A single man does not decide the historical destiny of a whole people."][38] In our day, Paraguay no longer exists as a special phenomenon, and Latin American history books do not always (nor deeply) dedicate their pages to the *sui generis* character of its historical process during the nineteenth century. There is a relative lack of studies about the country; the interest in its history, literature, and culture seems to have vanished.

My intention throughout these pages has been to point out some narrative operations that seek to reinaugurate debate, which is always welcome and so frequently absent. These novels struggle to destroy silences and different forms of invisibility. They are fictional discourses that continue to construct by being "counter"—that seek to reread, appropriate, and discuss some key figures in Latin American history. I believe that, in this sense, it is urgent to carefully observe, once again, certain processes that always have something to tell us and that help us to think of ourselves as Latin Americans.

NOTES

1. I would like to acknowledge here the invaluable comments made by Sibylle Fischer and Marcos Rohena Madrazo regarding different aspects of this chapter.

2. When I speak of "symbolic battles" in this chapter, I refer to discursive struggles for the appropriation of a given symbol. It is clearly not about physical struggles, but about opposing readings of history and national symbols (corresponding to national projects that are also opposed to each other) that struggle to obtain a major role in the public sphere, in intellectual debates, or in the writing of history.

3. Helene Weldt-Basson also adopts the idea of "counter-history" as a point of departure in order to analyze the different ways in which intertextuality is present in *I the Supreme*. The author distinguishes, according to the *Webster's New Universal Unabridged Dictionary*, three possible uses of the word "counter": "A) opposite, contrary to, as in counter-clockwise; B) in retaliation, as in counterplot; C) opposed to but like, complementary, as in counterpart" (112). Even if I am not intending to work from an intertextual perspective, this definition is still pertinent to my work, since the idea of "counter-history" (in the three senses that Weldt-Basson analyses in detail) will constitute a permanent presence throughout these pages.

4. It is important, however, to make clear in this introduction that Fignolé's character cannot be referred to unproblematically as a "dictator" or a "tyrant." I shall return to this crucial discussion later.

5. Of course, this word did not have at that time the highly negative connotations it has acquired today, mainly since the last dictatorships in the Southern Cone. It would be interesting to think, in this respect, about some specific and popular readings of *I the Supreme*. For example, on the occasion of Roa Bastos' recent death, the obituaries published in some newspapers in the Hispanic world referred to the central character of the novel in rather problematic ways. The following quotation by Ricardo Pacheco Colín on the internet site of *La crónica de hoy* (see "Se rompió Augusto y no hay repuesto: Eduardo Galeano") is a good example: "Este personaje, cultivado por cierto, gusta de la sangre, de los olores nauseabundos, del sexo con las niñas. Anastasio Somoza en Nicaragua; Augusto Pinochet en Chile; Ubico en Guatemala; Porfirio Díaz en México; Getulio [sic] Vargas en Brasil, todos son y no son el Doctor Francia" ["This character, well educated, likes blood, nauseating smells and to have sex with little girls. Anastasio Somoza in Nicaragua; Augusto Pinochet in Chile; Ubico in Guatemala; Porfirio Díaz in Mexico; Getulio [sic] Vargas in Brazil, all of them are and are not, at the same time, Doctor Francia"]. Also, the very well know Spanish newspaper *El País* (*see* elpais.com), on the occasion of Roa Bastos's death affirmed that "Augusto Roa Bastos se introdujo en la piel, los huesos, el pasado y el presente de un tirano—José Gaspar de Francia—un dictador que en el

siglo XIX mantuvo la soberanía paraguaya a fuerza del aislamiento total de sus súbditos. Un desalmado tirano que llevó a su país al oscurantismo" (Augusto Roa Bastos got himself into the skin, the bones, the past and the present of a tyrant—José Gaspar de Francia—a dictator that in the nineteenth century maintained Paraguay's sovereignty by dint of the total isolation of his subjects. A soulless tyrant who lead his country to obscurantism). These and many other examples of misreading, originate, as I see it, in the hasty inclusion of *I the Supreme* within the group of the "novels of Latin American dictatorship," which is regarded—as the dictators themselves—as monolithic and homogenous

6. As it will become clear later, both processes are complementary and at some points cannot be completely distinguished from each other. These two moments are sometimes the same one, since they are interdependent and impossible to conceive in isolation from each other.

7. The Supreme seems to be aware of this logic: "lo peor de lo malo en cuanto a pretextos, las fechas. Esta del 12 de octubre, Día de la Raza, una de ellas. En la tabla de los calendarios parecen inmortales. Rigen la ilusión de la realidad. Menos mal que, por lo menos en el papel, el tiempo puede ser comprimido, ahorrado, anulado" (295) ["the worst of all as far as pretext go: dates. This one of October 12, the Day of the Race, one of them. In the square boxes of the calendars they appear to be immortal. They rule the illusion of reality. Luckily time, on paper at least, can be compressed, saved, done away with" (241)]. Beyond theory, another proof—in this case, a historical one—of the awareness of Francia regarding the importance of commemoration is objectified in the fact that his own birthday was a national holiday during his government, in a moment in which annual celebrations dedicated to heroes were almost inexistent in the continent (462, Spanish version; 385, English version).

8. These problems have been extensively discussed in my article "Las fechas y la invención del sistema simbólico nacional en América Latina." Trouillot also analyses the symbolic implications of commemoration.

9. When I write "the Supreme" in this article (without inverted commas or any special typeface), I am always referring to the narrative voice that dominates Roa's text (I also identify it as the "main character"), which is the particular reading of a historical character (with whom it should not be confused) carried out by the author throughout the text. This expression is used by some authors to refer to the biographical Dr. Francia, but never by me.

10. Note that all translations of *Yo el Supremo* are taken from Augusto Roa Bastos, *I The Supreme*, translated by Helen Lane.

11. Fischer's article shows the fissures that the presence of the indigenous voice causes within a discourse that presents itself as uniform and definitive. That other's "voice" makes the contradictions within The Supreme's discourse evident, and remains untouched by its manipulative

and interpretative strategies. To a certain extent, the indigenous voice operates in relation to the Supreme's voice in the same way as the latter operates in relation to the official historical discourse. In this article, I am more interested in the mythical discourse as a *form* within the process of autoconstruction performed by the Supreme than in the ways its *content* is read by his voice during the same process, even though both strategies cannot be sharply distinguished.

12. Note that all translations of Fignolé's text are mine. I would like to thank Alexandre Bonafos for his help with the English translation of Fignolé's novel.

13. There are, as a matter of fact, various "openings." Toussaint narrates how he acquires his surname and erases the original one, "Bréda," which brought him memories of his own origin, now forgotten and hidden: "l'état-major du général Laveaux m'appella Toussaint l'ouverture. Affectueusement. Je gardai le nom. Ma foi, il était plus sympathique que Bréda qui me rappelait trop mon passé. Trop de mauvais souvenirs" (163) ["the Joint Chiefs of Staff under General Laveaux named me Toussaint l'ouverture. With affection. I kept the name. My goodness, it was much nicer than that of Bréda which made me remember my past too much. Too many bad memories"]. The surname "l'ouverture" is thus a new beginning, an "opening" to new (auto) constructions.

14. Alejo Carpentier's version, in his novel *The Kingdom of this World*, 50–51, tries to show the way in which Mackandal was conceived within the imaginary of Haitian slaves: "What did the whites know of Negro matters? In his cycle of metamorphoses, Macandal had often entered the mysterious world of the insects, making up for the lack of his human arm with the possession of several feet, four wings, or long antennæ. He had been fly, centipede, moth, ant, tarantula, ladybug, even a glow-worm with phosphorescent green lights. When the moment came, the bonds of the Mandingue, no longer possessing a body to bind, would trace the shape of a man in the air for a second before they slipped down the post. And Macandal, transformed into a buzzing mosquito, would light on the very tricorne of the commander of the troops to laugh at the dismay of the whites." Although the narrator makes clear later on that Mackandal did really die on that occasion, what matters is that mythical thinking was stronger than "facts." For the slaves who attended the execution there was no doubt: Mackandal had managed to escape, transforming himself once again.

15. We could compare Mackandal's discourse, in this respect, to that of the Indigenous peoples in *I the Supreme*. Both voices are subsequently interpreted, appropriated, and erased by the central respective voices.

16. The aforementioned essay by Pacheco, where he realizes an analysis of *I the Supreme* within the Bakhtinian conception of dialogism, turns out to be very useful from this perspective, although this is not exactly the point of view I assume here.

17. In this sense, the novels by Roa and Fignolé also have in common the absence of an action that is exterior to the voices. If we were to sum up the novels' anecdote, we could only say that both texts are about voices that narrate (themselves). None of the central characters (who are, more precisely, voices) "performs" any action: they just speak (the inverted commas refer to the fact that, as we know, language can also "do" things; that is, it can have a performative function).

18. See:Diccionario de la Real Academia Española, http://buscon.rae.es/draeI/SrvltConsulta?TIPO_BUS=3&LEMA=vocero].

19. Mitre is also partly responsible for another "black legend," according to which José Artigas, whose relations with Buenos Aires during the process of independence has some points in common with those of Dr. Francia, was considered a "bandit" and a "barbarian" until the last decades of the century. I shall come back to the relationship between Artigas and Francia, to which Ana Ribeiro has dedicated her book *El caudillo y el dictador.*

20. It is worth remembering, in this respect, the genocidal War of the Triple Alliance (1864–1870), in which Brazil, Argentina, and Uruguay joined their forces against Paraguay. As a result, the latter's population was reduced to half of what it was prior to the war, and the masculine population almost disappeared: "Although reliable statistics do not exist, we can accept the estimate of 525,000 as Paraguay's population in 1865 with relative equanimity . . . A count made in 1871, under supervision of the victors, found 221,079 people in the country. Of these survivors, 106,254 were women, 86,079 were children, and 28,746 were men" (Warren 243). Mitre was President of Argentina during the first years of the war, and Roa's novel refers to this (108).

21. The historian criticizes Dr. Francia very harshly from a liberal and democratic perspective, and calls him "sinister" (105) and "bizarre" (110). Basing his own account largely on that of the brothers Robertson (who throughout *I the Supreme* are constantly considered as holding misleading opinions in the service of imperial interests), Lynch dismisses the idea of considering Dr. Francia's dictatorship as revolutionary, and affirms: "In fact social reform was alien to the dictator's mentality, and he did nothing to disturb the basic structure of society" (116). Besides, he criticizes the inexistence of a commercial agriculture and of a landowner class, and points out an extraordinary delay in the abolition of slavery (116). Lynch states that even if Francia maintained independence and national sovereignty, this was done to the detriment of industrial development, liberties, and commerce. However, I actually see in Lynch's analysis a certain uneasiness regarding the absence of a real capitalist development in Paraguay (104–17). It would be interesting to ask ourselves to which "revolutions" does Lynch's title refer, since, if there were no structural changes in Paraguay, it is highly questionable to affirm that they existed somewhere else in the continent.

22. Rubén Bareiro Saguier refers as well to this situation in "Estructura autoritaria y producción literaria en el Paraguay" (533), and includes, as an appendix, a terribly written manifest by the "Anti-Communist Paraguayan Centre 'General Rogelio R. Benítez,' which claims to continue to be faithful to Francia's "spiritual energies" (538). In relation to the different Paraguayan approaches to Dr. Francia's figure, I would like to mention here the kind help provided by Mr. Oscar Centurión, the Cultural Attaché at the Paraguayan Embassy in the United States, with whom I had illuminating conversations while preparing this essay.

23. As a matter of fact, the text subtly makes this appropriation impossible. The mention of "The Great Tutelary Toad" who "ha mandado extraer las piedras para pavimentar esta maldita ciudad" (342) ["has ordered to quarry stones from it to the streets of this accursed city" (281)] could be read as a reference to Stroessner. Furthermore, there is an allusion to the construction of the Itaipú dam, under his presidency, a mistake that benefited Brazil economically and militarily: "Los saltos de agua. Las presas. Sobre todo las presas que quieren convertirnos en una presa ao gosto do Imperio mais grande do mundo!" (288) ["The waterfalls. The dam sites. Above all those damned sights fixed on Paraguay by the Imperio mais grande do mundo" (235)]. Finally, in the appendix, we can see the contradictions into which historians fall while trying, in 1961, to appropriate Francia through the recovery of his mortal remains. Through these contradictions and the parodic tone used here, we can read a rejection of these appropriative efforts.

24. Yegros and Francia ruled together for a brief period at the beginning of the revolutionary process. Once the perpetual dictatorship had been established; however, the former—who was the latter's cousin—was accused of planning a conspiracy against the government and executed on July 17, 1821. It is worth noticing that the erasure of Yegros' discourse that takes place in the novel is a textual parallel to the historical and performative erasure carried on by the dictator.

25. For example, in Roa's novel, Paraguay proposes to Buenos Aires that a federation should be the only possible political alliance between Latin American peoples, and situates it in a context close to Pan-Americanism: "Esta fue la primera vez en la historia americana que resonó la palabra Federación, tan famosa después en las guerras civiles, en sus congresos constituyentes y en sus destinos futuros. Esta célebre nota puede considerarse como la primer acta de Confederación levantada en el Río de la Plata. El Paraguay regalaba pues a los porteños esta idea que podía resolver de golpe todos sus problemas. Proyectaba para América toda, antes que ningún otro pueblo, la forma de su destino futuro" (237) ["This was the first time that there had resounded in the history of the American continent the word Fede-ration, so famous later in its civil wars, its constituent congresses, its future destinies. This celebrated note may be considered to be the first act of Confederation proposed in the

Río de la Plata. Paraguay freely offered the Porteños this idea that could resolve all its problems at one stroke. It projected, for all of America, before any other people, the form of its future destiny" (192)]. Francia not only rejected proposals from Buenos Aires, but also refused to be a part of the Federación de Provincias Unidas whose leader was, around 1815, José Gervasio Artigas, and which projected a federal system that would unite the provinces of Northern Argentina, the Banda Oriental— as the territory that is now Uruguay was known by then—and Paraguay against Buenos Aires.

26. Like almost every national hero (including, of course, Francia), Artigas has also been appropriated by the right. The Uruguayan dictatorship (1973–84) maintained a totally pro-Artigas discourse, augmenting his mythical dimension.

27. "Foreigners caught in the trap, especially after 1820, remained in Paraguay year after year, dead to the rest of the world. The French naturalist, Aimé Bompland, was held for eight years; Artigas never returned to his native Uruguay" (Lynch 112).

28. Besides the specific mention of the Iraq war, there are some expressions that clearly refer to this nightmarish conflict while ironically identifying Napoleon and G. W. Bush. The former would have initiated a "preventive war" because the latter supposedly possessed "weapons of mass destruction" (70). Like in *I the Supreme*, these kinds of references transform the act of enunciation into an almost atemporal or eternal present. The difference would be that while the Supreme's voice is for the most part anchored in 1840, from where it repeatedly travels to different points in the future to come back again, Toussaint's voice in Fignolé's novel comments on the historical events from an invariable contemporary perspective. The 1840 perspective is mobile, while that of 2003 (we could situate the present of writing presumably in that year) is much more stable.

29. The Supreme tries, inversely, to deny some genealogies, as shown above.

30. The erasure of the family we analyzed above includes also the children, by whom the character feels betrayed. He accuses them of being Francophiles because they prefer the metropolis to Haiti. Regarding Napoleon, it is worth noting that there is also his engraving in the Supreme's room, next to that of Robespierre (160, 198–99, Spanish version; 58, 89–90, English version). While he recognizes both Napoleon and Robespierre as possible "fathers," in what seems almost a contradiction (only if we consider their political ideas, since both of them were in different ways liberators and tyrants), he also vindicates certain independence with respect to Bonaparte: "No sabía yo que en los días de aquella época el gran Napoleón había pronunciado iguales o parecidas palabras" (134) ["I didn't know that around that time the great Napoleon had uttered the same or similar words" (38)].

31. Apart from the classical account by C. L. R. James, intellectuals such as Aimé Césaire, Franz Fanon, or Édouard Glissant have expressed similar interpretations. Laurent Dubois, writing in the twenty-first century, goes one step further and states that the Haitian Revolution was not only the founder of the African processes, but that "it was itself in many ways an African revolution" (Dubois 5).

32. Frank Moya Pons (249) confirms this: "Henry Christophe pursued the policies of his predecessor, Toussaint, attempting to preserve the plantations and their labor force intact." Henri Christophe has been also represented in interesting ways, generally as an excessive, tyrannical oppressor, although the different versions show slightly different approaches. I think here mainly of Alejo Carpentier, who devotes the third part of *The Kingdom of this World* to the rise and fall of Christophe's reign. Ti Noel, the character who acts as a connecting thread between the different moments in the Haitian revolutionary process, thinks that he is under "a slavery as abominable as that he had known on the plantation of M. Lenormand de Mézy. Even worse, for there was a limitless affront in being beaten by a Negro as black as oneself, as thick-lipped and wooly-headed, as flat-nosed; as low-born; perhaps branded, too" (122). In Aimé Césaire's *La tragédie du roi Christophe*, written in 1963, it is possible to find a shocking scene in which the king beholds in the distance a worker who is sleeping at an improper time and immediately has him shot from the fortress (78–79).

33. While doing research for this essay, I found something particularly curious and relevant in this sense. In a 2003 open letter to Roa Bastos, Yolanda Huerga, wife of a Cuban "dissident" who was by then a prisoner in Cuba, quotes the condemnatory words that close the novel and asks for his support, since he has been able to represent in his work "los rasgos y características propios de una dictadura que mutila todas las libertades y desangra al pueblo por una lucha por la supervivencia" (www.cubanet.org) ["the characteristics and features typical of a dictatorship that mutilates all liberties and lets its people bleed to death for a struggle for survival"]. Thus, *I the Supreme* is also appropriated by the Cuban dissidence with the opposite sense to the one Fernández Retamar reads in it, and at the same moment in which Roa expresses his support for the regime with his visit. Each of them performs a different interested reading of the text and interprets the central character as a tyrant or a liberator. This is, in a certain sense, what I have shown here: the novel makes it possible for the reader to find both images. That is to say, both tyranny and liberation are present *simultaneously* in the same character. As I have suggested above, this ambiguity exists also in relation to the historical character, since Francia has been not only an exemplary figure for leftist groups and thinkers in Latin America (Fernández Retamar and Ares Pons are two samples of this position), but also regarded as Paraguay's national hero during Stroessner's dictatorship.

34. The figure of Francia is completely ignored in texts in which we could expect to find, if not a complete analysis, at least a mention of him. I am thinking of Lucía Sala de Tourón's article "Jacobinismo, democracia y federalismo" ["Jacobinism, Democracy and Federalism"]. Considering the closeness of the historian to Marxist thinking, this omission seems almost shameful. As I see it, this is telling about the silencing that surrounded the Paraguayan process.

35. The very definition of "revolution" is problematic in relation to these processes, and it seems obvious to me that its connotations are not the same for both of them. For example, while the presence of extreme violence in Haiti is evident, in Paraguay, Francia's government was characterized by an absolute peace and stability from its very beginning, and violence appeared only to *break* the process many years after his death. When I suggest that there was no violence during the Paraguayan "Revolution," I think of violence as a massive phenomenon, as a popular revolt, since it is undeniable that there were public executions and repression during Francia's dictatorship. In any event, here I am trying to expose the complexities that the word "revolution" implies in these cases—and, actually, in every case—with an almost banal example that omits the ideological, theoretical, and political connotations of the concept, which I cannot discuss in depth here, even if I believe to have implicitly discussed the problem from different angles throughout this essay.

36. The official Cuban discourse during colonial times intended to ignore the revolution at all costs (Fischer 3–6). The dimensions of the terror generated by the ghost of the Haitian Revolution in Cuba are also visible in *Sab* (1841), by Gertrudis Gómez de Avellaneda, the canonical antislavery novel of nineteenth-century Cuba: "-En sus momentos de exaltación, señor, he oído gritar a la vieja India: -La tierra que fue regada con sangre una vez lo será aún otra; los descendientes de los opresores serán oprimidos, y los hombres negros serán los terribles vengadores de los hombres cobrizos. –Basta, Sab, basta, -interrumpió don Carlos, con cierto disjusto [sic]; porque siempre alarmados los cubanos, después del espantoso y reciente ejemplo de una isla vecina" ["In her moments of exaltation, Sir, I have heard the old Indian woman shout: -The land that was flooded with blood once, will be again; the descendants from the oppressors will be oppressed, and black men will be the terrible avengers of the copper-coloured men. –Enough, Sab, enough, -interrupted don Carlos, with a certain uneasiness; since Cubans, always alarmed after the horrifying and recent example given by a neighbouring island"] (*Sab* 93). The presence of the Haitian Revolution continues to be—not "recently," but forty years later—terrifying and unspeakable though inevitable, a trauma that helped to justify the gradual and considerably slow changes toward abolitionism by Cuban intellectuals.

37. In the article in which I discuss the construction of the Latin American symbolic system, I refer to a very well known book, precisely about the

abolition of slavery, in which the Haitian Revolution is not studied. See Uriarte 372–73.

38. Pangrazio, 60. This polemic and revealing fragment goes on somehow ambiguously, since immediately after the quoted words, the author admits that the "el mérito de haber administrado el delicado proceso de nuestra independencia" (60) ["merit of having administered the delicate process that was our independence"] corresponded to Francia, the author immediately points out again that "no es pertinente identificar nuestra autonomía política con la personalidad del Dr. Francia, ni menos atribuirle la formación de nuestra nacionalidad" (60) [it isn't appropriate to identify our political autonomy with Dr. Francia's personality, let alone to attribute to him the formation of our nationality]. The identification and attribution to which Pangrazio refers are exactly the ones that *I the Supreme* carries out.

WORKS CITED

Ares Pons, Roberto. *El Paraguay del siglo XIX: Un estado socialista*. Montevideo: Nuevo Mundo, 1987. Print.

Bareiro Saguier, Rubén. "Estructura autoritaria y producción literaria en el Paraguay." *Lectura crítica de la literatura americana. Actualidades fundacionales*. Ed. Saúl Sosnowski. Caracas: Biblioteca Ayacucho, 1997. 526–38. Print.

Borges, Jorge Luis. "Nota sobre Walt Whitman." *Obras completas. 1923–1972*. Buenos Aires: Emecé, 1974. 249–53. Print.

Carpentier, Alejo. *The Kingdom of this World*. Trans. Harriet de Onís. New York: The Noonday Press, 1994. Print.

Césaire, Aimé. *La tragédie du roi Christophe*. Paris: Présence Africaine, 1970. Print.

Dubois, Laurent. *Avengers of the New World. The Story of the Haitian Revolution*. Cambridge: Belknap Press of Harvard University Press, 2004. Print.

elpais.com. "Muere Augusto Roa Bastos, azote del poder." *Muere Augusto Roa Bastos, azote del poder*. April 27, 2005. http://www.elpais.com/articulo/cultura/Muere/Augusto/Roa/Bastos/azote/poder/elpepicul/20050427elpepicul_2/Tes. (October 2007). Web.

Ezquerro, Milagros. "Introduction." *Yo el Supremo*, by Augusto Roa Bastos. Madrid: Cátedra, 2003. 9–75. Print.

Fernández Retamar, Roberto. "Cuba defendida." *Cuba defendida*. Buenos Aires: Nuestra América, 2004. 199–228. Print.

Fignolé, Jean-Claude. *Moi, Toussaint Louverture . . . avec la plume complice de l'auteur*. Mont-Royal, Québec: Plume & Encre, 2004. Print.

Fischer, Sibylle. "El sujeto y su discurso: la construcción de la voz indígena en *Yo el Supremo*." *Revista Hispánica Moderna* 44.1 (June 1991): 93–107. Print.

————. *Modernity Disavowed. Haiti and the Cultures of Slavery in the Age of Revolution*. Durham: Duke University Press, 2004. Print.

Gómez de Avellaneda, Gertrudis. *Sab*. La Habana: Consejo Nacional de Cultura/Editorial Nacional de la Habana, 1963. Print.

Huerga, Yolanda. "Carta abierta a Augusto Roa Bastos." *Ola represiva. Carta abierta a Augusto Roa Bastos/ Yolanda Huerga. Prensa independiente de Cuba*. August 20, 2003. www.cubanet.org/CNews/y03/ago03/20a7 .htm (October 2006). Web.

James, C. L. R. *The Black Jacobins. Toussaint L'Ouverture and the San Domingo Revolution*. 2nd ed. New York: Random House, 1963. Print.

Lynch, John. *The Spanish American Revolutions. 1808–1826*. London: Weidenfeld and Nicolson, 1973. Print.

Moya Pons, Frank. "Haiti and Santo Domingo, 1790–c.1870." *The Cambridge History of Latin America. Volume III. From Independence to c.1870*. Ed. Leslie Bethell. Cambridge: Cambridge University Press, 1985. 237–55. Print.

Pacheco, Carlos. "*Yo el Supremo*: la insurrección polifónica." Introduction to Augusto Roa Bastos, *Yo el Supremo*. Caracas: Biblioteca Ayacucho, 1986. ix-liii. Print.

Pacheco Colín, Ricardo. "Se rompió Augusto y no hay repuesto: Eduardo Galeano". *La crónica de hoy*. April 27th 2005. www.cronica.com.mx/nota .php?id_nota=178643 (Octubre 2006). Web.

Pangrazio, Miguel Ángel. *Historia política del Paraguay*. Vol. I. Asunción: Intercontinental, 1999. Print.

Real Academia Española. *Diccionario de la lengua española. Vigésima segunda edición*. http://www.rae.es. (May 2007). Web.

Ribeiro, Ana. El caudillo y el dictador. Buenos Aires: Planeta, 2003. Print.

Roa Bastos, Augusto. "Algunos núcleos generadores de un texto narrativo." *Escritura* 2.4 (1977): 167–93. Print.

————. *I the Supreme*. Trans. Helen Lane. Normal, IL: Dalkey Archive Press, 2000. Print.

————. *Yo el Supremo*. Madrid: Alfaguara, 1984. Print.

Saer, Juan José. "La mayor." *Cuentos completos (1957–2000)*. Buenos Aires: Seix Barral, 2001. 125–44. Print.

Sala de Tourón, Lucía. "Jacobinismo, democracia y federalismo." *Calidoscopio latinoamericano*. Coord. Waldo Ansaldi. Buenos Aires: Ariel, 2004. 33–50. Print.

Tovar, Francisco. *Las historias del dictador. Yo el Supremo, de Augusto Roa Bastos*. Barcelona: del Mall, 1987. Print.

Trouillot, Michel-Rolph. *Silencing the Past: Power and the Production of History*. Boston: Beacon, 1995. Print.

Uriarte, Javier. "Las fechas y la invención del sistema simbólico nacional en América Latina." *Derechos de memoria. Actas, actos, voces, héroes y fechas: nación e independencia en América Latina*. Ed. Hugo Achugar. Montevideo:

Facultad de Humanidades y Ciencias de la Educación, Universidad de la República, 2003. 345–400. Print.

Warren, Harris Gaylord. *Paraguay. An Informal History.* Westport: Greenwood, 1949. Print.

Weldt-Basson, Helene Carol. *Augusto Roa Bastos's* I the Supreme. *A Dialogic Perspective.* Columbia: University of Missouri Press, 1993. Print.

Rewriting in Roa Bastos's Late Fiction

"El ojo de la luna," *El fiscal*, and *Los conjurados del Quilombo del Gran Chaco*[1]

Jorge Carlos Guerrero

Roa Bastos's practice of rewriting has been diversely viewed, with some critics regretting it and others applauding his efforts. Tomás Eloy Martínez's stands out among the critics upholding a negative view.[2] In his 2005 obituary, entitled "Roa Bastos todavía está aquí," ["Roa Bastos is Still Here"] this writer and old friend since the early days of Argentine exile was particularly blunt in this regard. He suggested Roa Bastos's writing of recent years had diminished in quality, and he attributed it to the author's return to Paraguay after decades of exile. Paraguay, the recovered home, was not a place of writing, but rather the last stage in Roa Bastos's existential journey, a place of farewells and death. Martínez tells us he expressed his disappointment to the author in one of their intermittent telephone conversations: "Después del *Supremo*, me pareció que su camino de narrador navegaba con las velas caídas, y se lo dije" (After the *Supreme*, it seemed to me his writing had gone adrift, and I told him so).[3] Martínez, however, judged very favourably as "otra de sus obras maestras" (another masterpice) a text that Roa Bastos had sent him in 2002. It was "Frente al frente argentino," part of a larger text published in 2001 with three other writers and entitled *Los conjurados del Quilombo del Gran Chaco* (2001) [*The Conspirers of the Shanty of the Greater Chaco*].[4] *Los conjurados* is peculiar, even sui generis, on several counts. It is a collective project that involves authors from Argentina, Brazil, and Uruguay. It delves into the issue of the War of Paraguay, but from a perspective that transcends the national framework from which Roa Bastos traditionally approached the subject. It also responds to the frustrations and hopes generated by unprecedented transformations in the geopolitics of the Southern Cone, namely, regional integration. Finally, it is part of an intellectual engagement that posits the need to address nationalism and the common past as a necessary step for cultural, economic, and political integration in Latin America.

Roa Bastos' critical intratextuality in *Los conjurados* refers to "El ojo de la luna" (1991) and *El fiscal* (1993). I will examine the author's rewriting with the objective of establishing the extent of the transformations, and of showing how they meaningfully develop recurrent themes in his fiction. I propose to show that the author's act of rewriting in the three texts is part of a creative process that in its self-referentiality seeks to attain a synthesis or overall fictional coherence. I share the position of critics who have rejected the notion of a "pointless rehashing of his previous work" and emphasize the creative dimension of Roa Bastos's critical intratextuality (Weldt-Basson, "Augusto Roa Bastos's *Contra-vida*," 93). Furthermore, Roa Bastos's practice provides an insight into autobiographical presence in his writing as the author engages critically with his previous texts and transforms them in a process of metafictional reflection.

"EL OJO DE LA LUNA"

"El ojo de la luna" is divided into seven parts. Three sections center on Sir Richard Burton as a character who is both a diplomat travel-ing in Paraguay during the war and the author of the *Letters from the Battlefields in Paraguay* (1870), and four sections revolve around the biography of the Argentine painter Cándido López. Both historical figures turned literary characters are described as witnesses and narra-tors of the war (13). In a postmodern fashion, the third person narrator announces from the outset a narration about narrations, a multiplica-tion of discourses that will ultimately question the notion of truth and the possibility of representing the past. The narrator explains (13) that the "hechos" ("facts") witnessed and narrated by Cándido López and Burton are absent from "la historia oficial de los vencedores" ("the official history of the victors") and "la desmemoriada contrahistoria de los vencidos" ("forgetful version of the defeated"). These "facts," which should be interpreted in the sense given by Hayden White to them (elements in the historian's plot) in opposition to "events" (elements in the historical record before narrativization), are essential ingredients of the new plot of "El ojo de la luna" (17).

According to the narrator, his account of Burton's actions and writing derives from the *Letters from the Battlefields in Paraguay* (1870). However, he introduces the story with a statement that blurs the distinction between history and fiction: "Y es verdad que en esas cartas-crónicas flota . . . el aire mágico e irreal de *Las Mil y Una Noches* . . . El mismo parecía un personaje escapado de ese libro" (14) ["And it is true that in those letters . . . the magical and imaginary air of *The One Thousand and One Nights* flows . . . He himself looked like an escaped character from that book"]. Burton travels through the battlefields enjoying the "descenso a los infiernos en el corazón de la selva tropical" (13) ["descent to hell in the heart of the tropical forest"]. He witnesses atrocities, observes the artist Cándido López painting at the end of combats, and spends time with Solano López and Elisa Lynch in their camp.

The narrator appeals to textual authority to support his narration. He quotes or comments on letters with reassuring statements (14) such as "escribe el ex capitán de la campaña de Egipto" ["the ex capitan of the Egyptian campaign writes"] or "explica Burton en una nota" ["Burton explains in a note"]. None of these references appears in the actual *Letters*, but the reader's lack of acquaintance with the document does not constitute an obstacle to understanding the irony since much of the account relies on missing notes (15). Based on lost, and therefore inaccessible, notes, the narrator describes Burton's conversations in the Paraguayan leader's headquarters. The text centers on the parody of Paraguayan historical revisionism. In Burton's interview with Solano López, the latter anachronically expresses the historiographic thesis developed in the twentieth century to explain the war and legitimize authoritarianism in Paraguay. Solano López explains

> que la inicua guerra que estaba devastando el país había sido instigada y financiada por el Imperio británico . . . el imperio trocó la enseña corsaria de Sir Francis Drake y sus congéneres, por la patente de corso de la 'independencia protegida' y del 'libre cambio,' y la ha entregado a las fuerzas de Buenos Aires y el imperio del Brasil. Inglaterra necesita destruir el Paraguay, el único obstáculo en su invasión piratesca. (16)
>
> that the wicked war that was devastating the country had been instigated and financed by the British Empire . . . the Empire exchanged

the pirate flag of Sir Francis Drake and others like him for the letter of marquee of 'supervised independence' and 'free trade' and has handed it to the forces of Buenos Aires and the Empire of Brazil. England needs to destroy Paraguay, the only obstacle in its pirate-like invasion.

In addition to this parody of historical revisionism, the text carnavalizes the national hero. Burton has set his eyes on Solano López's wife. Under the spell of a veritable "coup de foudre" (15), he represents the Paraguayan leader, the obstacle to the realization of his sexual fantasy, as a grotesque figure: "Lo ve de baja estatura, abultado abdomen, nariz chata de leopardo, los ojos ribeteados de una orla de sangre, la cara enormemente hinchada por el dolor de muelas" (15) ["He sees him as having a short stature, bulging belly, flat leopard nose, blood-shot eyes, his face enormously swollen by his tooth ache"].

This carnavalization extends to all the historical figures in the text. In the third section, the narrator refers to the story of a globe sent by Solano López in a secret mission to eliminate the Marquiz de Caxias. The Brazilian general was saved by a "mero azar, pues se hallaba negociando necesidades íntimas en el retrete" (18) ["pure chance, only because he was negotiating his intimate needs on the toilet"]. The hero is grotesquely reduced to "negotiating" his very human needs; his bodily functions are what save him, not any heroic deeds. Later, in a metafictional comment, the narrator will clarify the narrative excess of Burton's writing. He tells us that Burton "hizo, en este punto, sin quererlo quizá, lo único que se puede hacer con la historia: no parafrasearla sino parodiarla" (21) ["made at this point, perhaps, without intending it, the only thing that can be done with history: namely, not to paraphrase it, but rather parody it"]. This explains the proliferation of narrations called to support other narrations.

The story of the assassination attempt serves as a transition to Cándido López's pictorial representation as authoritative source on the event. The narrator informs that "Hay un testimonio irrefutable de esta hazaña de fantasmas" (17) ["There is an irrefutable testimony of this ghostly exploit"]. There are two paintings where the globe appears and in one of them:

> se ve el centelleo de los sables entrando sigilosamente . . . Un imperceptible efecto óptico produce la impresión de que la cabeza del jefe, demudada de horror, se halla separada del tronco por una delgada estría. Se ha vuelto, implorante, hacia sus invisibles asaltantes, es decir, hacia el relumbrar de los sables. (18)

the glint of the sabers can be seen entering stealthily . . . An impercep-
tible optical effect produces the impression that the head of the leader,
altered by fear, is separated from the body by a slim striation-like line.
He has turned, imploring, toward his invisible assailants, that is, toward
the glare of the sabers.

These paintings are among the artist's "centenares de escenas de la
guerra" (hundreds of war scenes) that are all exhibited today in the
National Museum of Asunción "donde el público puede verlas" (18)
["where the public can see them"]. The historical record conflicts
with this statement; the painter's entire collection is in Argentina, not
Paraguay, and consists of seventy paintings (Pacheco 8). Moreover,
the paintings described above contradict Burton's contention that
the Brazilian general was "negotiating his intimate needs." This is
all the more problematic when considering, as the narrator is careful
to emphasize, that Cándido López is obsessed with photographic or
realist representation.

Furthermore, we soon learn that the hundreds of paintings were
illegally copied by the Paraguayan painter Ignacio Núñez Soler during a month-long exhibit organized by the Argentine government
to commemorate the "cincuentenario de la unidad argentina de la
que fue árbitro y arquitecto el extinto mariscal Solano López; triunfo
diplomático inaugural que no impidió la derrota y la destrucción
del pueblo paraguayo" (22) ["fifty years of Argentine national unity
whose arbitrator and architect was the deceased marshal Solano López;
an inaugural diplomatic triumph that did not prevent the defeat and
destruction of the Paraguayan Nation"]. There is not only a proliferation of narrations, but also of paintings and painters. Additionally, the
incident underscores Solano López as responsible for a geopolitical
order that dooms him. In an ironic twist of poetic justice, the collection sent back to Buenos Aires is made up of "los cuadros copiados
en secreto por Ignacio Núñez Soler y no los originales de Cándido
López" (23) ["the pictures copied secretly by Ignacio Núñez Soler
and not Cándido López's originals"].

Cándido López is also an embodiment of the figure of the artist.
As a former assistant to Bartolomé Mitre, Cándido appeals to him for
help. He despairs in "la afligente miseria material y espiritual en que
me ha sumido la muerte de mi hermano Teo, el único que cuidaba de
mi despedazada y ya ruin persona" (19) ["the distressing material and
spiritual misery in which I was plunged by the death of my brother
Teo, the only one who looked after my battered and despicable
being"]. The reference points to Van Gogh and his relationship with

his brother Theo. Mitre does not heed the call for help of a painter whose works "le recordaban errores" ["reminded him of mistakes"] made during the war, such as the defeat in the battle of Curupaytí or the high price paid for the provocation involving the delivery of the globe to Solano López that resulted in the aforementioned assassination attempt (19). In fact, the narrator informs that Mitre "mandó ocultar expresamente el cuadro que reproduce con inocente ironía . . . la escena de donación del globo" (19) ["ordered to hide the picture that reproduces with naive irony . . . the scene of the globe's donation"]. Availability and access to historical documentation crucial for the historian's task is thus largely dependent on power, an element that also underscores the narrator's possible access to documentation.

Cándido López loses the General's favor owing to his "instinto . . . pictórico pero también moral" ["pictorial but also moral instinct"] and to his stay in the theater of war until the very end, a decision that Mitre "no perdonó" ["did not forgive"] because for him the attitude of the assistant represented a desertion (19). For the narrator, Mitre is unable to understand the painter's "inquebrantable sentido de entereza moral en total aleación con la integridad de su conciencia artística" (19) ["unshakable sense of moral fortitude fused with the integrity of his artistic conscience"]. Roa develops the theme of the artist's mutilation, alluded to by the reference to Van Gogh, and also in the biographical reference to the historical Cándido López, who lost his right hand during the war. Cándido López becomes the "mutilado pintor" ["mutilated painter"] who is both "una metáfora corporal del daño de la guerra y su propio comentario" (19) ["a corporal metaphor of the damage caused by war and his own commentary"]. However, the narrator subtly suggests that the artist's integrity is explained by his literary origins. We are told about his provincial soul ("provinciano de alma") despite being a "porteño" ["from Buenos Aires"]; this inhabitant of Buenos Aires is a good *gaucho* ["gaucho bueno"], a sort of Martín Fierro: "Había en él un gaucho rebelde a la injusticia y a los privilegios" (19) ["He exhibited the gauchos' typical rejection of injustice and privilege"]. It is his gaucho soul that leads Cándido López to embrace "el dolor paraguayo" (20) ["Paraguay's suffering"]. He commits himself to depicting the war in the middle of the battlefields as all his limbs are slowly blown apart: "El pintor decrece en la misma medida en que va siendo mutilado ese pueblo al que ve sucumbir" (21) ["The painter's mutilated body mirrors the mutilation of the nation that he himself is witnessing"]. Cándido López is partly the victim of a mysterious unmerciful eye who always watches on ["el ojo implacable que lo vigila"] (20).

The relentless eye suggests an intratextual reference. In "El sonámbulo," a novella published in 1976, the narrator is haunted by a memory of the War of Paraguay and an enemy soldier who painted in the middle of the battlefields:

> sospeché que se trataba de una nueva forma de alucinación. Le disparé un tiro que levantó un poco de tierra detrás del caballete. No se alteró, giró fugazmente la cabeza en dirección a mi escondite, lanzó un escupitajo y siguió pintando impasible. No fui el único que lo vio, muchos otros lo avistaron pintando con el mismo coraje el desarrollo de los combates, sentado en la cima de los despojos. Le dieron el nombre de tá angá apohá [artífice de figuras]. (33)

> I suspected that I was dealing with a new form of hallucination. I fired a shot that rose a bit of earth behind the easel. He was not shaken, he turned his head briefly in the direction of my hideout, spitted and kept on painting impassively. I was not the only one who saw him, many others caught sight of him painting the combat's development with the same courage, sitting on top of the mortal remains. They named him tá angá apohá (maker of figures).

Silvestre Carmona's remembrance in "El sonámbulo" partly explains the title of "El ojo de la luna." However, the narrator activates the intratextual reference only to relate it to a subsequent development in the story. In section five, the narrator claims Cándido López witnessed the end of Solano López, and depicted an identical crucifixion to Mathias Grunewald's altarpiece "The Crucifixion." Burton saw the painting and wrote about Mitre's reaction to it:

> El jefe austero—dice de Mitre—celoso de su honor militar, francmasón y liberal, respetuoso del credo de los demás, no perdonó, sobre todo, a su asistente, un sacrilegio histórico, religioso y militar: el que hubiese pintado la crucifixión del cadáver de Solano, el jefe enemigo derrotado y asesinado, izado por manos anónimas la misma noche de la victoria final ante la tienda del mando aliado, en el pétreo anfiteatro de Cerro-Corá. (21)

> The severe leader—says about Mitre—zealous of his military honor, freemason and liberal, respectful of the creed of others, did not forgive, above all, his assistant, for an historical, religious and military sacrilege: the fact that he had painted the crucifixion of the Solano's cadaver, the enemy leader defeated and assassinated, hoisted by anonymous hands during the night of the final victory before the allied command tent, in the rocky amphitheatre of Cerro-Corá.

However, the narrator, after having stated that Burton "no supo o no quiso declarar que el cuadro es una exacta reproducción del Cristo de Grunewald" (did not know or refused to declare that the picture is an exact replica of the Grunewald's Christ), adds later that it is not an absolutely exact replica ("reproducción absolutamente exacta"), owing to slight dissimilarities ["leves disimilitudes"] (21). However, the ensuing enumeration of differences suggests little resemblance. One salient contrast is a moon that waxes or wanes, mirroring the real moon (22). It is also, then, this "eye of the moon," as the title suggests, that both witnesses and represents the crucifixion and also represents itself. The artist, the narrator, *a la Velazquez*, represents the war and himself, very much like the representation of the historical Cándido López, who, in the painting entitled "La batalla de Curupaytí," depicts himself with his arm being blown apart by a hand grenade (Pacheco 78) Furthermore, the narrator informs that, beyond his version of Burton's account, there is no evidence of the existence of the painting. The only evidence is literary and limited to the fleeting moment of reception before the text, as in other instances, abolishes its existence. During that brief instant the story reproduces the same "misterio de la transmisibilidad de la energía creativa" ["mystery of the contagiousness of creative energy"] that explains the Paraguayan painter Ignacio Nuñez Soler's ability, "una especie de transmigración pictórica" ["a kind of pictorial transmigration"], to make the perfect replicas of Cándido López's paintings that will travel back from Paraguay to Argentina in greater number than the originals (23).

"El ojo de la luna" blurs the distinction between history and literature. The proliferation of narrations in the story mimics the multiplication of contending histories about the war. The story that comes in between "the official history of the victors" and "the counterhistory of the vanquished," carnavalizes all heroes and parodies its intertexts.

EL FISCAL

Critics have established *El fiscal*'s postmodern affiliation and emphasized the "crisis of the future" embodied in the plight of the main character and first person narrator. The novel, structured mainly around Félix Moral's diary in France, and then the letters from Paraguay to his companion Jimena, reveals his obsession with delivering his homeland from dictatorship by executing its ruler. For Weldt-Basson, *El fiscal* "closes Roa Bastos's postmodern cycle of novels on power and dictatorship" (Weldt-Basson, "Augusto Roa Bastos's Trilogy," 352). The critic identifies some of the postmodern characteristics I have discussed in relation to "El ojo de la luna" in the novels *Yo el Supremo*, the second version of *Hijo de hombre*, and *El fiscal*.[5] Weldt-Basson also underscores the novel's "rejection of utopia in favor of the recognition of the impurity and partiality of any process" (Weldt-Basson, "Augusto Roa Bastos's Trilogy," 344). For Kraniauskas, "*El Fiscal* exhibe la impotencia, en sus varios sentidos, para compartir una crisis de futuro" (shows the impotence, understood in all its connotations, to share a crisis of the future). This "crisis of the future" is felt by the "intelectual tradicional, idealista y exiliado (como Roa Bastos mismo) que siente la pérdida del poder ético-cultural, la capacidad 'dirigente' (hacia el futuro) o política de la categoría social a la cual pertenece, la imposibilidad de aliarse a un sujeto de cambio histórico" (211) ["traditional intellectual, both idealist and exiled (as Roa Bastos himself) who feels the loss of ethical and cultural power, of both the leadership and political ability of his own social status, the impossibility of establishing an alliance with any agent of historical change"]. This novel expresses the crisis of postmodern culture personified in the exiled Paraguayan intellectual, whose obsession with political agency condemns him to a tragic end.

El fiscal reveals its conclusion from the outset. The narrator refers to his "posthumous letters" and reveals an ambivalent and dangerous relationship with Paraguay's nationalist history. While trying to write a script about Solano López and Madama Lynch with the greatest objectivity possible, he felt the overwhelming power of the myths of his "race" and experienced a "revelation" (30). Despite his initial goal of intellectual rigor, he begins to depict Solano López's crucifixion, something absent from the historical record. Writing stirs in Moral a powerful identification with the national hero. As a result, Moral claims to experience Solano Lopez's emotions before his Brazilian executioners (31). This self-recognition in the hero blinds any critical thinking and, possessed by the evocation, he embraces the nationalist myth: "Todos mis prejuicios y viejos anatemas contra López y la Lynch . . . se borraron como bajo un soplo demasiado fuerte" (34) ["All my prejudices and old insults against López and Lynch . . . were erased by an overwhelming gust"]. The character is unable to break off his close proximity to the regime via the identification with the same nationalist myth, that is, the narrative that establishes a legitimating genealogical relationship between the dictator, Solano López, and the War of Paraguay.

Naturally, it is not this authorized revisionist script (36), but his involvement in the shooting of an American film about the war that leads to his imprisonment and exile. According to the narrator, the director's script follows Hollywood's demands for success by center-ing on the conflict between Madama Lynch and Pancha Garmendia. The latter undergoes horrible torture and execution at the hands of a jealous Madama Lynch, who deeply envies her beauty and noble qualities. The dictatorship reacts to the film's depiction of its national heroes by putting an abrupt and violent end to what it interprets to be antihistorical and anti-Paraguayan pamphlet (39). Despite its com-mercialism, the film is subversive because in it, Pancha Gamendia is interpreted as a metonymy of the people who have suffered at the hands of López and Lynch. She is seen as the opposite of Solano López through the representation of her crucifixion (43–44). In this perspective, the cultural industry is not so much a competitor for the task of the intellectual (Krauniaskas 210), but rather the provider of another story about the war that, despite its commercialism, ironically disrupts official dogma.

Furthermore, taking intratextual elements into consideration, the film's script in *El Fiscal* is remarkably similar to Roa Bastos's *Pancha Garmendia y Elisa Lynch* (2006), which the author describes as an "Opera en cinco actos inspirada libremente en los personajes históri-cos del mismo nombre" ["An opera in five acts inspired freely by the historical characters of the same name"].[6] As in the case of the trilogy of which *El fiscal* is part, Roa Bastos's intratexts establish connections that generate possible new readings. In any case, this emphasizes the contention that the film's script ironically contrasts with Moral's script and underscores the narrator's ambivalent identification with revision-ist history, because, after all, his script was the only one officially sanc-tioned for the film (36).

Moral's nationalism explains his authoritarian tendency. He con-sciously adopts the role of judge and executioner, and, despite his doubts about the need or consequences of his actions, he returns to Paraguay to liberate his people (246). He is not only different from the people, the oppressed, owing to his shared vision of the founding myths of authoritarian nationalism with the state, but also owing to his exile. He acknowledges that he does not recognize himself any longer in his fellow countrymen (247). Among the letters sent to his companion, there is one that rewrites "El ojo de la luna." In it, Moral discusses the difficulty in gaining an understanding of the War of Paraguay; he blames mainly the "historia oficial de los vencedores" (264) ["official history of the victors"]. In contrast to "El ojo de la luna," where Paraguayan history also contributes to the confusion, in *El fiscal*, Moral does not mention it as questionable.

Moral comments and quotes Burton's *Letters* in order to present "elementos no tratados por los profesionales de la historia" (265) ["things professional historians have not studied"]. According to Moral, Burton is a privileged witness and narrator who "siguió con sus catalejos los últimos combates" ["observed with his telescope the last combats"] and produced a chronicle that is of questionable "calidad literaria y magia creativa" ["literary quality and creative magic"], but superior to all others "como crónica del holocausto de un pueblo" (265) ["as a chronicle of the holocaust of a nation"]. He had access to Cándido López's paintings and even saw the artist at work sitting among the dead at the end of a battle. Letter three, dedicated to López, might explain, the narrator tells us, the quality of Burton's account, which he probably owes to the artist's "visiones de delirio" (266) ["delirious visions"].

In Moral's account, the perspective is different from "El ojo de la luna." Whereas the narrator of the short story accentuates the literariness of historical characters, in *El fiscal*, the narrator insists on their historicity and generally underscores the veracity of the documentation. In Burton's interview with the Paraguayan leader, Solano López discusses the revisionist theory in great detail, but perception of the anachronism implied depends largely on the reader's acquaintance with the historiography of the conflict (266–69). As for the story of the globe, central in the short story, López takes Burton to view the globe used by the allies to spy on the Paraguayan front. The narrator's clarification of the meaning of the word globe in Buenos Aires becomes a metafictional comment about his reading of Burton's text. The narrator explains that "globo" is an idiom from Buenos Aires that means "embuste, inflada mentira" (270) ["lie, an exaggerated lie"]. When finally a globe is seized, not delivered by Bartolomé Mitre, as happens in "El ojo de la luna," one questions the narrator's claims of "irrefutable" proof (283). The evidence is postponed: it comes either from Burton's account of Cándido López or from the Paraguayan double of the painter who is also depicted as painting in the middle of the battlefields under the watchful eye of the hunter (285).

The character's very personal reading of Burton's *Letters* becomes apparent when comparing his diary with the letter to Jimena. Burton's account in Moral's letter largely coincides with Moral's views. For instance, in a moment of exaltation during the writing of the film script, Moral imaginatively addresses Solano López on the cross: "Has vencido al azar mediante una locura desaforada! . . . . ¿Era necesario este espantoso delirio?" (33) ["You have defeated destiny through an outrageous madness . . . Was this terrible delirium necessary?"].

Moral later quotes comparable lines from Burton's text: "Necesitaba seguir derramando ríos de sangre . . . Tomarse a sí mismo como destino era su peor desatino" (269) [He needed to keep spilling rivers of blood. To think of himself as destiny was his worst foolishness]. Moral assesses Burton's writing negatively because "se inflamaba de un arrebato trágico de segunda mano" (270) ["he became overwhelmed by a secondhand tragic outburst"]. However, this assessment also reveals Moral's reaction to his own script about Solano López; Moral's writing exhibits the same tragic rapture and reveals his input in commenting on Burton's account. The commonalities between the diary and the letter underscore the character's appropriation of the *Letters*. For instance, both Burton's and Moral's account share the same revisionist view of Solano López. In the diary, the character has placed López among the continent's heroes (Che, Bolívar, Martí) and commented that, in Latin America's revolutions, heroes always end up "asesinados o derrotados" (170) ["assassinated or defeated"]. Burton's account establishes the same comparison: "Más que amo de su pueblo era su semidiós. Sabía que estaba arando en el mar, como dijo Bolívar" (273) ["More than the master of his nation he was his demigod. He knew that he was plowing in the sea, as Bolívar said"]. In Moral's account of Burton's *Letters*, the latter not only seems to express unvarying views but also utilizes the same wording. In the diary, for instance, the character had likewise referred to the "semidiós de un pueblo" (33) ["a people's demigod"].

Even if several paragraphs from the short story find their way into the novel, the ironic tone is naturally different. In the novel, it involves Moral's parody of Burton as Orientalist, something that also reveals the narrator's own personality traits. In "Ojo de la luna," Burton explains that an upset López spoke to him in a "germanía inextricable" (16) ["an impenetrable slang"]. In *El fiscal*, Moral delights in commenting that Burton did not understand very well the bilingual discourse of the marshal despite "bragging" about his ability to speak thirty-five languages, including its dialects (267). Burton's extraordinary knowledge of all things is overturned as he becomes the object of irony and ridicule.

The brief reference to Madama Lynch in the short story is further developed in *El fiscal*. Moral announces that "notas extraviadas" (missing notes) unveil Burton the womanizer and his quest to seduce Lynch or Ela. Burton undermines the masculine opponent by describing the small, white, and almost feminine feet that an assistant washes and massages with aromatic ointments (69). Additionally, his account carnavalizes Solano López by contrasting the delicate feminine feet with the grotesque description of the body (69). Burton's fantasies involving Ela, an Irish woman, are only activated through his oriental eroticism. Ela is Tintoretto's Queen of Sheba, a popular object of inspiration in nineteenth-century pictorial representation of oriental imaginings. Moral quotes letters nineteen and twenty in which Burton speaks of a love affair with an Ethiopian princess who resembles the divine Ela (74). He appeals to *The Thousand and One Nights* and oriental eroticism through spicy stories narrated in a "delicada gradación" (71) ["delicate gradation"] that place them, as a dervish and Scheherazade, at the center of an erotic plot.

Notwithstanding the fact that, despite his literary skills, the seduction plan fails miserably, Burton takes pride in the "hallazgo narrativo" ["narrative discovery"] of having turned the narrator into a character of a story unknown to her (73). This is a *mise en abyme* of Burton the narrator as character in Moral's letter to his companion and also of Moral the narrator as character in *El fiscal*. This mirroring suggests the multiple layers at play in the novel. The deeply contradictory Moral mocks a Burton who is a product of his own imagination. In the appropriation of the *Letters* and his account of Burton's obsession with Elisa Lynch, Moral is also describing his own sexual obsessions. He warns us that Burton was a skillfull "manipulador del subterfugio narrativo" ["manipulator of narrative subterfuge"] and mastered the art of "insinuación capciosa" (280) ["cunning insinuation"]. In Moral's account, Burton shares the same favorite themes: "la guerra y los placeres prohibidos" (281) [war and forbidden pleasures]. Toward the end of this letter, the narrator contradicts his initial evaluation of Burton's account to accommodate the imaginative flight that has taken over his narrative. Burton's *Letters* are no longer inferior in literary quality and creative magic. He now reassesses them, underscoring their value as both historical documentation and fiction. They are "delirante fantasía" (291) ["feverish fantasy"], much superior to the translation of the *Thousand and One Nights*. Moral's interpretation is evidently a mimetic rendering of his own obsessions.

Kraniauskas argues that Moral "literally" feels the crisis of the future, as opposed to Roa Bastos, who "possibly" sees it "ironically" (Kraniauskas 212). My understanding of irony is the pragmatic one taken by Linda Hutcheon, who also emphasizes the social and political edge of irony.[7] Irony permeates the dramatic, or rather melodramatic, representation of Moral's contradictions and crisis. The character heads to self-destruction; an alternate self-realization cannot be found in any realm, private or public, including in his own professional vocation, as he even rejects literature (69). However, the novel takes a different stand on the possibilities of writing. The preface refers to the implied author's belief in literary utopia. In it, he affirms his position vis-à-vis *El Fiscal*: "era el acto de fe de un escritor no profesional en la utopía de la escritura novelesca" (9) ["the act of faith of a nonprofessional writer in the utopia of fictional writing"]. Literature's function in the novel is to represent the crisis of utopia, the impossibility of its realization, given the complexity of any historical process, as embodied in Moral's contradictory and incongruous reaction to this crisis.

Even if the parallels with the biographical author are evident, the perspective is different. Acquaintance with Roa Bastos's intratexts, such as "El ojo de la luna" or *Pancha Garmendia and Elisa Lynch*, certainly contributes to capturing the intentionality of the novel. The proliferation of narrations in the short story underscores the possibility of knowing the past; this proliferation in Moral's letter to Jimena is a mimetic rendering of his obsessions. It is the lack of ironic distance that completely escapes Moral that leads to the horrible filmic and literary death in Cerro Corá, one that does not replicate history (the crucifixion of Solano López) but rather his own identification with an authoritarian nationalist myth.

LOS CONJURADOS DEL QUILOMBO DEL GRAN CHACO

Los conjurados is intimately associated with the turn of the century in Latin America. In the era of unprecedented regional integration, old issues gained momentum: inter-Latin American relations in the Southern Cone, the conflictive pasts constructed by self-absorbed national historiographies, and the possible function of the intellectual and of literature. Roa Bastos's engagement with the project of integration both at the Latin American and Ibero-American level was clearly articulated in his essay "El dilema de la integración iberoamericana" (1986). The document underlined the author's vision of history and the place of cultural identity underpinning what he termed this "concrete utopia" (39). For instance, he advocated an ethics of historical knowledge (26), which he defined as an understanding of the past that is linked to the present and the future. The author's promotion of integration coincided with the emergence of economic and political regionalization in the Southern Cone. In 1991, the Mercosur project of integration became official with the Treaty of Asunción (1991). The signing ceremony in Paraguay was a highly symbolic occasion, an event that referred back to the War of Paraguay (1865–70), and opened a new beginning for the region and Paraguay.[8]

Roa Bastos's contribution to *Los conjurados* responds directly to this new epochal episteme by deconstructing his oeuvre and producing a text that supplements it with the new concerns of the present. Although the book is a collection of texts, its internal coherence is evident in the common theme and plot elements developed in all four texts. The stories are subplots of the text's larger plot of conspiracy against the War of Paraguay. It narrates the tale of a group of officials and soldiers from the allied armies of Argentina, Brazil, and Uruguay that, together with their Paraguayan counterparts, founded a community of deserters and conspired to put an end to the war.

It is no coincidence that Roa Bastos, the avid reader of Burton, had never developed the potential of this story. The author had carnivalized and parodied Burton's letters and biography to varying degrees in his fiction, but it is only in the context of regional integration that Burton's reference to this community becomes a fictional text. In letter thirteen of his *Letters*, Burton actually makes passing reference to a settlement of deserters from the conflict: "In the Gran Chaco opposite exists a large quilombo or maroon settlement, where Brazilians and Argentines, Orientals and Paraguayan fugitives, dwell together in mutual amity, and in enmity with all the world" (Burton 430). In "Fundación, apogeo y ocaso del Quilombo del Gran Chaco" ["Foundation, Apogee and Fall of the Shanty of the Greater Chaco"]. Alejandro Maciel's contribution, the narrator explains that "El 'Quilombo del Gran Chaco' es una república de la selva nacida del armisticio voluntario de un grupo de oficiales de las cuatro naciones que afuera siguen enfrentándose, invocando oscuros intereses" (127) ["The Shanty of the Greater Chaco is a republic in the jungle born of the voluntary armistice entered by officials from the four nations that are confronting each other, alleging obscure interests"]. The dissident community intends to defeat the war (129).

I place *Los conjurados* in line with Mihai Spariosu's view of literature as an essentially nonantagonistic and irenic commitment to positing alternate worlds to history's impasses.[9] This perspective coincides with *El Fiscal*'s preface: "Sólo el espacio imaginario del no-lugar y del no-tiempo permite bucear en los enigmas del universo humano de todo tiempo y lugar. Sin esta tentativa de busca de lo real desconocido, el trabajo de un autor de ficciones tendría apenas sentido" (9) ["Only the imaginary space of nonplace and nontime allows to delve in the enigma of time and place. Without an attempt to search for the unknown real, the work of the fiction writer would not make sense"]. The "quilombo" is a liminal place opposed to the historical dynamics confronted in the war. The name "conjurados" and "quilombo" describe the meanings ascribed to the community. "Quilombo" (brothel and illegal settlement) points to the carnivalization of norms and to a community formed by those escaping an oppressive sociopolitical order as in the case of what is normally denoted by the term: a runaway slave settlement in Brazil during the colonial period.[10] "Conjurados" connotes both a rejection of the sacred (covenanter) and of the political (conspirator). All these meanings are activated in the novel, where the world of the Quilombo rejects states' power, their monopoly on violence, and their discourse of nationalism. Save for general and contextual commentary, I will restrict my analysis to Roa Bastos's text in *Los conjurados*.

Roa Bastos's text in *Los conjurados* consists of two sections entitled "Frente al frente Argentino" ("In Front of the Argentine Front") and "Frente al frente Paraguayo" ("In Front of the Paraguayan Front"). The former is a long text that develops, to great length, the brief reference to exchanges between Bartolomé Mitre and Cándido López in "El ojo de la luna"; the latter, as the implied author explains in a footnote, comes from *El fiscal*. It is in fact Moral's entire letter to Jimena. However, "Frente al frente paraguayo" also contains six new additional pages at the end. The intricate relationship between both sections goes beyond the mirroring suggested by the titles; it actually underscores their identity. The story in each section narrates exactly the opposite of what the title announces: "Frente al frente argentino" does not refer to a story about the Argentine front, but rather to the Paraguayan front, while "Frente al frente Paraguayo" refers to the Argentine Front, not the Paraguayan. These subtitles thus emphasize the book's rejection of difference and nationalism; the stories about both fronts are interchangeable—discourses, historiographies, representations are all subsumed under the universal identity of the "enemy." In this way, Roa Bastos sets the stage for the following texts that will develop stories about the community of deserters. The opposing historical, literary, or pictorial narratives about the war are all essentially the same: a celebration of a questionable difference (100). Only in overcoming these contending narratives, as in the liminal space of el "quilombo del Gran Chaco," is it possible to form an alternate new community.

As I have shown elsewhere (Guerrero 237–52), "Frente al frente argentino" is a polyphonic text where, without a narrator's intervention, Bartolomé Mitre and Cándido López debate their mutual modes of representation. The former is translating the *Divine Comedy*, and Cándido López is critical of Mitre's penchant for the literal in his craft. He argues for a cultural translation that is a true dialogue between the spirit of the original text and the cultural context and language of South America. Cándido López is ultimately pessimistic about Mitre as a translator. The artist's vision of translation involves the ability to live in-between cultures, something contrary to the nature of the general who wages war. On the other hand, Bartolomé Mitre rejects Cándido López's art for his commitment to a photographic realism, instead of an epic representation of Argentina's participation in a war that could contribute to the new national imaginary. The dialogue, which seemingly takes place in the afterlife, is endless.

The text does not address the fictional or the historical. Any reference to the epistemological status of the dialogue lies solely in the reader's knowledge of history. "Frente al frente argentino" transforms the historical figures into literary characters whose words and actions respond to a particular reading of their work, that is, the implied author's interpretation of Mitre's translation of the *Divine Comedy* as well as of Cándido López's paintings. In "Frente al frente paraguayo," acquaintance with *El fiscal* alone explains the symmetry of both sections in terms of voices. The third-person narrator, although not mentioned in the text, is probably dead. The narrator is akin to Moral, a self-absorbed voice, like Cándido López's and Bartolomé Mitre's in the "Frente al frente argentino," who speak from the afterlife.

Moral's letter to Jimena in *El fiscal* now carries the title "Frente al frente paraguayo." However, we do not know the identity of the narrator. The difference with Moral's letter lies in the six added pages that serve as a conclusion to Roa Bastos's contribution to *Los conjurados*; these pages are subtitled "El guerrero y su doble" ("The Soldier and his Double"). This new text can be read as a metafictional comment, the author's intervention with the objective of underscoring the place of Cándido López in his fiction and providing hints about *Los conjurados*. In this short essay, the narrator explains that Cándido López transcends nationalism for refusing to "hacer alegorías" (96) ["make allegories"] of war; the painter rejects "la exaltación épica del vencedor" (97) ["epic exaltation of the victors"] and the "desdeñoso desprecio del vencido" (97) ["disdainful slight of the vanquished"]. His art is not an "apología de la guerra" (97) [defense of war] but rather "su plácida y serena negación" (97) ["its placid and serene negation"]. It is this reading, independent of the historical record, which has guided the representation of Cándido López.

The essay also allows for the multiplication of Cándido López. The narrator emphasizes his belief in the power of literature by also positing a "versión legenderia" ["folk legend"] about a Paraguayan double or "transmigrante de su homónimo argentino" (99) ["transmigrant of his Argentinean homonym"]. The Paraguayan painter "recrea lo descreado con un nuevo credo que reconstruya los pasos extraviados" (101) ["recreates the destruction of war with a new creed that reconstructs the missing steps"]. In this regard, *Los conjurados*, along the same lines as Spariosu's view of literature, comments on its "playfully staging" of "an imaginary world" and expresses the utopian belief in the transmission of the "ethical choices open to a certain community" (Spariousu xvi).In *Los conjurados*, and specifically in Roa Bastos's contribution, literature thus posits a transcendental fraternity of popular origins, a powerful legend: "Desde la leyenda (los artistas) se abrazan, y por encima del horror celebran ambos la fraternidad de dos pueblos" (100) ["In the legend (the artists) embrace each other and above the horror celebrate the fraternity of two nations"]. Furthermore, if I have been stressing the autobiographic presence in the fictional, it is because, in fact, the narrator's concluding remarks to his contribution in *Los conjurados* extend beyond the book. In his preface to *Cándido López. Proyecto Cultural Artistas del Mercosur* (1998), Roa Bastos presents the same short essay of *Los conjurados* and entitles it "Transmigración de Cándido López" ("Transmigration of Cándido López"). In it, he presents, by blurring the non-fictional dimension of this type of preface, the legend his texts had been elaborating since 1991 with the publication of "El ojo de la luna" and developed in *El fiscal* and *Los conjurados*. The legend, having moved from the literary to folk culture, is now presented as originating in the popular imaginary (3–5).

In conclusion, it is possible to trace the author's concerns and critical literary development in the nineties and early turn of the century. While "El ojo de la luna" problematizes the representation of the past and carnavalizes national narratives, *El fiscal* ironically underscores a contradictory intellectual position that rejects authoritarianism, but is ambivalent about the state's national narratives. Conversely, *Los conjurados* posits an alternate community that transcends these contending national narratives. Despite representing the crisis of utopia and of a modern form of intellectual agency in *El fiscal*, the novel promotes the role of literature. This is even more evident in *Los conjurados*, where the decision to collectively write a literary narrative and publish a Portuguese and Spanish edition reveals not only an engagement with regional integration, but also perhaps a strategy on the part of literary intellectuals to gain visibility in a city, or rather, cities, that are no longer lettered. Finally, in all three of Roa Bastos's texts, albeit more specifically in *Los conjurados*'s metafictional evaluation of his own reading of Cándido López's paintings, popular culture is intimately related to literary culture; literary culture is nothing less than the provider of the legend that fills popular culture's imaginary. It sums up a constant and definite commitment to literary utopia on the part of Roa Bastos.

Notes

1 My special thanks to Dr. Guillermo Renart for his careful reading of this paper and his many valuable suggestions.
2. In "Augusto Roa Bastos's *Contravida* and *Madama Sui*. An Archetypal Interpretation," Helene Weldt-Basson, who positively interprets Roa Bastos's rewriting, reviews the contrasting views of Aldo Albónico and Carlos Pacheco on the author's critical intratextuality. The latter considers *Contravida* an uneven and pointless patchwork" whereas the former values it as a transgressive practice of critical counter-reading ("transgresiva práctica de contralectura crítica"). In "¿Augusto Roa Bastos en sus últimas novelas: evolución o involución?" (21), Albónico goes as far as to posit an involution in the author's late fiction.
3. All translations of Roa Bastos's works are mine, unless otherwise noted.
4. I will shorten the title in this paper to *Los conjurados*.
5. Weldt-Basson, in "Augusto Roa Bastos's Trilogy," enumerates the following postmodern characteristics: "questioning of historical and literary knowledge," "a lack of separation of the aesthetic and the political, the mixing of various genres and disciplines . . . the questioning of the relationship between language and its referents (as well as the examination of) the relationship between different texts" (338)
6. Although published recently, according to Milagros Esquerro, who writes the preface to this first edition, she received the script from Roa Bastos in 1995 just before his return to Paraguay (9).
7. For Hutcheon, irony is an event inferred by the reader: "Irony, therefore, is like all other community acts in that it is always culture specific, relying on the presence of a common memory shared by addresser and addresee. While this means that an ironist may presuppose in the interpreter 'a determined type of cultural formation' that will permit 'particular allusions, particular ellipses' without endangering comprehension, so too might an interpreter infer the same from the text of the ironist" (98).
8. In "Revisionismo histórico y autoritarismo," the Paraguayan writer Guido Rodríguez Alcalá argued that Paraguayan isolation, in all its forms, came to an end owing to the arrival of democracy and the greater contact with the rest of the world made possible by new technologies and regional integration in Mercosur. Isolation had been a refuge for the growth of *lopizta* nationalism, which strengthened ideologically the country's isolation through the propagation of xenophobia. For the author, Paraguay faces the challenge of exercising a form of nationalism that is capable of promoting both the country's culture and international integration.

9. In *The Wreath of Green Olive*, Spariosu argues that "since literary discourse belongs to a playful, liminal mode of being, it is not bound by the logical and analytic methods of philosophical and scientific discourse and, therefore, can also propose alternative models based on irenic principles. Furthermore, literature as a form of aesthetic play can both involve and transcend the sociocultural context in which it arises. Unlike other types of discourse, it can adopt an *as if* stance toward the ethical norms of a certain community or culture. Consequently it can produce, in the imagination, new sets of values that can later be adopted by ethical and sociopolitical thought as well. By playfully staging a real or an imaginary world and presenting it from various perspectives, literature contributes to a better understanding of the ethical choices open to a certain community and hence can assume an important role in bringing about historical change" (1997xvi).

10. The connotation of the word in both Portuguese and Spanish is relevant since the text is linguistically hybrid. The authors speak one or the other language and, in fact, translation is an important feature of the novel. It was almost simultaneously published in both Spanish and Portuguese. Its title in Brazil is *O livro da Guerra Grande* (Rio de Janeiro: Editora Recorde, 2002).

WORKS CITED

Albónico, Aldo. "¿Augusto Roa Bastos en sus últimas novelas: evolución o involución?" *Studi di letteratura ispano-americana* 30 (1997): 21–26. Print.

Burton, Richard. *Letters from the Battlefields in Paraguay.* London: Tinsley Brothers, 1871. Print.

Guerrero, Jorge Carlos. "Augusto Roa Bastos y *Los conjurados del Quilombo del Gran Chaco* (2001): un legado literario para la integración latinoamericana." *Revista Iberoamericana* 218–19 (2007): 237–52. Print.

Hutcheon, Linda. *Irony's Edge: The Theory and Politics of Irony.* London: Routledge, 1995. Print.

Kraniauskas, John. "Retorno, melancolía y crisis de futuro: *El fiscal* de Augusto Roa Bastos." *Las culturas de fin de siglo en América Latina.* Ed. Josefina Ludmer. Buenos Aires: Beatriz Viterbo editora, 1994. 209–17. Print.

Martínez, Tomás Eloy. "Roa Bastos todavía está aquí." *La Nación.* April 28, 2005. http://www.lanacion.com.ar/nota.asp?nota_id=699702. Web.

Pacheco, Marcelo. *Cándido López. Proyecto Cultural Artistas del Mercosur.* Buenos Aires: Banco Velox, 1998. Print.

Roa Bastos, Augusto. "El sonámbulo." *Cándido López. Imágenes de la guerra del Paraguay, con un texto de Augusto Roa Bastos.* Milano: Franco María Ricci, 1984. Print.

———. "El dilema de la integración iberoamericana." *Cuadernos hispanoamericanos.* 427 (1986): 21–42. Print.

———. "El hijo de la luna." *Cuadernos Hispanoamericanos.* 493–94 (1991): 13–24. Print.

———. *El fiscal.* Madrid: Alfaguara, 1993. Print.

Roa Bastos, Augusto, *et al. Los conjurados del Quilombo del Gran Chaco.* Buenos Aires: Alfaguara, 2001. Print.

Rodríguez Alcalá, Guido. "Revisionismo histórico y autoritarismo." *Revista Multipla.* 7.11 (2001): 9–27. Print.

Spariousu, Mihai. *The Wreath of Wild Olive. Play, Liminality, and the Study of Literature.* New York: State University of New York Press, 1997. Print.

Weldt-Basson, Helene. "Augusto Roa Bastos's Trilogy as Postmodern Practice." *Studies in Twentieth-Century Literature* 22.2 (Summer 1998): 335–55. Print.

———. "Augusto Roa Bastos's *Contravida* and *Madama Sui*: An Archetypal Interpretation." *Confluencia: Revista Hispánica de Cultura y Literatura.* 3.1 (2007): 93–106. Print.

White, Hayden. *The Content of the Form: Narrative Discourse and Historical Representation.* Baltimore: Johns Hopkins University Press, 1987. 1–25. Print.

ALL WOMEN ARE WHORES

PROSTITUTION, FEMALE ARCHETYPES, AND FEMINISM IN THE WORKS OF AUGUSTO ROA BASTOS

Helene Carol Weldt-Basson

Although over four hundred articles and several books have been written about Augusto Roa Bastos, very few of these studies focus upon the role of women in his fiction.[1] Female characters have not appeared central to the author's work until his last novel, *Madama Sui* (1996), in which the protagonist is courtesan to the dictator modeled on Alfredo Stroessner, who governed Paraguay from 1954 through 1989. However, if we now look back over Roa Bastos's six novels populated by very strong male characters, such as Cristóbal Jara, El Supremo, and Félix Moral, among others, it is clear that women have always been present and occupied a significant role in his narrative.

What struck me as I pondered the question of how Roa Bastos portrays women in his fiction is that almost every female character is a prostitute. This superficially suggests a rather stereotyped view of women. However, Roa Bastos's fiction, although frequently constructed on the basis of Christian symbols and Jungian archetypes,[2] is never quite that simple. Just as his Christian symbolism in *Hijo de hombre* paradoxically communicates a socialist message of faith, not in God, but in the power of man, and in men's ability to perform "miracles" on the basis of solidarity, on closer examination, so does Roa Bastos's portrayal of women as prostitutes fail to result in a stereotyped portrait of women. Indeed, the object of this analysis is to illustrate how Roa Bastos paradoxically employs the figure of the prostitute, as well as other fixed female archetypes, to achieve a complex, postmodern view of women, as well as to communicate a feminist message to the reader, in his novels *Hijo de hombre* (1960), *Yo el Supremo* (1974), *El fiscal* (1993), and *Madama Sui* (1996). I will also consider in this light Roa Bastos's posthumous work, *Pancha Garmendia y Elisa Lynch* (2006), which bears a direct intertextual relationship to *El fiscal.*

Before we can approach the role of prostitutes and archetypal figures in the Roa Bastos's narrative, it is important to define what we mean by the terms "feminism" and "postmodernism," which have been subject to a variety of definitions in contemporary discourse. I employ "feminism" here in a very general sense, in accordance with the following statement by Jane Freedman: "Any attempt to provide a baseline definition of a common basis of all feminisms may start with the assertion that feminisms concern themselves with women's inferior position in society and with discrimination encountered by women because of their sex. Furthermore, one could argue that all feminists call for changes in the social, economic, political, or cultural order, to reduce and eventually overcome this discrimination against women" (Freedman, *Feminism*, 1). As I hope to show below, this feminist concern lies at the heart of many of Roa Bastos's novels.

As Raquel Olea points out, postmodernism and postmodernity are imprecise terms with multiple meanings (Olea 192). However, some broad definition of postmodernism is required in order to facilitate a discussion of Roa Bastos's postmodern employment of archetypes to deconstruct traditional dichotomies surrounding women. Jean-François Lyotard defines postmodernism "as incredulity toward metanarratives . . . The postmodern would be that which in the modern, puts forward the unpresentable in presentation itself . . . A postmodern artist or writer is in the position of a philosopher: the text he writes, the work he produces, are not in principle governed by pre-established rules, and they cannot be judged according to a determining judgment, by applying familiar categories to the text or the work" (Lyotard xxiv, 81). Madan Sarup adds that postmodernism is characterized by "a rejection of narrative structure in favor of simultaneity and montage; an exploration of the paradoxical, ambiguous, and uncertain, open-ended nature of reality; and the rejection of the notion of an integrated personality in favor of an emphasis upon the Freudian 'split' subject" (Sarup 172). These broad definitions encompass many of the characteristics we have come to associate with postmodern literature, such as conflation of different disciplines and genres, and a deconstruction of socially established categories, such as woman versus man and heterosexual versus homosexual. In other words, postmodernism evinces doubt about the objectivity of all discourse and the validity of traditional categories and dichotomies. Roa Bastos does the same with regard to the discourse of psychoanalytical archetypes, which form a metanarrative that defines women in terms of stereotypical, limiting, fixed dichotomies such as good versus bad and pure versus impure. Roa Bastos deconstructs such discourses by blending various archetypal figures and focusing on prostitutes (who are the impure female figure *par excellence*) in order to illustrate how his women characters transcend such dichotomies and stereotypes and reveal a deeper, more complex, postmodern identity.

Traditionally, the literary use of archetypes tends to reinforce dominant patriarchal ideology with regard to women and their societal roles. Michele Barrett speaks of three principal tendencies in literary and mass media portrayals of women: stereotyping, compensation, and collusion. Stereotyping refers to the presentation of women in limited, traditional roles. In this sense, the Jungian archetype of the Great Mother, or presentation of women as nourishing, maternal figures, has been used by writers to foster this stereotyped view of women. Similarly, Barrett's "compensation" refers to the tendency to "elevate the moral value of femininity" (Barrett 109). The archetype of the spiritual virgin incarnates this type of compensatory work in fiction. Finally, Barrett defines collusion as attempts to "parade women's 'consent' to their subordination and objectification" (Barrett 110). Many literary portrayals of prostitutes exemplify how male authors may emphasize women's complicity with their own oppression. By "choosing" to become prostitutes, women demonstrate their acceptance of their exploitation and their internalization of this debased role.

Although Neumann's psychoanalytical discourse acknowledges the coexistence of various female archetypes in the feminine psyche, these archetypal images tend to be isolated and dichotomized by men so that women are represented either as pure virgins or evil, devouring, sexually aggressive witches in various media. In contrast with many other writers, Roa Bastos employs archetypes in a new way that subverts such dominant ideological practices in favor of a postmodern, feminist vision. Roa Bastos achieves this portrayal in two manners: first, he recovers certain female archetypes, such as that of the sacred prostitute, that are complex rather than monolithic, and second, he blends a variety of female archetypes to suggest a more varied and less stereotyped image of women. Roa Bastos's use of the archetype of the sacred prostitute in his first novel, *Hijo de hombre*, is a paradig-matic example of this postmodern, feminist approach. Although some deny the existence of the sacred prostitute in antiquity (Budin 9), Nancy Qualls-Corbett states, "The sacred prostitute . . . was a reality of ancient times. Inscribed clay tablets, unearthed relics and excavated temples tell of religious ceremonies celebrating the potent goddess of love and fertility . . . Her sexual nature was an integral aspect of her spiritual nature" (Qualls-Corbett 26–31). In other words, the archetype of the sacred prostitute, unlike other unidimensional female archetypes, fuses sexuality with spirituality and thus contests a mono-lithic, stereotypical portrait of women. In *Hijo de hombre*, this fusion can best be observed in the development of the character Salu'i. Salu'i blends some elements of the sacred prostitute with others related to Christian symbolism. Although Salu'i may be seen as the repentant whore and thus associated with Mary Magdalene in Chris-tian theology, she also exhibits various characteristics that relate her to the sacred prostitute. The first of these characteristics is Salu'i's association with spirituality and her paradoxical nature. We are told that she "había olvidado todo lo que estaba detrás. Hasta su antiguo nombre, María Encarnación" (287) ["She had forgotten everything that had happened to her before she came there, even her name, María Encarnación"].[3] "Encarnación" means "adoption of a mate-rial or carnal form by a spiritual being."[4] Thus, from the outset, Salu'i's real name suggests her relationship to spirituality, despite her material form as a prostitute. This supposed paradox, which was not really a contradiction in ancient times, is emphasized by Salu'i's dual role as transmitter of venereal disease (which is how she received the ironic name Salu'i, or "good health"), but also as the nurse who aids the victims of the Chaco War.

Another important characteristic of the sacred prostitute is that she was a moon goddess (Qualls-Corbett 58). Salu'i's connection with the sacred prostitute is thus established in the following passage in which her sexuality is emphasized by the brilliance of the moonlight: "De tanto en tanto, ella salía a ventilarse semidesnuda, el cabello en desorden, pequeña pero inmensa ante los hombres excitados, el vien-tre y los senos *henchidos de luna* bajo la enagua rotosa" (288; my emphasis) ["From time to time she would come out to get some air, half-naked, her hair in disorder, her small figure larger than life to the men's excited eyes. The moonlight emphasized her stomach and breasts. Her torn petticoat was stained with sweat" (200)].

A third connection between Salu'i and the sacred prostitute can be found in the emphasis placed on Salui's transformative capacity.

Qualls-Corbett notes that for Jung, the feminine archetype is associated with both a static and transformative principle. The static aspect of the feminine archetype is woman's maternal nature (the Great/ Terrible Mother archetypes). However, the "moving, changing, transformative aspect of the feminine is that associated with the goddess of love and with which the sacred prostitute is identified" (Qualls-Corbett 57). Salu'i is equally identified with transformative power. For example, when the men in the village begin to get sick with venereal disease and give her the nickname Salu'i, she is not upset: "Le gustó el marcante. Le gustó que la gente pudiera cambiar aunque más no fuese de nombre. No se había convertido aún en enfermera. Por entonces sólo era la *enfermedora*" (288) ["She liked the name. She liked to think that people could change, even if only in name. She had not begun to nurse the sick at that time. She only made them sick" (200)]. Not only does Salu'i change names and occupations, but the novel suggests that through her love of Cristóbal Jara, she also recovers her virginity:

> Quedaba limpia, nueva. Sentía retoñar su muñón de mujer en una sensación algo parecida a la de los heridos de guerra que continúan por algún tiempo con la ilusión de que el miembro amputado todavía está allí, pegado a las carnes deshechas. En lo más hondo de su degradación habría sentido resucitar su virginidad como una glándula . . . en un momento imprevisible para todos, la inconcebible regeneración comenzó. La glándula incorruptible revivió en su feminidad ardiente y destruida. Nadie volvió a traspasar la estera. Pero nadie creyó en su voluntad de purificación. (289–90)
>
> Her regeneration, which had seemed inconceivable, began. Something in her ardent, abused femininity, something which had never got quite corrupted, began to grow. No one was allowed into her hut. But, alas, no one believed in her change of heart (201).

According to Qualls-Corbett, the woman who is conscious of the goddess of love or sacred prostitute within her "is virginal. This has nothing to do with a physical state, but with an inner attitude. She is not dependent on the reactions of others to define her own being . . . She is not governed by an abstract idea of what she 'should' be like or 'what people will think'"(Qualls-Corbett 62). This is an apt description of the process Salu'i undergoes when she meets Cristóbal Jara. Moreover, the novel emphasizes how Salu'i's transformation is an interior process that resists skepticism and judgment from without. Despite the general disbelief in her purification, and derogatory comments by such characters as Otazú, who is dubious about her new saintly comportment, Salu'i now sees herself as a virgin.

Finally, the sacred prostitute's primary function was that of welcoming the stranger to the temple, and this stranger was thought to be "the emissary of the gods or perhaps the god incarnate" (Qualls-Corbett 39). Furthermore, the sacred prostitute is likened to mother Mary of Christian tradition because "like Mary, the sacred prostitute is considered virginal (psychologically): just as Mary's virginal womb brought forth the Christ child, so does the womb of the sacred prostitute, as anima, give birth to man's Christ-like nature, his higher consciousness"(Qualls-Corbett 104). This may explain the intimate connection established in the novel between Salu'i and Cristóbal Jara. Jara, as both his actions and his first name, containing "Cristo" imply, is clearly developed as a Christlike figure in the novel.[5] Salu'i can be seen as welcoming him to the temple, first, because she witnesses his arrival in town, and second, because although he is the only male in the village who does not come to her tent for sexual services, she repeatedly invites him to do so: "Lo mandaba llamar con Silvestre Aquino y los otros" (289) ["She asked him to come with Silvestre Aquino and the others" (201)]. Salu'i can also be seen as a Mary Magdalene icon. However, her role in the novel is closer to the figure as portrayed in Gnosticism as opposed to the Christian bible: "In sources other than Christian scripture, we find quite a different image of the Magdalene and her function . . . The Gnostic Gospel of Philip . . . describes Mary Magdalene as Jesus's most intimate companion and the symbol of Divine Wisdom. This image of Mary Magdalene as a chosen, even favored disciple contrasts greatly with the orthodox view of her as a penitent whore" (Qualls-Corbett 49). In *Hijo de hombre*, Salu'i also becomes Cristóbal's "favored disciple" by donning the clothing of a dead soldier, hitching a ride on his water truck, and serving as his faithful and final companion until her death minutes before Cristóbal's completion of his mission (of bringing water to the Chaco soldiers) and his own demise. Qualls-Corbett views this gnostic Mary Magdalene as a figure akin the sacred prostitute, who has transformative, spiritual power over man.

The most important aspect of Roa Bastos's development of Salu'i is the fact that prostitutes in *Hijo de hombre* are not seen as totally negative, evil, and degraded women, but rather as spiritual beings. In this instance, rather than deconstructing the archetype, Roa Bastos recovers it from antiquity in order to show how its blend of sexuality and spirituality breaks monolithic barriers and creates a more balanced portrait of women. Although Salu'i eventually abandons prostitution, as does María Rosa, these women were always spiritually pure and carried the seed of kindness and solidarity within. In a postmodern vein, the employment of the myth of the sacred prostitute seeks to destabilize established categories and dichotomies such as that of the virgin versus the prostitute, or the good girl versus the bad girl, which results in a more realistic portrait of women.[6]

Roa Bastos's second and most famous novel, *Yo el Supremo* (*I The Supreme*; 1974) has two main female characters, *La Andaluza* and María de los Ángeles. Each exhibits transformative powers, although different in nature than those of the sacred prostitute in *Hijo de hombre*. The first of these two women is an ambiguous figure. *La Andaluza* appears to the dictator, El Supremo, when he recalls an episode from the past in which he granted her audience, but did not actually receive her, limiting himself to observing her through his telescope. *La Andaluza* is a contraband runner sent by Buenos Aires politicians to assassinate the nineteenth-century dictator who presided over the Paraguayan nation during its early independence stage. El Supremo admires *La Andaluza* for her courage and bellicose tendencies, but rejects her as a traitor:

> Ah traidora, astuta, bella Deyanira-Andaluza! . . . Piensas que voy a desvestirme de mi piel de león para que la tela fatal roce mi cuerpo con su hechicería de sangre monstruosa-menstrual? Con muy poco dinero han comprado . . . mi muerte por tu mano . . . Ah si pudiera poblar mi país de mujeres belicosas como tú mas no traidoras, belicosa contra el enemigo, las fronteras del Paraguay llegarían hasta la Asia Menor . . . Dicen las malas-lenguas que todos los tripulantes de tu barca elegidos por ti se acuestan contigo uno por vez . . . No traes armas para mi ejército. Nada más que tu rojo pañuelo . . . Lujurioso, sensual, lúbrico, libidinoso, salaz, voluptuoso, deshonesto, impúdico, lascivo, fornicatorio . . . Sultán estuvo muy bien en echar a la puta de la Andaluza!" (146–51)

> Ah treacherous, clever, beautiful Deyanira-Andaluza! . . . Do you think you're going to strip me of my lion's skin so that the fatal cloth will brush my body with its black magic of monstruous-menstrual blood? . . . They have bought . . . my death by your hand for very little money . . . Ah, if I could populate my country with women warriors like you, though without your traitorous nature, ones who would wage war on the enemy, the frontiers of Paraguay would extend to Asia Minor . . . Malicious gossips say that . . . the entire crew of your boat, personally chosen by you, goes to bed with you, one at a time . . . You have brought no arms for my army. Nothing but your red rag . . . Lustful, sensual, lubricious, libidinous, salacious, voluptuous, dishonest,

shameless, lascivious, fornicatory . . . Sultan was quite right to throw out *La Andaluza*, that whore![7] (47–51).

El Supremo emphasizes *La Andaluza's* sexual nature, calling her a prostitute and accusing her of bedding all the sailors on her ship. She has allegedly been sent to seduce and murder the dictator. Her dangerous sexual nature likens her to Neumman's archetype of the young, seductive witch, which is considered a negative transformative figure. The young witch destroys men by seduction and sexual allurement.[8] This is clearly the case of *La Andaluza*, who is described as beautiful and voluptuous, and plans on using these qualities to attract and kill El Supremo in the novel. Her "red handkerchief" is another sign of the young witch archetype, since this figure is usually associated with vivid colors, especially red or black (McManus, n.p.). Furthermore, the dictator speaks of *La Andaluza's* "hechicería de sangre monstruosa-menstrual" ["black magic of monstruous-menstrual blood"]. The allusion to witchcraft further reinforces the young witch archetype based on negative enchantment; however, the reference to blood retains some strains of the terrible mother, associated with castration and destruction.[9] In either case, the *Andaluza* as prostitute, although a largely negative, traitorous figure, is also much admired for her courage and willingness to fight her enemies. The dictator expresses his desire to populate the country with women warriors modeled after la Andaluza. This lends a positive aspect to the traitorous prostitute, and the character's dual or ambiguous nature once again belies traditional good/bad dichotomies and suggests the ultimate complexity of women and inability to pigeonhole them into certain preestablished categories.

The other major female figure, María de los Ángeles, is el Supremo's goddaughter. When she returns to Paraguay (albeit only in El Supremo's imagination, since she left with her father José Isasi under false pretenses and never returned), El Supremo charges her with the directorship of the *Casa de Muchachas Huérfanas y Recogidas* (Home for Orphan and Foundling Girls). El Supremo claims that this institution "no funciona desde que en 1617 murió Jesusa Bocanegra" (486) ["it hasn't been a working institution since Jesusa Bocanegra died in 1617" (326)], but El Supremo wants María de los Ángeles to make it perform its original function. He warns her that she may find some of his own children there "si están todavía y no se han maleado por malos casamientos y esas tristes cosas que ocurren a las mujeres que han nacido para ser sometidas" (486) ["if they are still there, that is, and have not gone wrong by making bad marriages and all those sad things that happen to women born to be subdued" (326)]. Subsequent to

María de los Ángeles's appointment, Patiño informs the dictator that the orphanage has turned into a brothel. Almost one hundred pages later (573), the orphanage is referred to as a special school ("Escuela Especial: Casa de Huérfanas y Recogidas"), and one of its students, Telésfora Almada, demands popular elections and the dissolution of the corrupt army in a statement to El Supremo. These demands are followed by Patiño's comment that:

> A propósito de la casa de huérfanas y recogidas, Excelentísmo señor, me permito informar que en este establecimiento están ocurriendo cosas muy extrañas . . . Allí reina el mayor libertinaje que se pueda uno imaginar. De noche la Casa: un prostíbulo. De día, un cuartel. Han formado un batallón de todos colores, edades y condiciones . . . Antes de romper el alba se van a los montes. Capaz que se dedican a ejercicios de combate. Durante todo el día hasta la caída de la noche se oyen tiros lejanos. (573)
>
> Most Excellent Sire, I take the liberty of informing you that very strange things are going on in that establishment . . . the greatest libertinage that anyone can imagine reigns there . . . By night the Home is a brothel. By day a barracks. They've formed a battalion of every color, age, and estate . . . Before dawn breaks they take off into the wilds. It could be that they practice combat maneuvers. From dawn to dark you can hear distant rifle fire (405).

In other words, the supposed orphans are not orphans at all, but have been transformed, first, into prostitutes by night, and then into revolutionaries by day, presumably under the guidance of María de los Ángeles. María de los Ángeles is associated in the novel with revolution first, through her ability to set El Supremo's broken clock in motion (suggesting a temporal moving forward toward political change after the dictator's death), and second, by his giving his rifle to her as a gift. Once again, the novel subverts dichotomies by demonstrating that women simultaneously occupy both a passive and an active role. The occupation of prostitute is an icon of the exploited, dominated female previously referred to by El Supremo, while women's revolutionary activity suggests female power and subversion of the current patriarchal order. María de los Ángeles is thus herself seen as a dual figure, both madam and revolutionary leader. Once again, the prostitute is not simply the traditional, stereotyped, exploited whore, but a more dynamic and ambiguous figure who contains the ability to transform herself and transform man's destiny. The successive conversion of the Home for Orphan and Foundling Girls from orphanage to brothel, to special school, to revolutionary barracks underscores how female identity is not a question of fixed nature but of performative role—a series of endless shifts according to context and circumstance.

The image of women in the third novel of Roa Bastos's trilogy, *El fiscal* (1993), is projected through two parallel love triangles. The principal figures of the first triangle are the protagonist, Félix Moral, his partner, Jimena Tarsis, and his graduate student, Leda Kautner. The second triangle is constituted by three historical figures: the dictator Francisco Solano López, president during the Triple Alliance War (1864–1870), his Irish concubine, Madame Lynch, and the native Paraguayan woman, Pancha Garmendia, whom López had unsuccessfully tried to seduce prior to his relationship with Lynch (Ezquerro, n.p.). A series of complicated connections and allusions exist between these two sets of triangles as well as within each triad.

To a certain degree, both Jimena Tarsis and Leda Kautner are archetypal figures that represent two fundamental dimensions of the feminine archetype: Jimena is the incarnation of Neumann's positive female transformative character. She is not only the nurturing mother of the elementary plane (The Great Mother), but also, spiritual Sophia. According to Neumann, Sophia, who is the Judeo-Christian God's female soul, has an "overflowing heart [that] is wisdom and food at once. The nourishing life that she communicates is a life of the spirit and of transformation, not one of earthbound materiality" (Neumann 331). In *El fiscal*, Jimena is equally responsible for Félix's material and spiritual well-being. In addition to Jimena's physical salvation of Félix when the doctors have given him up for dead, we are told by the narrator that she totally transformed his character and ended his days as a "nómada del neolítico" (18) ["Neolithic nomad"][10] through her spiritual influence.

Despite Félix's ideal relationship with Jimena, he is importuned by his infatuated graduate student, Leda Kautner. Kautner is presented as an extremely ambiguous figure in the novel. One night, she appears at Félix's house, and sexually accosts him. Félix is never sure whether this episode actually took place, or is in fact imagined by him, and the novel presents a variety of clues that support both interpretations. The encounter is described in the following manner, in which once again, Leda is equated with a prostitute:

> Empezó a ondular . . . con la habilidad y plasticidad de la ramera
> más experimentada en las magias y manipulaciones de la cópula . . .
> Ella me hacía entrar en su cuerpo con la fuerza de succión del suyo,
> cada vez más poderosa. Sólo con su muerte iba a poder liberarme de

esa representación diabólica del pez-útero . . . que ahora estaba allí
devorándome a través de su ombligo-vagina. (123)

She began to undulate . . . with the ability and plasticity of a whore
who was experienced in the magic and manipulations of copulation . . .
She made me enter her body with the force of suction of her own, each
time more powerfully. Only with her death could I free myself of this
diabolical representation of the fish-uterus . . . which now was there
devouring me through its navel-vagina.

In this passage, Leda exhibits all the characteristics associated with
the Terrible Mother and the negative, transformative power of the
young witch. In his narration, Félix specifically associates Leda with
the transformative power of magic ("las magias y manipulaciones de
la cópula), while his emphasis on her suctioning power and devouring vagina, both suggest the ensnaring and devouring functions of
the Terrible Mother (Neumman 168). By associating Leda with the
prostitute, the latter acquires her dimension of dangerous, devouring
female, in a manner similar to *La Andaluza* in *Yo el Supremo*.

If we were to stop here, it would seem that *El fiscal* subscribes to
traditional female archetypes in a way that reinforces one-dimensional
portrayals and archaic stereotypes. However, the character of Leda is
transformed and developed throughout the rest of the novel in a manner that negates such a stereotyped portrait.

Leda's first transformation occurs when Félix flics back to Paraguay on a mission to assassinate the dictator, Alfredo Stroessner. After
a bomb scare on the plane and sudden landing, the passengers exit
the aircraft in a panic, and one of the passengers, the dissident Pedro
Alvarenga, disguised as a priest, is strangled. In the ensuing confusion,
Leda Kautner appears as a stewardess who guides Félix to safety:

Giré . . . y vi a Leda Kautner en uniforme de azafata . . . Leda llevaba
del brazo a una anciana y a una niña de corta edad. Me ordenó . . . que
las ayudara a descender del avión. . . . Buscó protegerme a mí con el
escudo de la anciana y la niña, convirtiéndome en la imagen del res-
petable pater-familias. (234-235)

I spun around . . . and saw Leda Kautner dressed as a stewardess . . . Leda carried by the arm an elderly woman and a young girl.
She ordered me . . . to help them descend from the airplane. . . . She
sought to protect me with the shield of the old woman and the child,
converting me into the image of the respectable head of the household.

Leda is no longer the devouring female, but rather the nurturing
mother who preserves Félix and ensures his safety. Leda's portrayal

defies traditional dichotomies and suggests a more multidimensional view of women because she is simultaneously the devouring female and the nurturing mother. Moreover, Leda is portrayed as adopting and abandoning distinct roles according to varying situations that cause her to "perform" her gender according to different aspects of her identity and personality.

Leda's multidimensionality is further developed in a subsequent section of the novel in which the reader learns that the name of the stewardess on the plane is not Leda Kautner, but Paula Becker. A discussion between Félix and his friend Clovis reveals to the reader who might be unfamiliar with Leda's new identity, that Paula Becker was a love interest of the famous poet, Rainer Maria Rilke, whom Rilke platonically worshipped for her virginity until Paula married Otto Modersohn and died in childbirth. According to Clovis, "Paula murió al ser madre. Lo que por doble motivo produjo en Rilke una profunda depresión. Por perder a una de sus vestales y también porque el fin de Paula contradecía y desacreditaba su doctrina de 'la muerte propia'" (330) ["Paula died upon becoming a mother. Which for a double motive produced a profound depression in Rilke. Because he lost one of his maidens and also because Paula's end contradicted and discredited his doctrine of 'one's own death'"].

These comments locate Leda Kautner within yet a third archetype—that of the mana figure, spiritual virgin or Sophia, according to Neumann (Neumann 325). Suddenly Leda incarnates all of Neumann's archetypes: Great and Terrible Mother, young witch and spiritual, virginal Sophia. Moreover, this identification between Leda Kautner and Paula Becker, besides emphasizing the postmodern character of women by underscoring her contradictory nature (she is at once prostitute and virgin), serves two other important purposes within the novel. First, Leda/Paula is associated with Rilke's theory that each person should have a death of one's own, based on the character of his/her own life, and not a generic death, such as a woman dying in childbirth, which is the death that Paula Becker actually suffered.[11] This theory is expounded in Rilke's prose work *The Notebooks of Malte Laurid Brigge*, which Roa Bastos specifically mentions in *El fiscal* (330). The Rilkean context is highly significant for interpreting Roa's novel. Although the protagonist, Félix, appears to die in vain, attempting to murder the dictator who will be deposed shortly after Félix's death, nonetheless, this death is not seen as a useless martyrdom but rather as Félix's "death of one's own," or the way in which his death plays out the significance of his life. This idea is reinforced by Félix's comments when he first decides to undertake the mission to kill Stroessner: "Podía ser este el instante único y excepcional en el que vengo pensando desde hace bastante tiempo . . . este momento definitivo en el que, en un fogonazo infinitesimal, uno se convierte en lo que debe ser y hace lo que debe hacer" (167) ["This could be the unique and exceptional moment about which I have been thinking for awhile. All my being extended itself toward this definitive moment in which, in an infinitesimal blast, one is converted into what he should be and what he should do"].

Leda Kautner/Paula Becker undergoes one final transformation in the novel, which tenders a bridge to the second love triangle, the historical one between Solano López, Pancha Garmendia, and Madame Lynch. Toward the end of *El fiscal*, when Félix is trying to flee further persecution, and Jimena is trying to carry him to freedom across the Brazilian border, the protagonists endeavor to blend in with a reenactment of Solano López's defeat at Cerro-Corrá during the Triple Alliance War. The actress who is performing the part of Madame Lynch is none other than Leda Kautner: "A los pies de la cruz se hallaba Madama Lynch . . . Pero esa actriz no era otra que Leda Kautner . . . [Félix] Levantó los brazos hacia ella y la llamó vagamente . . . pero . . . cayó de bruces sobre el suelo rocoso (349). ["At the foot of the cross was Madame Lynch . . . But this actress was no other than Leda Kautner, the strange girl and ex-student of Félix . . . He raised his arms toward her and vaguely called to her . . . but . . . fell flat on his face on the rocky ground"]. By the end of the novel, Leda Kautner has come full circle. She is no longer the nurturing Paula Becker, but is now identified with Madame Lynch, who, as we are about to see, was also a prostitute and bears a resemblance in the novel to the archetype of the devouring woman. Leda is unresponsive to Félix's gestures as he falls on the ground. She does not aid him or save him. Once again, she is the negative, devouring prostitute through her identification with Madame Lynch.

The link between Leda Kautner and Madame Lynch leads us to the second, historical love triangle between Pancha Garmendia, Francisco Solano López, and Madame Lynch. From the purely historical perspective, Madame Lynch is a contested figure. She has sometimes been viewed as the heroic Paraguayan mother who stood by Solano López throughout the Triple Alliance War, while other times has been seen negatively as the controlling, ambitious, greedy female, hated by the Paraguayan people, and who sexually seduced Solano López to obtain wealth and power (Rees 315–19). Roa Bastos develops the figure of Madame Lynch both in *El fiscal*, and, more recently, in his posthumously published work *Pancha Garmendia y Elisa Lynch*, which the author conceived of as potentially a play or opera. This libretto serves as an important intertextual reference point for comprehending how Roa Bastos views the figure of Lynch within *El fiscal* and adds an important dimension to his overall portrayal of women characters.

As suggested with regard to Leda Kautner, in *El fiscal*, Madame Lynch is principally seen as the incarnation of the young witch archetype who casts a sexual spell over Francisco Solano López. The alleged notes of Sir Richard Burton state that "La 'mariscala' ejercía sobre él [Solano López] ese tipo de dominio que se asemeja al hechizo" (275) [The "female marshal" exerted over him (Solano López) that type of control that is similar to a spell"].[12] Just like *La Andaluza* in *Yo el Supremo* and Leda Kautner, Madame Lynch is a sensual beauty who magically dominates and transforms men. Her evil, sexual beauty is constructed in direct opposition to the pure and virginal attraction of Pancha Garmendia: "La hermosura de la nativa era suave y lunar . . . su rostro [tenía] un halo de candor y de misterio" (39) ["The beauty of the native was soft and lunar . . . her face (had) the halo of candor and mystery"]. Garmendia is established as the archetype of the spiritual, virginal Sophia. Her virginal and saintly qualities are suggested by the words "suave," "espíritu," "halo," and "candor." Pancha Garmendia incarnates good, the positive, spiritual transformative power of the feminine, while Lynch is its negative, transformative counterpart.

However, the validity of this initial archetypal interpretation is subverted through a reading of *El fiscal* in conjunction with Roa Bastos's libretto *Pancha Garmendia y Elisa Lynch*. This work expands on the relationship between Pancha, Solano López, and Madame Lynch in ways that negate one-dimensional archetypes and suggest a more complex and authentic portrayal of women.[13] Initially, the play continues the oppositional dichotomy between the two women established in *El fiscal*: "Sensual y carnal, Madama Lynch ama . . . en Panchita . . . su castidad y pureza de espíritu, su resistencia indomable a prostituirse o degradarse" (*Pancha Garmendia*, n.p.) ["Sensual and carnal, Madame Lynch loves . . . in Panchita . . . her chastity and purity of spirit, her indomitable resistance to prostituting or degrading herself" (my translation)]. The principal manner in which this archetypal vision is subsequently negated is through the ultimate identification that Roa Bastos establishes between his two female protagonists in the play. In the first act and scene, each woman is wearing a mask: "Las máscaras clásicas (las que cubren todo el rostro) se usarán solamente en los dos encuentros entre Pancha Garmendia y Madama Lynch, a fin de poner en evidencia el parecido idéntico de ambas: hermanas siamesas opuestas" (*Pancha Garmendia* n.p.) [The classical masks (those that cover the entire face) will be used only in the two encounters between Pancha Garmendia and Madame Lynch, in order to show the identical resemblance of the two: opposite siamese twin sisters (my translation)]. Similarly, in Act II, Scene I, the identical masks are also emphasized: "Madama Lynch se aproxima a Panchita alumbrándola con el farol. Sus máscaras son exactamente iguales. Se diría dos hermanas gemelas" (*Pancha Garmendia* n.p.) ["Madame Lynch approaches Panchita illuminating her with the lantern. Their masks are exactly the same. One would say two twin sisters" (my translation)]. Through these two descriptions, Roa Bastos fuses these two very opposite characters into one. Together they represent two sides of one woman: the spiritual and the carnal, kindness and cruelty. These two women share their common exploitation by Solano López; this is why we were told earlier that Lynch admired Pancha's resistance to degradation and prostitution. The real-life Madame Lynch could never marry López, first, because she was never able to divorce her first husband, Xavier de Quatrefages, and second, because she met with much opposition from López's family, who refused to accept her as anything more than a common prostitute. Lynch, after her marriage and abandonment of her French husband, served as a "lorette," or low-ranking courtesan in France (Rees 19). In Roa Bastos's play, despite Lynch's ambitious and calculating nature, she is also seen somewhat as a victim of her circumstances and female condition. In one scene Lynch states, "No soy mas que la concubina del Presidente . . . En mi honor circulan pasquines y canciones satíricas" (*Pancha Garmendia* n.p.) ["I am nothing more than the President's concubine . . . In my honor satirical pasquinades and songs are circulated" (my translation)]. Although it is difficult to feel sympathy for Madame Lynch, as she manipulates López into believing that Pancha has been conspiring against him (which ironically turns out to be true at the end of the play), nonetheless, the play creates some sympathy for Lynch because she is forced to occupy an inferior social position due to her status as concubine. Father Maíz refuses to baptize her son in the cathedral, and the society women turn their noses up at her. In this sense, she can be seen as the exploited prostitute, and her fusion with Pancha suggests the general exploitation of all Paraguayan women.

This fusion between Pancha and Madame Lynch is ultimately confirmed by the final scene of the libretto. In this scene, Pancha, who in an earlier episode refused to participate in the conspiracy against López, extricates from her blanket "el inmenso anillo, contraseña de la conspiración, con las iniciales bien visibles F.S.L." (*Pancha Garmendia* n.p.) ["the immense ring, password of the conspiracy, with the very visible initials F.S.L." (my translation)]. This act creates an ambiguity in the text because Pancha's initial refusal to participate in a conspiracy against the dictator was seen as a sign of her rectitude and purity, while her ultimate involvement (possession of the conspirators' password) suggests that perhaps Pancha is not as loyal and honest as originally implied. Thus, once again, Roa's works develop female characters on the basis of the deconstruction of traditional dichotomies and stereotypes, focusing on postmodern contradictions rather than pure archetypes.

Finally, in *El fiscal,* Roa Bastos also blends prostitution with the archetype of the Great Mother or nourishing female. The novelist attributes the following commentary to Sir Francis Cochelet as cited in Richard Burton's historical account of Paraguay: "Estos batallones de "prostitutas patrióticas" . . . No eran rameras profesionales. Eran madres lactantes voluntarias" (294) ["These battalions of 'patriotic prostitutes' . . . were not professional prostitutes. They were voluntary, lactating mothers"].

In this passage, prostitutes are seen as mothers who give sustenance in the form of sex to their dying sons during the war. They are prostitute-mothers, who, at first, voluntarily offer sexual solace to the men, but are later seen as forced into prostitution as a means of survival during the war and the subsequent occupation of Paraguay. In this instance, prostitutes are not negative, devouring females, the antithesis of pure virgins, but rather generous, loving, exploited, and desperate mothers. Once again, stereotypes and traditional dichotomies are destroyed in favor of more complex, postmodern vision. Women are not exclusively either prostitutes or mothers, but can be both, as was the case during the War of the Triple Alliance in the novel. This view humanizes prostitutes and sympathizes with their plight, thus suggesting a feminist criticism of female exploitation and the inferior female condition dictated by patriarchy.

In Roa Bastos's last novel, *Madama Sui* (1995), the author explicitly problematizes the institution of prostitution through the title character. Madama Sui is one of the dictator's young mistresses, and her plight is seen as emblematic of that of the Paraguayan woman in general. In the novel's preface, Roa Bastos states:

> La protagonista se convirtió en una víctima propiciatoria del proceso de degeneración social y nacional que produjo la tiranía. La estrategia del poder unipersonal encontró en la prostitución de la mujer el elemento primario, el más vulnerable, pero también el más eficaz, que le permitió implantar la corrupción generalizada de una sociedad atrasada e inerme.

En el contexto de este fenómeno masivo, a la vez político y social, el destino de la protagonista adquiere su perfil verdaderamente trágico, su pleno valor de documento humano. (11)

The protagonist was converted into a propitiatory victim of the process of social and national degeneration that tyranny produced. The strategy of personal power found the primary element, the most vulnerable element, but also the most efficacious, in the prostitution of women, which allowed the implantation of generalized corruption of a backward and defenseless society. In the context of this massive phenomenon, at once political and social, the destiny of the protagonist acquires its truly tragic profile, its complete value as human document.[14]

Through the novel's protagonist, women are presented as innocent victims of a patriarchal political and social system that they are powerless to control. Despite the fact that Sui is a prostitute, the novel's narration repeatedly underscores her purity, as does the author in the preface: "El vértigo del poder no logró prostituir su dignidad intrínseca de ser humano y su innata inocencia" (12) ["The vertigo of power did not succeed in prostituting her intrinsic dignity of a human being and her innate innocence"]. Sui, although degraded and exploited through her prostitution, is shown to maintain her integrity, refusing to participate in a plot against Stroessner, similar to Pancha Garmendia's initial rejection of the conspiracy against Solano López.[15] The novel clearly indicts patriarchy for its role in sustaining prostitution and the inferior social position of women: "[Sui] no estaba segura de que la mujer pudiera convertirse algún día en un ser humano porque el hombre no le permitiría ganar esa dignidad, mientras él no se convirtiese en un ser humano. Lo cual era casi imposible. Y lo más seguro: totalmente imposible" (37) ["Sui was not sure that women could some day be transformed into human beings because man would not permit her to earn that dignity, as long as he did not become a human being himself. Which was almost impossible. And the surest thing: totally impossible"].

If we momentarily return to *El fiscal*, it is possible to observe how *El fiscal* and *Madama Sui* articulate a clear feminist viewpoint. *El fiscal's* protagonist, Félix Moral, claims to have written an article on feminism that is also an obvious indictment of patriarchy. In this piece, he admonishes man for his anguish faced with women's acquisition of independence and concludes that the world suffers from "una enfermedad incurable, llamada hombre" ["an incurable illness, called man"].

If we now examine these novelistic discourses within the context of current feminist views on prostitution, the novel's ideological stance becomes clear. According to Maggie O'Neil,

> Feminist analyses of prostitution inevitably challenge the ways in which sexual and social inequalities serve to reproduce ideology, patriarchy, and the structuration of gender relations. The central ideological problem for feminism is the exchange of money for sex is taken to be the exchange of equivalents. This is a socially created illusion and is central to the commodification of women's bodies as use objects and our subsequent oppression by society . . . Rooted in capitalism, commodification, and as Pateman argues, the structure of sexual relations between men and women, it is a major task for feminists to develop better understanding of the complex issues involved.[16]

A second way in which Roa Bastos implicitly rejects patriarchal domination of women in his novels is through his portrayal of lesbianism. This can primarily be seen through Sui's lesbian relationship with Friné, the German guard to Stroessner's harem of prostitutes. Sui's relationship with Friné is described in the following manner:

> Acogió desaprensivamente ese amor clandestino y desconocido que le ofrecían; "El más maravilloso de todos—le aseguró Friné—el más tierno, el más puro—¿Más que el amor del hombre y la mujer—preguntó con deslumbrada ingenuidad.—Mucho más—musitó Friné con un soplo caliente en su oído . . . "El hombre sólo sabe hacer el amor para su goce personal. La mujer no existe para él sino como objeto de su propio placer . . . mientras está poseyendo a una, piensa en otras dos o tres más, en un espejeo de cuerpos desnudos de mujer que estimulan su libido . . . Del amor sólo sabemos nosotras, las mujeres. (236–238)
>
> She received this clandestine and unknown love that they offered her neglectfully; "The most marvelous of all"—Friné assured her—the most tender, the most pure—More than the love between a man and a woman—she asked with dazzling ingenuousness—Much more—mused Friné with a hot blow of air in her ear . . . "Man only knows how to make love for his personal pleasure . . . while he is possessing one, he thinks of two or three more, in an optical illusion of naked female bodies that stimulate his libido . . . About love, only we women know.

Sui's reaction to her affair with Friné is clearly one of rebellion against Stroessner:

> Por otra parte le divertía igualmente esa especie de sediciosa trasgresión que envolvía una burla sutil y sensual del poder.

> —Ponerle cuernos al hombre todopoderoso pero impotente sobre sí mismo! Ponerle cuernos con una mujer al Gran Hombre convertido en eunuco . . . !—se rió con ganas. (239)

On the other hand, she equally enjoyed that type of seditious transgression that involved a subtle and sensual mockery of power.

> —To be unfaithful to the Great Man, converted into a eunuch, with another woman—she laughed with gusto.

Sui's sentiments bring to mind Cheryl Clarke's comments on lesbianism: "To be a lesbian in a male-supremacist, capitalist, misogynist, racist . . . culture . . . is an act of resistance. . . . No matter how a woman lives out her lesbianism—in the closet, in the state legislature, in the bedroom—she has rebelled against becoming the slave master's concubine"(Clark 155). Although Sui's rebellion may appear somewhat ironic in light of Clarke's words, because she is in fact the slave-master's concubine in the novel, she is forced into this position for her own safety (there is no way to refuse), and thus her relationship with Friné is the only means she has to manifest her dissidence with her socially delegated position.[17] Hence, it is legitimate to speak of lesbianism as a form of rebellion against patriarchy and prostitution in the novel.

Roa Bastos's decision to focus on a female protagonist in his last novel is the culmination of a lifetime of writing in which the deconstruction of female stereotypes emerges as a recurrent subplot of his fiction. Madama Sui suggests a new, feminist woman, despite her subordinated, exploited role as prostitute. In *Metaforismos*, Roa Bastos's collection of axioms extracted from his own fictional works, he highlights the following passage taken from *Madama Sui*:

> La joven se mostraba segura de sí misma, digna pero no altanera. Símbolo de la nueva posición de la mujer en un viejo relato. "Mi manera de tener," dijo, "es no pedir. Mi manera de encontrar es no buscar. Mi manera de ser es vivir mi verdad íntima hasta sus últimas consecuencias." (*Metaforismos* 147).

> The young girl was sure of herself, dignified but not arrogant. Symbol of the new position of women in an old story. "My way of having" she said, "is not asking. My way of finding is not looking. My way of being is living my intimate truth to its final consequences" (my translation).

Perhaps Roa Bastos isolated this quotation from *Madama Sui* because it posits a new role for females within "the old story," and thus a more progressive future for women. Undoubtedly, his utilization of archetypes throughout his fiction is geared toward an identical goal. Moreover, through his fiction, Roa suggests the ultimate contradictory, postmodern nature of all men and women, who cannot be constricted by limiting dichotomies such as vicious versus virtuous: "La mujer y el hombre sólo pueden ser virtuosos cuando se entregan a un vicio que los absorbe por completo y los devuelve como una pasión mística a la naturaleza de lo sagrado" (*Metaforismos* 25, originally from *Yo el Supremo*) ["Women and men can only be virtuous when they engage in a vice that completely absorbs them and returns them like a mystical passion to the nature of the sacred" (my translation)]. Salu'i, *La Andaluza*, María de los Ángeles, Leda Kautner, Madame Lynch, Pancha Garmendia, and Madama Sui all have complex, multidimensional, and contradictory natures, as do all human beings.

Notes

1. See María Elena Carballo, "Lo femenino y lo absoluto en *Yo el Supremo*," *Las voces del karaí: Estudios sobre Augusto Roa Bastos*, ed. Fernando Burgos (Madrid: Edelsa-Editores, 1988), 101–8; Kathleen N. March, "Las figuras femeninas en *El trueno entre las hojas*," *Cuadernos Hispanoamericanos* 493–94 (1991): 177–85; Rivas Rojas, Raquel, "'Kurupí' y 'Madera quemada': La progresión cuestionadora de Augusto Roa Bastos," *Escritura: Revista de Teoría y Crítica Literarias* 15.30 (1990): 373–88; Alain Sicard, "Del incesto al parricidio Escritura y sexualidad en la obra de Augusto Roa Bastos," ed. Alain Sicard (Madrid: Centre de Recherches Latino-americaines/Fundamentos, 1990), 337–47.

2. For studies that illustrate the use of Christian symbolism and archetypes, see Rosa Audubert, "El estigma de la cruz en *Hijo de hombre* de Augusto Roa Bastos," *Espéculo: Revista de Estudios Literarios* 21 (2002) [no pagination]; Jacqueline Baldrán and Rubén Bareiro Saguier, "Las dos caras del mito en *Hijo de hombre* de Augusto Roa Bastos," *Letterature d'America: Rivista Trimestrale* 6.26 (1985): 35–62; Loreto Busquets, "El realismo impresionista de *Hijo de hombre*," *Cuadernos Hispano-americanos* 493–94 (1991): 199–215; David William Foster, *The Myth of Paraguay in the Fiction of Augusto Roa Bastos* (Chapel Hill: University of North Carolina Press, 1969); David William Foster, *Augusto Roa Bastos* (Boston: Twayne Publishers, 1978); Adriana Valdés and Ignacio Rodríguez, "*Hijo de hombre*: El mito como fuerza social," *Homenaje a Augusto Roa Bastos: Variaciones Interpretativas en torno a su obra*, ed. Helmy F. Giacoman (Long Island City, NY: Anaya-Las Ameritas, 1973), 97–154; Helene C. Weldt-Basson, "Augusto Roa Bastos's *Contravida* and *Madama Sui*: An Archetypal Interpretation," *Confluencia: Revista Hispánica de Cultura y Literatura* 23.1 (2007): 93–106.

3. This translation of *Hijo de hombre*, and all future ones, are taken from Roa Bastos, *Son of Man*, 199.

4. This is my translation of the definition provided in *El Pequeño Larousse Ilustrado* (Mexico, D.F., Ediciones Larousse, 2005), 383.

5. The indices of this association between Jara and Christ are too extensive to enumerate here and have been studied elsewhere as indicated in a prior footnote. Suffice it to say, in addition to his name, Jara is associated with Christ's dissemination of love among the people, through his bringing of water to the Chaco War soldiers, since water is developed as a symbol of love and solidarity throughout the novel. Moreover, before he and Salu'i undertake their final mission, the character Gamarra speaks of their "última cena." Finally, once wounded, in order to arrive at his destination, Jara has Salu'i tie his arms in a cross-like fashion to the truck's steering wheel. He dies a martyr, delivering water to the sole survivor of the battle, Miguel Vera, the novel's Judas-like traitor.

6. Indeed, all the female characters in *Hijo de hombre* are portrayed as bearers of love for their fellow man and protestors against injustice. Such is the case of the *aloja* vendors, who insist upon giving water to the political prisoners. They impose their will on the guards: "—Mejor es que te calles de una vez. Dame sí un jarro bien lleno de tu aloja—oyeron que le dijo—Sí. Te voy a dar. Pero me vas a dejar dar también a los presos. El cabo estuvo a punto de darle un culatazo, pero se contuvo ante la actitud tranquila de la mujer, dominado por las miradas que brotaban del semblante cobrizo—E'a, un mozo tan buen mozo y tan enojado! Manda sí abrir el vagón! Nei pue, che karaí (*Hijo de hombre* 198) [—It would be better if you would finally shut up. Give me a very full jar of your aloja, they heard that he said. Yes, I am going to give it to you. But you are also going to let me give some to the prisoners. The lieutenant was going to give her a smack, but contained himself faced with the tranquil attitude of the woman, dominated by the looks that sprouted from her copper face—Such a nice looking young man and so angry! Order the wagon to be opened! Agree then, my master!] As can be seen from this passage, women are far from passive figures in *Hijo de hombre*.

7. This translation, as all others of *Yo el Supremo*, is taken from Roa Bastos, *I The Supreme*, 47–51.

8. Neumann 80. Also see the very interesting article by José Colmeiro, who analyzes figures similar to La Andaluza as the Carmen archtetype in literature in "Exorcizing Exoticism: Carmen and the Construction of Oriental Spain."

9. Neumann 71. Another episode in *Yo el Supremo* relates directly to the archetype of the Terrible Mother. The dictator's dog relates the story of the *Vieja-Demonio* (Old Woman-Devil), from Guarani myth, who is "armada de doble dentadura, una en la boca, otra en el bajo vientre . . . ¿Qué significa la vulva-con-dientes si no el principio devorador, no engendrador de la hembra?" (258) [armed with a double set of teeth, one in her

mouth, the other iin her sex . . . What is the meaning of the vulva-with-teeth if not the devouring nonengendering principle of the woman? (138)]. This myth is incarnated in a minor character, Juana Esquivel, an elderly neighbor of the British traveler (234–35) Juan Robertson, who falls in love with him and tries to seduce him (her story runs parallel to the myth of the vagina dentata, in a footnote at the bottom of the page). According to Erich Neummann "the destructive side of the feminine, the destructive and deathly womb, appears most frequently in the archetypal form of a mouth bristling with teeth . . . This motif of the vagina dentata is most distinct in the mythology of the North American Indians . . . the hero is the man who overcomes the Terrible Mother, breaks the teeth out of her vagina . . ." (Neumann 168).

10. Note that all translations of *El fiscal* are mine. Jimena appears to be the only exception to Roa Bastos's blending of archetypes. She remains totally idealized according to the great mother and spiritual Sophia archetypes, perhaps because she is based on Roa Bastos's second wife, Iris Giménez.

11. Note that Roa Bastos's use of the figure of Paula Becker is even more complicated than stated here. Although Clovis claims that Rilke did not sustain a sexual relationship with Becker, historical works on the pair indicate that such a relationship, though never proven, was entirely possible. At one point after Becker's marriage to Moderhson, she abandoned him and lived in Paris. During this time, Rilke posed for a portrait for Becker, and it is possible that a sexual relationship ensued. Becker's relationship with Rilke, just like Leda's with Félix, is shrouded in mystery and uncertainty, and the parallels do not end there. The history of Rilke's life suggests three more love triangles that follow the archetype outlined with regard to the novel: Paula, Rilke, and Rilke's wife Clara Westhoff constitute one triangle; Paula, Otto Modersohn's first wife, Helene, and Otto constitute another; while Otto, Paula, and Rilke constitute the third (see Torgersen, *Dear Friend*).

12. Although the narrator claims to quote Sir Richard Burton, upon reference to Burton's historical work, we learn that these quotations are totally invented. See Burton's *Letters from the Battle-fields of Paraguay*.

13. *El fiscal* also suggests some ambivalence toward Madame Lynch and the possibility of some positive aspect to the character, through the narrator's (Félix Moral's) attitude with regard to this figure. He vacillates between rejecting Lynch as an ideological tool of the Stroessner administration (in its attempts to present Lynch as a national heroine whose work the Stroessner administration continues), and embracing her as a courageous woman who stood by Solano López's side in his heroic albeit futile enterprise of defending Paraguay against Brazil, Argentina, and Uruguay during the war of the Triple Alliance.

14. Note that all translations of *Madama Sui* are mine.

15. Interestingly, the narration identifies Sui with other famous concubines, notably Madama Lynch (113) and Eva Perón (115).

16. O'Neill 31–32. It is important to note that there simultaneously exists a feminist position from which prostitution is viewed as legitimate work for women. Feminists adhering to this view have occupied themselves with the task of ensuring prostitutes' rights.

17. The novel makes this point clearly through the story of Purificación Capilla, one of the virgins destined to be the dictator's future mistress. Purificación escapes from the dictator's harem and goes into hiding, but is eventually tracked down by the dictator, raped and killed. This is the fate that awaits rebellious females under Stroessner. See *El fiscal* 219–20.

Works Cited

Barrett, Michele. *Women's Oppression Today.* London: Verso, 1980. Print.

Budin, Stephanie Lynn. *The Myth of the Sacred Prostitute in Antiguity.* London: Cambridge University Press, 2008. Print.

Burton, Sir Richard. *Letters from the Battle-fields of Paraguay.* London: Tinsely Brothers, 1870. Print.

Clarke, Cheryl. "Lesbianism: An Act of Resistance." *Feminism and Sexuality: A Reader.* Ed. Stevi Jackson and Sue Scott. New York: Columbia University Press, 1996. 155–61. Print.

Colmeiro, José. "Exorcizing Exoticism: Carmen and the Construction of Oriental Spain." *Comparative Literature* 54.2 (2002): 127–44. Print.

Ezquerro, Milagros. Prefacio. *Pancha Garmendia y Elisa Lynch.* www.cabildoccr .gov.py/libros/Pancha%20Garmendia%20y%20Elisa%20Lynch.pdf. Web.

Freedman, Jane. *Feminism.* Buckingham (England): Open University Press, 2001. Print.

Lyotard, Jean-François. *The Postmodern Condition: A Report on Knowledge.* Trans. Geoff Bennington and Brian Massumi. Minneapolis: University of Minnesota Press, 1984. Print.

McManus, Barbara F. "Structure of the Feminine Archetype." www.cnr.edu/ home/femarchstructure.html. Web.

Neumann, Erich. *The Great Mother.* Trans. Ralph Manheim. Princeton, NJ: Princeton University Press/Bollingen Mythos Series, 1991. Print.

Olea, Raquel. "Feminism: Modern or Postmodern?" *The Postmodernism Debate in Latin America.* Ed. John Beverley, José Oviedo and Michael Aronna. Durham, NC: Duke University Press, 1995. 192–200. Print.

O'Neill, Maggie. *Prostitution and Feminism: Towards a Politics of Feeling.* Cambridge: Polity Press, 2001. Print.

Qualls-Corbett, Nancy. *The Sacred Prostitute: Eternal Aspect of the Feminine.* Toronto: Inner City Books, 1998. Print.

Rees, Sian. *The Shadows of Elisa Lynch.* London: Headline Book Publishing, 2003. Print.

Roa Bastos, Augusto. *El fiscal.* Madrid: Alfaguara, 1993. Print.

———. *Pancha Garmendia y Elisa Lynch.* www.cabildoccr.gov.py/libros/ Pancha%20Garmendia%20y%20Elisa%20Lynch.pdf. Web.

———. *Hijo de hombre*. Buenos Aires: Editorial Sudamericana, 1990. Print.

———. *I The Supreme*. Trans. Helen Lane. New York: Alfred A. Knopf, 1986. Print.

———. *Madama Sui*. Madrid: Alfaguara, 1996. Print.

———. *Metaforismos*. Buenos Aires: Seix Barral, 1996. Print.

———. *Son of Man*. Trans. Rachel Caffyn. New York: Monthly Review Press, 1988. Print.

———. *Yo el Supremo*. Madrid: Cátedra, 1983. Print.

Sarup, Madan. *An Introductory Guide to Post-Structuralism and Postmodernism*. Athens: University of Georgia Press, 1993. Print.

Torgersen, Eric. *Dear Friend: Rainer Maria Rilke and Paula Modersohn-Becker*. Evanston, IL: Northwestern University Press, 1998. Print.

Contributors

Fernando Burgos is Professor of Latin American Studies at the University of Memphis. His area of research includes nineteenth- and twentieth-century Latin American narrative. He has published ten books, including *La novela moderna hispanoamericana: un ensayo sobre el concepto literario de modernidad* (Madrid), *Vertientes de la modernidad hispanoamericana* (Caracas), *Cuentos de Hispanoamérica en el siglo XX* (Madrid), and *Los escritores y la creación en Hispanoamérica* (Madrid). He has also published more than fifty articles in European, North American, and Latin American professional journals.

David William Foster is Regents' Professor of Spanish and Women and Gender Studies at Arizona State University, where he is the former chair of the Department of Languages and Literatures. His research focuses on urban culture, with an emphasis on gender construction, women's history, and Jewish Diaspora culture, with particular reference to fiction, theater, film, and photography. He is currently preparing a monograph on Latin American documentary filmmaking.

Jorge Carlos Guerrero is Assistant Professor Spanish American Literature and Director of Latin American Studies at the University of Ottawa. He received his Ph.D. in Latin American Literature from the University of Toronto in 2006. He has published articles on Brazilian and Spanish American literature.

Katie MacLean received her Ph.D. in Spanish/Latin American Studies from Duke University and is Associate Professor of Romance Languages and Literatures at Kalamazoo College. Her scholarly interests include early modern women in the Hispanic world, women and gender in Hispanic literatures, and mysticism in the Spanish empire. She has published articles on the relationship between Spanish mysticism and imperial ideology.

Tracy K. Lewis is a Professor of Spanish at the State University of New York at Oswego. He has written extensively on Roa Bastos and many other Paraguayan writers, and has published English translations of Juan Manuel Marcos's novel *El invierno de Gunter* and Renée Ferrer's poetry collections *Peregrino de la eternidad* and *Sobreviviente*. A poet himself, Lewis writes verse in English, Spanish, and Guarani, and has published work in *Qualitative Inquiry, Confluencia, Elysian Fields Quarterly*, and the Paraguayan journals *Takuapu* and *Ñe'engatú*. In 2002, he received the Poetry Prize of the Society for Humanistic Anthropology.

Fatima R. Nogueira is Assistant Professor of Spanish and Portuguese at The University of Memphis with a specialization in twentieth-century Latin American literature. Her publications include articles in *Revista Chilena de Literatura, Alpha: Revista de Arte, Letras y Filosofía, Confluencia: Revista Hispánica de Cultura, INTI: Revista de Literatura Hispánica, Luso-Brazilian Review, Káñina: Revista de Artes y Letras de la Universidad de Costa Rica, Afro-Hispanic Review*, and *Arizona Journal of Hispanic Cultural Studies*. She is currently working on a book addressing the issue of postmodernity in the work of Lispector, Roa Bastos, Cortázar, and Valenzuela

Javier Uriarte is a Ph.D. student at New York University. He has published two book chapters in Uruguay: "Las fechas y la invención del sistema simbólico nacional en América Latina," included in *Derechos de memoria*, edited by Hugo Achugar; and "La configuración identitaria en *The Purple Land*," included in *William Henry Hudson y "La tierra purpúrea." Reflexiones desde Montevideo*, edited by Vegh and Jean-Phillipe Barnabé. In 2009, he coordinated a special issue of the Université Paris VIII's literary journal "LI.RI.CO.," dedicated to Uruguayan literature, which will appear in 2010.

Gustavo Verdesio is an Associate Professor in the Department of Romance Languages and Literatures and the Program in American Culture at University of Michigan. He teaches courses on colonial Latin America, indigenous societies, and popular culture. A revised English version of his book *La invención del Uruguay* (1996) has been published as *Forgotten Conquests* (Temple University Press, 2001). He is also the coeditor (with Álvaro F. Bolaños) of the collection *Colonialism Past and Present* (SUNY Press, 2002). His articles have appeared in *Trabajos de Arqueología del Paisaje, Arqueología Suramericana, Bulletin of Hispanic Studies, Revista de Estudios Hispánicos*, and *Revista Iberoamericana*, among other journals.

Helene Carol Weldt-Basson is an Associate Professor of Spanish at Michigan State University. Her area of specialization is twentieth-century Latin American literature, with an emphasis on Paraguay, the historical novel, the Boom, and feminism. Her work includes two books: *Augusto Roa Bastos's I The Supreme: A Dialogic Perspective* (Missouri Press, 1993) and more recently, *Subversive Silences: Nonverbal Expression and Implicit Narrative Strategies in the Works of Latin American Women Writers* (Fairleigh Dickinson University Press, 2009), as well as numerous articles on Latin American fiction.